Lighthouses of Lake Michigan

Past and Present

by Wayne S. Sapulski

Wilderness Adventure Books
Manchester, Michigan

© 2001 by Wayne Sapulski

ISBN: 0-923568-47-6
LCCN: 2001-126916

Printed in Canada

Unless otherwise indicated, all photographs and picture postcards
are from the author's personal collection.

On the cover: Chicago Harbor Light

Wilderness Adventure Books
P.O. Box 856
Manchester, MI 48158
800-852-8652

Library of Congress Cataloging-in-Publication Data

Sapulski, Wayne S.
    Lighthouses of Lake Michigan : past and present / by
Wayne S. Sapulski. —1st ed.
    p.cm.
    Includes bibliographical references and index.
    ISBN: 0-923568-47-6

    1. Lighthouses—Michigan, Lake. I. Title.

VKI023.3.S27 2001   387.1'55'09774
                          QBI01-200920

*This book is dedicated to Jennifer Tregembo, whose
unfailing support aided its completion*

Contents

Foreword: Lightkeeping in the 21st Century

Lighthouses: Why build them? Why visit them? Why save them? Navigational aids have been a necessity from the moment man went to sea. For more than 2300 years, lighthouses have guided mariners through dangerous waters and into safe harbors. Two of the seven ancient wonders of the world served as lighthouses: Pharos of Alexandria, Egypt and the Colossus of Rhodes, both built around 300 B.C.

In the United States, there were twelve Colonial lighthouses built before our country was formed. The first was on Brewster Island in Boston Harbor in 1716. Recognizing that commercial shipping was crucial to our developing nation, President George Washington created the U.S. Lighthouse Service as one of his first public acts in August 1789. Thirty-five years later, the U.S. expanded its dependence on water transportation routes with the opening of the Erie Canal in 1825. The canal opened the Great Lakes to the East Coast and international trade, fostering development of America's Midwest. Establishment of the first two lighthouses on Lake Michigan soon followed in 1832 at Chicago, Illinois and St. Joseph, Michigan. The pace of development increased rapidly with the opening of the locks at Sault Ste. Marie, Michigan in 1855. Raw materials such as coal, iron ore, limestone, copper, timber, and grain could flow more freely. Vessel traffic increased as industry and agriculture flourished, necessitating the lighting of busy shipping lanes and growing harbors.

Why build them? Shipping needed to be safeguarded. Why and when the lighthouses of Lake Michigan were built where they were built will be detailed in the tour that follows. Think of it as a historic site review. Over the last eight years Wayne Sapulski has visited, often more than once, every remaining light station site on the Great Lakes. In addition, he remains fully licensed by the U.S. Coast Guard to pilot ships of unlimited tonnage upon the waters of the Great Lakes. These credentials have given him a unique perspective on the development and current status of Great Lakes lighthouses.

Why visit them? The reasons are many: to fully understand their intended function; to study the architecture; to appreciate the hardships faced by the people who built and staffed them; to marvel at the beautiful locations. Visit them and you will soon come to realize they are endangered. Some have already been lost. Many more are in danger of being lost.

The days of the manned light station on the Great Lakes are over. The last two U.S. lighthouses were automated in 1983. Both are on Lake Michigan: Point Betsie in Michigan and Sherwood Point in Wisconsin. Our Canadian neighbors to the north completed their automation program in 1991. The technological evolution from whale oil lamps to fully automated solar-powered electric lights has been a long and difficult process. Yet major lighted aids to navigation like lighthouses are no longer crucial. In recent years, electronic aids to navigation like the Global Positioning System (GPS) have become affordable for even the smallest boats. Lighthouses serve as a backup system to the more precise electronic aids. The Coast Guard has made it quite clear that they have neither the budget nor the training to maintain lighthouses as historic structures. By the year 2005 most of the light stations will be leased or transferred to new stewards, be they other governmental agencies, nonprofit organizations, or other eligible entities.

In 1986, Representative Gerry Studds of Massachusetts chaired a Congressional hearing in Washington, D.C. to determine what should be done with lighthouses as historic maritime monuments. During the next fourteen years of legislative inaction, many nonprofit groups stepped up to care for these historic structures. These groups put hard labor and scarce funds into derelict light stations converting them into museums and tourist attractions. However, to take ownership of their recently restored lighthouse, the nonprofit had to pay 50% of the newly appraised value. In other words, a group that took a valueless structure, restored it and gave it value, then had to pay again to buy the value they created…a totally unfair proposition which dissuaded other preservation-oriented non-profits from taking on projects.

Finally in 2000, an amendment to the Historic Preservation Act called the National Historic Lighthouse Preservation Act 2000 passed and eligible nonprofit organizations are no longer required to pay for the value they have created. Cosponsors of the legislation in the Senate were Frank Murkowski, R-Alaska and Carl Levin, D-Michigan. On the House side the cosponsors were Mark Souder, R-Indiana and Bart Stupak, D-Michigan. Many called the legislation the "fairness legislation." The Secretary of the Interior, who sets the standards for historic preservation, is responsible for implementing this legislation, which is Public Law 106-355.

To facilitate this monumental transfer task in Michigan, the state with the largest number of lighthouses, the Michigan Lighthouse Project (MLP) was formed. Based on the Maine Island Institute, the MLP is a collaboration of the many agencies and organizations that "touch" or are interested in these transfers.

The group includes the U.S. Coast Guard, State Historic Preservation Office, National Park Service, Bureau of Land Management, General Services Administration, National Trust for Historic Preservation, Department of Natural Resources, Nature Conservancy, the Great Lakes Lighthouse Keepers Association, state and federal legislators, and others. For the first time, all of these interested parties have come together to resolve the many intricate steps that are necessary in the transfer process. The MLP will focus on two primary questions: Who has the capacity to care for and protect these retired sentinels? And what is needed to help make an efficient transition to new ownership and secure the lighthouse's future? The answers to these questions will vary from site to site, as will the parties involved. It is hoped the process developed by the MLP will serve as a useful example for lighthouse transfers carried out in other states bordering the Great Lakes and beyond.

Finally, why save them? They are an important part of our regional history...our maritime heritage.

After decades of neglect, lighthouses are again being cared for. If the effort is to be meaningful, however, it must be a sustained one. The Great Lakes Lighthouse Keepers Association has devoted major resources to develop a curriculum guide for maritime heritage education that is available to teachers and youth leaders. GLLKA has used its award-winning restoration of the remote St. Helena Island Light Station as a laboratory to develop this guide. Our job is not just to restore lighthouses, it is to develop the next generation of historic preservationists. We must light a fire in others who follow in our footsteps. Today's youth are the ones who must continue after we are gone and keep the lights burning for future generations of Americans.

Dick Moehl, President
Great Lakes Lighthouse Keepers Association

St. Helena Island Light—currently undergoing restoration by Great Lakes Lighthouse Keepers Association volunteers

Regarding the southern shores of Lake Michigan:

"The total absence of harbors around the southern extremity of the lake has caused the wreck of many a vessel, as the action of the storm from the northward upon such a wide expanse of fresh water is tremendous; and from the great height and violence of the surf, which then thunders in upon the base of the sand hills, and the utter solitude of this coast, lives are seldom if ever saved."
—English Author Charles Joseph Latrobe, 1833

Regarding the Great Lakes in general:

"On the lakes there is at all times a dangerous proximity of coast, upon which vessels must be thrown in a long continued gale, whilst on the ocean there is generally room to drift until the storm is over."
—Lake Surveyor Captain William G. Williams, 1842

Regarding the U.S. Lighthouse Establishment:

"The lighthouse and lightship appeal to the interests and better instinct of man because they are symbolic of never-ceasing watchfulness, of steadfast endurance in every exposure, of widespread helpfulness. The building and keeping of the lights is a picturesque and humanitarian work of the nation."
—Commissioner of Lighthouses 1910-1935, George R. Putnam

Introduction

Lighthouses of the Fourth Coast

For people unfamiliar with the Great Lakes, the tall towers of the East, West, and Gulf Coasts generally spring to mind when lighthouses are mentioned. Counting both American and Canadian sites, there are over 350 lighthouses on our Fourth Coast, the Great Lakes…the greatest concentration of these landmarks in North America. The number would be closer to 400 if all of the lights already lost to progress were also counted. Michigan, many miles from an ocean, has more lighthouses than any other U.S. state.

That there are so many lighthouses on the Great Lakes really should come as no surprise. Geographically, the region is a vast one, stretching for more than a thousand miles from Montreal on the St. Lawrence River to Duluth at the western end of Lake Superior. The Great Lakes define the borders of eight U.S. states and the enormous Canadian province of Ontario. With their numerous bays, coves, and islands, the Great Lakes contain over 10,000 miles of shoreline. Many Great Lakes lights are in areas so remote that knowledge of their existence is not common even by people residing in this region. Due to shifting patterns of commercial activity, once important lighthouses are now located far from commonly used shipping lanes. As a result, even professional mariners, a group the author once belonged to, are unfamiliar with some of them.

However, all of these lighthouses were established because they were deemed necessary aids to navigation. As such, they played an important role in augmenting the safety of men and ships at a time when waterborne transportation was the only viable mode of transportation available. Most of these lighthouses remain in use today, some are inactive, but all are important links to the maritime heritage of the Great Lakes.

Bringing it all Together

In traveling around the Great Lakes, a great deal of information about lighthouses was encountered. Some of the information was factual, some was anecdotal. Much of the information was incomplete. Some of it proved to be accurate, some was just plain wrong. Digging into lighthouse history is a frustrating business. Official government sources frequently disappoint. Records are missing and details remain sketchy. Worst of all, there is a lot of conflicting information floating around that must be dealt with. All of these factors tend to cloud the sequence of events at specific sites. Because there are so many

Chambers Island Light

lighthouses on the Great Lakes, the topic is best covered lake by lake.

This book is intended to present a comprehensive review of the lighthouses of Lake Michigan. Each site is presented from the viewpoint of the mariner. It simply makes no sense to discuss lighthouses without reference to the navigational hazards they were intended to mark. As much as possible, harbor lights

*Coast Guard cutter **Acacia** in Charlevoix*

are discussed within the context of concurrent harbor development. Emphasis is placed on the physical sites themselves and the architecture of the lighthouse structures. Although a few keepers are mentioned, little has been provided about the human element at Lake Michigan light stations. Due to the large number of sites covered, there was neither time nor space to engage in nautical storytelling. Great storms, famous keepers, tragic shipwrecks, and heroic rescues have all been more than adequately covered by other authors. Nor was there room for any of the author's own adventures in getting out to many of the lighthouses. The site information presented has been culled from many diverse sources and supplemented by visits to municipal libraries, local historical museums, regional and national research centers, and photographic archives. Every attempt has been made to provide only the most accurate information. Some questions remain unanswered. Nevertheless, it is hoped the text will provide a lasting, unifying overview of the lighthouses of Lake Michigan.

Author's Note: A Sense of Place

After reading this book, it will come as no surprise that the author is an unabashed Great Lakes travel enthusiast. Like many people, once I was financially able to travel I tended to ignore that which was right under my own nose. It was not until after I had traveled to Europe and throughout the United States that I came to fully appreciate the unique history and beauty of my home region.

The Great Lakes have witnessed a rich and varied panorama of history over the last three and one-half centuries. Place names in this region reflect the mixed influences of British, French, and Native American forces. On Lake Michigan alone, names like Charlevoix, Seul Choix, Grosse Point, Suttons Bay, Cross Village, Fish Creek, and Old Mission produce a satisfying lilt when spoken aloud. Particularly pleasing are the mellifluous tones of the Native American names like Ahnapee, Algoma, Kenosha, Kewaunee, Macatawa, Manistee, Manitowoc, Menominee, Milwaukee, Oconto, Sheboygan and Waugoshance. I love the way these names roll off the tongue. This region is relevant to my life experience. The Great Lakes provide a sense of place and a feeling of belonging. Yes, I like it here. I like it more than words can say.

Acknowledgments

An idea here, a thought there, constructive criticism and technical advice…it all adds up. Knowingly or unknowingly, many people helped over the years in the quest that culminated with this book. The danger in naming names is to inadvertently omit someone, but to one and all, my heartfelt thanks.

Kathy Beeman—	Galley reviewer and educator
Joel & Mary Ann Blahnik—	Caretakers, Chambers Island Light
Francis Cornell—	Photo contributor (Green Island Light)
Jack Edwards—	Great Lakes journalist
Louraine Ham—	Delta County Historical Society
Barbara Hanson—	Galley reviewer and photographer
Timothy Harrison—	Publisher, *Lighthouse Digest Magazine*
Bruce Jenvey—	Publisher, *Great Lakes Cruiser Magazine*
Rich Katuzin—	Lighthouse artist and historian
George Kilborn—	Superintendent, Harbor Point Association
John & Ann Mahan—	Great Lakes photographers and authors
Dick Moehl—	President, GLLKA
Bruce Nelson—	Board member, GLLKA
Ted Nelson—	Nature photographer and educator
John Scripp—	Chairman, North Point Lighthouse Friends
Charles Stewart—	Photo contributor (Squaw Point Light)
Frederick Stonehouse—	Great Lakes historian
Dave Tinder—	Michigan historic photo collector and contributor
John Wagner—	Aerial photographer extraordinaire
Ken & Barb Wardius—	Lighthouse photographers and authors
Edward Werner—	Kenosha historian
Dave Wobser—	Galley reviewer and photographer

Special thanks for their help in the procurement of archival photos to:

Robert Graham—Archivist
Historical Collections of the Great Lakes
Bowling Green State University
Bowling Green, Ohio

Carla Lavigne—Archivist
Clarence S. Metcalf Library
Great Lakes Historical Society
Vermilion, Ohio

Paul Herold—Chief, Civil Engineering Technology Center
U.S. Coast Guard—Ninth District, Cleveland, Ohio

Dr. Robert Browning and Christopher Halvern—Historians
U.S. Coast Guard Historians Office
Washington, D.C.

Patterns of Development

Importance of Water Transportation

Mention the great Northwest today and the states of Washington and Oregon spring to mind. Two hundred years ago the Northwest Territories included portions of northern Ohio and Indiana, Michigan, and the western expanses of Illinois and Wisconsin. In an era before airports, railroads, or even rudimentary roads, rivers defined how people moved, where they settled, and how commerce was conducted. The importance of water transportation cannot be overstated. For the rivers and streams of the Great Lakes watershed, the open waters of the Great Lakes provided the central hub of the wheel of water transportation.

The modern era of water transportation on the Great Lakes began with the opening of the Erie Canal in 1825. For the first time, the Upper Lakes had a waterborne link with the eastern seaboard. The 363-mile long canal employed 83 locks as it extended its reach from the Hudson River across the Mohawk Valley to Lake Erie. Four years later in 1829, the Welland Canal bypassed Niagara Falls, making navigation possible between Lake Ontario and Lake Erie and opening the lower St. Lawrence River to shipping from the Upper Lakes. The 333-mile long Ohio and Erie Canal, connecting Cleveland to the Ohio River at Portsmouth, opened the lakes to river traffic from the continental interior in 1832. The 97-mile long Illinois and Michigan Canal opened in 1848. It connected Chicago with the Illinois River at the town of LaSalle, forming a link with the Mississippi River System. Other canals were built, all of which contributed to the expansion of shipping traffic on the Great Lakes.

Lake Michigan Ports

Most of the towns on Lake Michigan were established where small rivers empty into the lake. The lower reaches and mouths of the rivers served as unimproved harbors. Unfortunately, the rivers were usually obstructed at their mouths by bars of sand and clay. The bars were formed by soil run-off suspended in the river currents, which became deposited when the current met the still waters of

Fish tug at Gills Rock, Wisconsin. Many ports on Lake Michigan still support small commercial fishing operations.

the lake. These bars at natural river mouths frequently had little more than two or three feet of water over them. Some of the bars closed up the entrance completely only to find water depths of twelve to fifteen feet or more a short distance inside the bar. Similar conditions existed at towns established on smaller lakes connected to Lake Michigan along its eastern shore. Sometimes only a shallow creek connected the deep waters of the inland lake to the deeper waters of Lake Michigan. Often there was no connection at all, the two lakes being separated by an expanse of solid beach.

On the western shore of Lake Michigan, the river channels also had a tendency to be deflected in a southerly direction from a straight course into the lake by shore currents driven before the prevailing

Process of Lightering

northerly winds. The shore currents bent the natural channel off at a right angle and carried it parallel to the shoreline to form a long spit of sand between the river and the lake. Thus deflected, the river quickly became much more shallow and would often run one-half mile or more before rejoining the lake.

If a ship was unable to enter a harbor due to shoal water, there was little choice but to stand offshore at anchor and discharge passengers and cargo from there. Smaller rowboats and scows would come out to make the exchange. Often large, flat-bottomed, shallow-draft barges called "lighters" were specifically built for this purpose as they provided more stability than a small boat for large amounts of heavy cargo. The process was called "lightering." Just getting the barge or lighter into position to be loaded posed problems as it either had to be towed out to the anchored ship or manually walked out by a number of men using long poles.

Loading and discharging cargo from a schooner in the early days of sail was always a physically demanding process. The process was sorely exacerbated if lightering proved necessary as the cargo had to be handled several times before reaching its final destination ashore. Obviously the whole process of unloading a ship swinging at anchor could only be accomplished under the calmest weather conditions. Lightering was dangerous but tolerated on the occasions it was needed as commerce continued to grow. Lightering, however, underscored the greater dangers of navigation on Lake Michigan. During storms, an impassable harbor entrance placed a ship and its crew in the untenable position of having no place to run for shelter. Improved harbors were urgently needed.

White Shoal Light

Early Lake Lights

While the work of improving harbor entrances progressed, "landfall" lights were established to help navigators find the general location of a port along the vast, undistinguished wilderness shoreline. By 1837, sixteen lake harbors had beacons or lighthouses for the safety of mariners. Typically, the lighthouses were placed on a high bluff adjacent to a harbor entrance. If no such high ground was available, they were built on a prominent point of land as close to the harbor entrance as possible. In both cases, especially at night or in times of reduced visibility, confusion caused groundings and/or complete wrecks as navigators unfamiliar with an area came too close to shore before realizing the actual harbor entrance was still some distance away. The job of entering a harbor became easier once entrance piers were constructed. Lights on the ends of the piers helped navigators discern how to approach and where to enter a harbor.

The early landfall light towers were usually of what is called rubble-stone or split-stone construction. The basic building material, rocks, were collected along the shoreline, in the shallow near-shore waters, or quarried locally so as not to have to be carried too far to the work site. In a few rare instances, locally kilned brick was available. Built by contractors submitting the lowest bid, these towers generally were inferior structures constantly in need of repair or replacement. They were equipped with a lighting system of lamps and reflectors that was grossly inferior to, but far less expensive than, the Fresnel lenses used in Europe. Poor mortar, unable to withstand repeated freeze and thaw cycles, often led to serious cracks in the towers, as did unstable foundations. Water leakage from above and around improperly fitted lantern rooms and their decks added to the problems. A combination of faults eventually brought down the early towers. Site erosion also caused the loss of some towers.

Given the bid process used to get the early towers built, there was no consistency in the quality of construction. It was possible for one party to submit the accepted bid and then subcontract with others for the actual construction. On Lake Michigan, most of the early towers were replaced between 1858 and 1860. Nevertheless, several examples of well-built early towers have survived into the present on the

Old Long Tail Point Light—a surviving rubble-stone tower

Great Lakes. Two have survived on Lake Michigan, one at Baileys Harbor and the other at Long Tail Point, although neither has been used as an aid to navigation for over one hundred and thirty years.

Quality control improved dramatically after the establishment of the Lighthouse Board in October 1852. Instead of using civilian contractors whose skills varied widely, qualified engineers from the ranks of Army Corps personnel were employed to design lighthouses and oversee their construction. In order to save time and money, several standardized lighthouse designs were developed that could be easily modified to fit a particular physical location. For this reason, many of the lights on the Great Lakes are virtually identical. Lighthouses on Lake Michigan whose design was repeated at several locations are indicated in the site review that follows. It should be noted, however, that each of the Great Lakes also saw lighthouses established with very unique designs.

Early Harbor Improvements

Where a river mouth was diverted to the south, the solution was to dredge a channel from the point of the bend across the neck of the sand spit straight into the deep water of Lake Michigan. Likewise, where a large inland lake was inadequately connected to Lake Michigan, a connecting channel was dredged. In all cases, harbors were improved by constructing nearly parallel piers from just upstream of a river's mouth or the start of a dredged channel into the deeper water of the lake. The piers were constructed two hundred feet apart or less, as close to one another as practical, so that river freshets would wash away any sand that tended to settle in the channel between the piers. The immediate goals were to deepen the channel entrance via dredging and to prevent the formation of another bar. As lake vessels became larger, they required a greater harbor depth, and the parallel piers were extended into still deeper water. However, it soon became apparent that extending the piers repeatedly would provide but temporary relief at disproportionate cost. The point of diminishing returns was soon reached as the natural processes that formed the original bars were still in operation. In later years, as piers fell into disrepair and needed to be reconstructed, they were actually shortened at some harbors with little ill effect. Dredging remains the only remedy adequate to maintain present harbor depths.

Initial harbor improvements were often funded by private business interests whose prosperity depended on consistent water transportation in and out of their particular ports. The Federal government got involved after a law was passed in 1826 making funds available for the examination, survey, and improvement of the harbors on the "northern lakes." Federal harbor improvements in the period from 1824 to 1839 and after the Civil War were carried out under the direction of the U.S. Army Corps of Engineers. After 1828 and until 1863, the improvements were under the direction of the Corps of Topographical Engineers. Army engineers were chosen to work on these civil projects because few qualified civilian engineers were available. Also, employment on civil works provided the military engineers with experience of benefit to the nation in time of war, and the harbor works came to be considered important to the national defense. Army engineers were responsible only for construction of the improvements, not their lighting. The onset of the Civil War interrupted harbor improvement work except at a few ports considered essential to the war effort. All projects resumed after the war ended.

Algoma North Pierhead Light

Grand Haven South Pierhead Light and catwalk at night

Pier and Breakwater Construction

In the early years of Great Lakes harbor construction, piers were built of square or rectangular timber cribs made of logs flattened on two sides and between twenty and thirty feet long. The crib logs were notched together in much the same way as the walls of a log cabin. Fastened with wooden pegs or iron bolts, the crib structure was strengthened inside with cross beams. Constructed on or near shore, the crib sections were floated into position, filled with stones gathered from the shore or nearby fields, and sunk upon the natural bottom of the lake. Once a string of cribs was in place, a superstructure, usually of sawed timber one foot thick, was built over them to a height of six to seven feet above the normal water level. The superstructure was then filled with stones and planked over to form a level deck. This planking is very evident in many of the old pier light photographs that follow.

There were variations in pier construction and much local experimentation to offset recurring problems. Very early piers, built higher than they were wide, were not strong enough to withstand beating by waves, wind, and ice. Construction methods evolved to solve these problems, but as long as timber was used in building piers, frequent repairs were required on all the above-water portions of the structure. Wooden piers were also susceptible to fires started by the exhaust cinders of passing steamers, which were usually fueled by wood or coal. In a few recorded instances, lightning strikes provided a source of ignition. Between 1916 and 1930, the U.S. Army Corps of Engineers rebuilt all of the wooden piers with stone and concrete, usually using the original timber cribs as a stable base, and reinforcing the vertical sides with corrugated steel sheet piling.

Breakwaters were later added offshore to better protect harbor entrances. Wind and waves building from the wrong direction often resulted in a storm surge that would funnel right up between the piers into the inner harbor and wreak havoc on ships already docked. After the Civil War, a modification of the basic pier plan included one or more breakwaters constructed offshore and set at angles to the harbor entrance in order to dissipate the storm surge.

Establishment of Pier Lights

Lake Michigan ports, more than any of the others on the Great Lakes, are known for their lighthouses on piers and breakwaters. Structures built to house lights on the outer end of a pier are referred to as "pierhead" lights. Early pierhead lights were built of wood as that material was readily available and easily worked. Wood was also light in weight and would not overstress a timber crib foundation. Pierhead lights had to be strong in order to withstand the impact of waves and vibrations, yet compact in size because of the limited space available on the piers. As piers were extended out into deeper and deeper water, the lights

Menominee Rear Range Light—September 14, 1941

at their ends were repeatedly picked up and moved out to the new end. At many ports, a system of range lights was established on one of the piers as an aid to navigators in lining up their approach to the harbor entrance. Usually, a rear range light structure was erected on the pier closer to shore with the pierhead light serving as the front light of the range.

The keeper assigned to maintain pier lights usually lived in a dwelling on shore near the base of the pier. To provide a means of access to the light structure during periods of stormy weather when large waves would break over the pier, an elevated walkway or catwalk was built back along the length of the pier to shore. Early catwalks were also built of wood. Using a catwalk to get back and forth from a pier light was no stroll in the park. Wind, waves, rain, ice, and snow often made their use a dicey business. Many keepers recorded harrowing experiences encountered while tending a pier light during inclement weather.

Wooden structures do not age well in a harsh marine environment and maintenance was a constant problem. In addition, the hazard of fire remained a concern as long as liquid fuel and an open flame served as the light source. A nearly ideal material was found in cast iron, which became a prominent building material after the mid-1850s. Cast iron was light when compared with stone and brick, in-

Sturgeon Bay Ship Canal North Pierhead Light

expensive, stronger than wood, watertight, and it had a very slow rate of deterioration. Eventually, cast-iron structures of various designs were used to replace the older wooden pier lights. Catwalks were also rebuilt using cast-iron supports.

Not Safe Yet

Once a harbor entrance was dredged, piers constructed, and lights established, a ship running before a storm still was not out of harm's way. In rough weather it was difficult for early lake vessels, many of which still navigated under sail, to proceed safely into a harbor entrance that was no more than two hundred feet wide. Liken the process to threading the eye of a needle while riding a roller coaster. Judging the combined effects of wind and weather along with the handling characteristics of a particular ship required an almost exquisite sense of timing on the part of lake captains. Once committed to entering a harbor, if a vessel was going to get into trouble it was going to happen right at the piers. Many did not make it. Some missed the opening altogether and ended up on the beach. Sometimes these ships could be salvaged after the storm if the surf had not beaten them to pieces. Some collided with the end of the pier and carried off the pier light in the process. The seriously wounded usually holed themselves and sank soon thereafter.

In an attempt to correct this problem, the parallel pier on the weather side was often extended beyond the other, thus acting as a breakwater behind which vessels could right themselves before proceeding into the harbor entrance. For this reason, most of the north piers at Lake Michigan ports extend farther out into the lake than their southern counterparts.

Offshore Breakwaters

After the Civil War, a modification of the basic pier plan included one or more detached breakwaters constructed offshore and set at angles to the harbor entrance in order to dissipate the force of wave action at the entrance. This would reduce damage caused by storm surges within the confines of the

Frankfort North Breakwater Light

inner harbor. Vessel captains soon observed that the protected area behind a well-placed breakwater was a good place to seek immediate refuge from a storm without the risk of approaching a harbor's entrance piers. The benefit of offshore breakwaters in protecting lakefront property also became apparent as they permitted the development of additional docking facilities outside the confines of a port's inner river harbor. The first breakwaters at Chicago were completed by the mid-1870s. During the 1880s, the construction of a large breakwater encompassing almost the entire Milwaukee lakefront commenced and in the 1890s breakwaters were provided for other harbors. The scope of these projects was later expanded as increases in commerce and vessel traffic dictated. The protected area enclosed behind offshore breakwaters at a given port came to define its outer harbor or Harbor of Refuge.

Later Enhancements

Gradually, the idea of a completely enclosed and protected outer harbor consisting of a wave-stilling basin emerged. A stilling basin is enclosed by breakwaters or piers that converge to an entrance opening in deep water beyond the original entrance piers. The basin allows waves that do get in past the breakwaters to expand and lose force instead of being conducted through the confined channel between the parallel piers. The stiller water inside the basin provides vessels with calmer conditions for making their approach to the inner entrance piers. A variation in this harbor design called the "arrowhead" was introduced on Lake Michigan after 1905. Such a harbor consists of two breakwaters connected to shore north and south of the original piers that converge at a ninety-degree angle offshore to form a new harbor entrance. Where necessary, the original piers were then shortened so as to clear the area comprising the outer harbor. Harbors of this type on Lake Michigan include Frankfort, Holland, Ludington, Manistee, and Muskegon.

Establishment of Breakwater Lights

Breakwater lights were established as breakwaters neared completion. As breakwater lights were the first encountered by approaching vessels, they soon became the prominent lights at many ports. Pier lights at many locations were scaled back in intensity or eliminated altogether. Between 1916 and 1930, Federal harbor improvement work on the Great Lakes mainly consisted of completing earlier projects, replacing wooden pier and breakwater superstructures with concrete, general repair and maintenance, and dredging to maintain harbor depths.

Gary Breakwater Light

Lighthouse Administration

The first Public Works Act and only the ninth law passed by the First Congress of the United States on August 7, 1789, was the creation of the Lighthouse Establishment. The law transferred authority over existing Colonial lighthouses and those subsequently to be established to the Federal government. The practice of charging dues or tolls to passing vessels was eliminated. Instead, lighthouses would be supported by general tax revenues and could be used by all vessels free of charge. Congress gave authority over lighthouses to the Treasury Department, which retained control until 1903, when jurisdiction went to the Commerce Department. The Secretary of the Treasury directly supervised lighthouse operations from 1789 to 1792 and again from 1802 through 1813, but delegated this responsibility to the Commissioner of Revenue from 1792 to 1802 and from 1813 to 1820.

*Steamer **Herbert C. Jackson**, 690 feet long and 75 feet wide, one of several lake freighters on which the author served.*

The Fifth Auditor

From 1820 through 1852, responsibility for constructing and operating lighthouses was vested in the Fifth Auditor of the United States Treasury, who held the title of "General Superintendent of Lights." During this entire period, the post was held by Stephen Pleasonton, who was responsible not only for lighthouses but also audited the records of a half-dozen Federal agencies. Pleasonton's time was divided among many unrelated tasks. He appears not to have had any interest in lighthouses other than to get them built as cheaply as possible and only if absolutely necessary. Pleasonton's period of lighthouse administration is often labeled the era of "the lowest bidder," during which many lighthouses of poor quality were built and whose lighting systems quickly became dated.

Part of the problem was Pleasonton's heavy reliance on Winslow Lewis, a former ship captain, for technical assistance. At the time, Lewis's credentials must have appeared impressive. In 1810, Lewis obtained a patent in the U.S. for a lighting system for lighthouses using Argand lamps backed with parabolic reflectors that intensified and directed the light. The system was virtually identical to the process Lewis had seen used in Europe. The Federal government purchased Lewis's patent rights in 1812 and awarded him a contract to convert the nation's lighthouses to his new system, a task he completed over the next three years. Thereafter Lewis retained the rights to manufacture and supply the system for new construction. Without a doubt, it was in the best financial interest of Winslow Lewis to ingratiate himself to Stephen Pleasonton when he arrived in office. Over the ensuing years, their cozy relationship effectively blocked from U.S. lighthouses the technically superior lighting system using Fresnel lenses that had been adopted in Europe. From a fiscal standpoint, Pleasonton was the consummate bureaucrat, but his policies were extremely short-sighted. Pleasonton never developed an appreciation for the importance of lighthouses to the safety of men and ships at sea.

Little Sable Light

The Lighthouse Board

By 1850, American lighthouses were among the worst in the world. Criticism of Pleasonton's administration had been building for years and peaked in March 1851, when Congress ordered a full-scale investigation to be conducted by the Secretary of the Treasury. The final report, some 760 pages long, came out in January 1852, and prompted Congress to create a completely new lighthouse administration. The resulting nine-member Lighthouse Board, composed mainly of military officers, formally came into existence on October 9, 1852. Between 1852 and 1860, 26 new lights were established on the Great Lakes, raising the total from 71 to 102.

Also during this time, in all the earlier towers deemed worth saving, the old Winslow Lewis lighting system was replaced by the brighter and more efficient Fresnel lenses already in use abroad. By the beginning of the twentieth century, the Lighthouse Board oversaw 334 major lights, 67 fog signals, and 563 buoys on the Great Lakes. The Lighthouse Board proved to be very successful in lighting U.S. waters, and American lighthouses came to be included among the best in the world.

Bureau of Lighthouses

Changes in lighthouse administration followed in later years. As the number of lighthouses and other aids to navigation increased, the Lighthouse Board became cumbersome. Various critics of the Board began to call for a more streamlined agency run by a single executive officer. In June 1910, Congress officially abolished the Lighthouse Board and replaced it with a Bureau of Lighthouses, commonly called the Lighthouse Service. The new Lighthouse Service was a civilian organization run by a single officer, the Commissioner of Lighthouses, who reported to the Department of Commerce. The first and longest serving Commissioner was George R. Putnam, who served in the post from 1910 until his retirement in 1935. A civil engineer and surveyor by training, Putnam proved to be a visionary leader who oversaw the continued expansion of the Service and kept it at the forefront of technical and scientific advances.

Cana Island Light

Return to Military Control

A governmental consolidation and reorganization inspired by President Franklin D. Roosevelt abolished the Bureau of Lighthouses on July 7, 1939. Oversight of the nation's lighthouses was transferred to the U.S. Coast Guard, then a part of the Treasury Department. Supposedly, the change in administration was done in the interest of efficiency and economy. More likely, Roosevelt probably sensed the coming world war and wanted America's vital aids to navigation back under military control. The Coast Guard was absorbed into the U.S. Navy on November 1, 1941 and remained there until January 1, 1946, when it returned to the Treasury Department. The Coast Guard became a part of the new Department of Transportation in 1967, where it remains today. Through all of these administrative changes, consistent quality control practices were established for the construction, lighting, and operation of the nation's aids to navigation.

Evolution of the Lighting Apparatus

System of Lamps and Reflectors

The light source is the heart of a lighthouse. Smoke, soot, and fumes were problems associated with wood, coal, and candles used in the earliest towers, none of which produced a very bright light when burned. Various oils burned brightly, but the smoke produced obscured the light. Aime Argand, a French scientist, developed a smokeless oil lamp in 1782. Prior to this design, the wicks in use were solid and either round or flat in shape. Smoke was produced as the outer edges burned before the center, which smoldered. Argand lamps used a tubular wick that burned brighter and cleaner as there was good air flow on both sides. The smokeless flame produced a light equivalent to seven candles. The use of an Argand lamp in combination with a parabolic reflector constructed of copper and coated with silver was first tested in 1784. The use of a reflector with a lamp is known as the "catoptric" system and it greatly improved the strength and directional control of the light. The lamp produced a steady flame from a wick needing only to be trimmed and adjusted a few times each night. The parabolic reflector directed the rays that reflected off its surface out to the mariner in a horizontal cone. The power of the light was increased by placing many lamps backed by reflectors around a metal frame. The resulting assembly was called an "array." The use of parabolic reflectors not only intensified the light produced, they also provided a means to alter its characteristic so it could be differentiated from other lights in the vicinity. The characteristic of the light displayed became a result of how the lamps and reflectors were clustered on the frame and how fast the entire array was rotated. Use of the catoptric system was quickly implemented in Europe.

Having spotted a good thing, Winslow Lewis, an opportunistic American sea captain, made minor design modifications to the European catoptric system and patented it for use in the U.S. in 1810. It came to be known, not surprisingly, as the Winslow Lewis Patent System and was placed in every U.S. lighthouse by 1816. Any catoptric system, however, was an inefficient one where even the best design available still allowed most of the light produced to escape vertically and to the sides of the reflector. Only 17% of the light from each lamp was reflected out to sea. Making matters worse, the reflectors required frequent cleaning and polishing, which quickly dulled their reflective surfaces. To make a lighthouse truly effective, it was necessary to snare the strong light and somehow direct it to the horizon. Working independently, several early experimenters developed a crude refracting lens that bent the light and therefore pointed it in a desired direction. The use

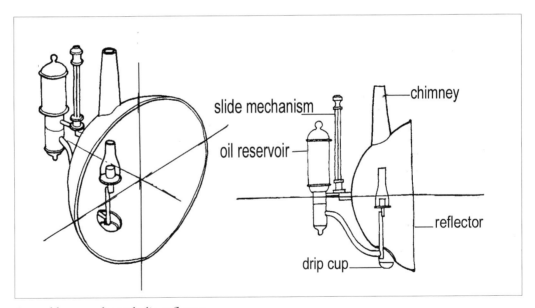

Argand lamp and parabolic reflector

of a refractive lens alone is known as a "dioptric" system. Unfortunately for mariners in American waters, the Winslow Lewis System remained in use through 1852, long after its inferiority to Fresnel lenses had been demonstrated.

The Fresnel Lens

Augustin Fresnel (pronounced: Frä-nel), a French physicist and civil engineer, developed an optical system for lighthouses in 1822 that was vastly superior to all systems previously known. Fresnel united in a single lens system, called "catadioptric," both the catoptric and dioptric approaches to focusing light. Fresnel abandoned the use of multiple lamps and reflectors and replaced them with a single larger lamp placed at the center, or focal point, of a cylindrical lens. Resembling a glass beehive with a brass framework, Fresnel's original lens was composed of a central panel of magnifying prisms. The panel was surrounded above and below by concentric rings of mirrors properly angled to gather the escaping light and intensify it into a narrow horizontal beam redirected seaward. After his death in 1827, rings of glass prisms that both refracted and reflected were substituted for the reflecting mirrors because they absorbed less light and required less maintenance. Unlike the simple refractive lenses of his predecessors, Fresnel's lenses included corrections based on formulas he had developed for spherical aberrations, light-wave interference, double-refractions, and polarization. This was pretty radical science for the early 1820s. Ultimately, a Fresnel lens transmitted fully 85% of the available lamp light, a considerable improvement over the catoptric system. The new lenses typically doubled the 5 to 8 mile visible range of the existing lighthouses to a range of 10 to 16 miles or more.

Third order Fresnel lens from Big Sable Light

The Fresnel lens was immediately adopted for use by England and France, where industries were launched to manufacture it. Well-known suppliers were Chance Brothers of England and the three French firms of Henry Lepaute; Sautter, Lemonier & Cie; and Barbier & Fenestre. French manufacturers supplied most of the Fresnel lenses eventually used in the U.S. Fresnel lenses were designed to produce identifiable characteristics if so ordered. A flashing lens had flash panels called bullseyes arranged around the focal plane of the lens to funnel light into separate beams, thus producing a flash. Flash panels outside the lens could also be used.

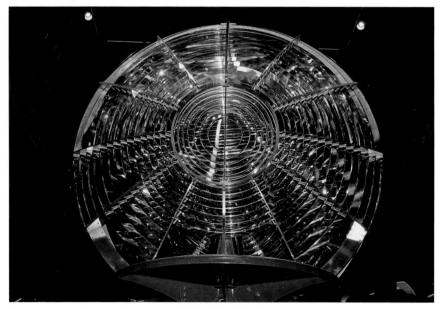

Second order Fresnel lens from White Shoal Light

To create a flash, only the lens or the external flash panel was rotated. The central lamp remained stationary.

Technical superiority aside, Fresnel lenses were very expensive to have manufactured in France, transported, and installed. The miserly Superintendent of Lighthouses, Stephen Pleasonton, blocked their adoption in the U.S. Pleasonton's resistance to the new lenses undoubtedly was influenced by his chief technical advisor, Winslow Lewis. Both had a vested interest in maintaining the status quo: Lewis to preserve a long-standing and lucrative government contract to supply his lighting system; Pleasonton to save money and face. Once Pleasonton was replaced by the Lighthouse Board late in 1852, the Fresnel lens was quickly put into service nationally...almost thirty years after its widespread use in Europe. Between 1852 and 1859, all of the older lighthouses—including those on the Great Lakes—were retrofitted with Fresnel lenses. Once in place, the lenses were cared for like precious jewels. Inventors had also been at work improving the central lamp and newer, more efficient designs replaced the old Argand type. Despite their initial cost, Fresnel lenses usually paid for themselves within a few years in reduced fuel costs as there was only one lamp to light.

Fresnel lenses were originally classified into six sizes or "orders" ranging from one to six with the numbers indicating the size and intensity of the light. However, seven sizes exist because a "third and one-half" order lens was later added. A first order lens has an internal diameter of six feet and stands almost eight feet tall without its pedestal and other supporting hardware. This size was used only in the largest seacoast lights. The second order lens, which stands about six feet tall, was the largest size ever used on the Great Lakes. Many coastal and harbor lighthouses on the Great Lakes employed third and fourth order lenses in their towers. A sixth order lens had an internal diameter of about one foot and stands just 18 inches high. Typically, this size of lens was used on pier and breakwater lights. Toward the end of the nineteenth century, a size larger than the first order called a "hyper-radical" lens was built but never installed in the continental United States. These lights were installed at significant landfall points like Cape Race, Newfoundland and Makapuu Point, Oahu, Hawaii.

Squaw Island Light

Plum Island Rear Range Light

Illuminants

Sperm whale oil burned cleanly and produced a bright light, thus remaining very popular until the mid-nineteenth century. The United States relied heavily on it until sperm whales became scarce due to over hunting. Disruptions in shipping caused by the Civil War also limited supplies. Those combined factors caused the cost of whale oil to increase sharply from $.50 per gallon in 1840 to $2.43 per gallon by 1863, forcing the Lighthouse Board to search for cheaper alternatives. Experiments by noted scientists were commissioned to analyze several grades and combinations of whale, shark, fish, seal, colza, lard, and mineral oils in search of a cheaper fuel. Colza oil, derived from cabbage seeds, had all the necessary properties of an inexpensive fuel source and was the primary fuel used in European lighthouses at the time. Unfortunately, it had to be imported as wild cabbages were not commonly grown in the U.S. and farmers could not be induced to grow enough of it. Continued testing of lard oil revealed it burned well if preheated and it certainly was cheap. Lard oil became the standard illuminant between 1864 and 1867.

Despite the standard use of lard oil, experimentation continued with other types of fuels. A new set of trials with mineral oil or kerosene proved successful and in 1877 the Lighthouse Board began to convert lights to the new fuel. Kerosene, however, did not become the standard illuminant until the early 1880s after the invention of the incandescent oil vapor (IOV) lamp. In an IOV, kerosene is mixed with air under pressure creating a fine volatile mist that soaks a mantle where it burns with a bright light, much like a modern Coleman lantern. Compared to wick type lamps, the IOV generated a brighter light with no increase in fuel consumption. Kerosene is highly flammable and its use necessitated the construction of oil storage houses outside and away from the dwellings and towers at most light stations.

Acetylene gas was pioneered in Sweden after 1900 and revolutionized lighting technology. It was contained in cylinders and made automated lights possible in remote areas. An acetylene gas lamp was controlled by a sun valve that turned on the flow of gas at night and turned it off during the day.

Before the incandescent electric light bulb was perfected, other forms of creating light with electricity were tried. One of these was the electric arc lamp. Carbon rods carrying the electric current created a very bright arc, but the rods had to be moved together gradually as the carbon burned away. The Lighthouse Board installed electric arc lights in the torch of the Statue of Liberty in New York Harbor in 1886, making it the first use of electricity in the United States for lighthouse purposes. The electrification of lighthouses on the Great Lakes began in the early 1920s, but did

Poverty Island Light

not become widespread until a dependable public utility power grid and inexpensive portable generators were available. Although many original Fresnel lenses remain in use, most have been replaced by modern optics that employ the same physical principles but require little maintenance as they are molded of clear acrylic plastic. All lights have automatic bulb changers. These changers hold several bulbs and automatically rotate a new bulb into position when the bulb in use burns out. Since there is no less expensive source of power than the sun, almost all of the lighthouses on the Great Lakes are now solar powered. A solar panel is composed of photovoltaic cells that convert sunlight into direct current electricity for recharging storage batteries that supply electricity to the light at the onset of darkness.

Pilot Island Light

Chronology of Great Lakes Lighthouses

1782

♦ *The first lighthouse on the Great Lakes was erected by the British on the roof of the old French Castle within Fort Niagara on Lake Ontario at the mouth of the Niagara River. This first of three lights at Fort Niagara, little more than a short wooden tower, remained in service until 1796 or later when the British relinquished the fort to American forces after the Revolutionary War. Thereafter, they retired to the opposite, western side of the river.*

1789

♦ *The first Public Works Act and only the ninth law passed by the First Congress of the United States created the Lighthouse Establishment as an administrative unit of the Federal government. Jurisdiction over the nation's aids to navigation, which were to be supported by appropriations out of general revenues, was vested in the Treasury Department. From 1789 until 1820, operational oversight alternated between the Secretary of the Treasury and the Commissioner of Revenue.*

1804

♦ *Newark Light, the first freestanding masonry lighthouse on the Great Lakes, was built by the British on Lake Ontario at Mississauga Point, opposite Fort Niagara at the mouth of the Niagara River. Useful to both sides during the War of 1812, it was spared by combatants and remained in operation throughout the war. The Newark Light was razed by the British after the war in 1814 to clear the site for the construction of Fort George.*

1808

♦ *Gibraltar Point Light was established on Lake Ontario at Toronto. Heightened in 1832, the lighthouse continued in service until 1958. Lovingly maintained by the City of Toronto, Gibraltar Point Light remains the oldest intact lighthouse on the Great Lakes.*

1812

♦ *Congress authorized the purchase of the patent held by Winslow Lewis for his lighting system consisting of Argand lamps and parabolic reflectors. Lewis was contracted to install the system in every U.S. lighthouse.*

1818

♦ *The first Canadian lighthouse on Lake St. Clair, located between lakes Erie and Huron, was established at the mouth of the Thames River. Heightened in 1867, by 1970 the Thames River Light was close to collapse due to a failing foundation. The lighthouse was completely dismantled, stone by stone, and rebuilt between 1973 and 1975. Returned to service thereafter, it remains the oldest Canadian lighthouse in operation on the Great Lakes.*

1819

♦ *The first two U.S. lighthouses on Lake Erie were established at Buffalo, New York and Presque Isle, now Erie, Pennsylvania.*

1820

♦ *The first U.S. lighthouse on Lake Ontario was established at Galloo Island.*

1820-1852

♦ *Responsibility for lighthouse administration was assigned to the Fifth Auditor of the Treasury, Stephen Pleasonton, who was given the title of General Superintendent of Lights.*

1822

♦ *Augustin Fresnel, French physicist, developed the lens that bears his name. The lens provided lighthouses with an optically superior lighting system that was quickly adopted throughout Europe.*

1822

- Sandusky Bay Light was established in Ohio on Lake Erie at the western entrance to Sandusky Bay. Renamed Marblehead Light in 1870, it remains the oldest lighthouse in continuous operation on the Great Lakes.

1825

- The Erie Canal was opened, connecting Buffalo, New York on Lake Erie to Albany, New York on the Hudson River. The canal opened the Great Lakes to the eastern seaboard and international trade.

- Fort Gratiot Light, the first U.S. lighthouse on Lake Huron, was established at the lake's southern outlet near the head of the St. Clair River. Located in what is now the city of Port Huron, Fort Gratiot Light was also the first lighthouse in Michigan.

1829

- The Welland Canal was opened, bypassing Niagara Falls to connect lakes Erie and Ontario.

1830

- The first Canadian lighthouse on Lake Erie was established at Long Point.

1832

- The first two lighthouses on Lake Michigan were established at Chicago, Illinois and St. Joseph, Michigan.

- The first lightship on the Great Lakes was stationed in northern Lake Michigan at Waugoshance Shoal.

1837

- Pottawatomie Light, the first lighthouse in Wisconsin, was established on Rock Island.

1837

- The first lighthouse in Indiana was established at Michigan City.

1838

- Windmill Point Light, the first U.S. lighthouse on Lake St. Clair, was established at the lake's southern outlet to mark the head of the Detroit River.

1839

- The first publication approaching what is known today as the "Light List" was "Lighthouses, Beacons, and Floating Lights of the United States" issued by the Treasury.

1841

- The first Fresnel lens in the U.S. was installed at Navesink Lighthouse, New Jersey to evaluate its effectiveness.

1847

- The first Canadian lighthouse on Lake Huron was established at Goderich.

1848

- The Illinois and Michigan Canal was opened, connecting Chicago to the Mississippi River System.

1849

- The first two U.S. lighthouses on Lake Superior were established at Whitefish Point and Copper Harbor, both in Michigan.

1850

- The rudiments of what would become the Lateral System of Buoyage were adopted for the U.S. by an Act of Congress.

1851

♦ *Waugoshance Light in northern Lake Michigan became the first offshore lighthouse built on a timber crib foundation on the Great Lakes.*

1852

♦ *The nine-member U.S. Lighthouse Board, which would administer the lighthouse system until July 1, 1910, was officially formed.*

1852-1859

♦ *Fresnel lenses were installed in all U.S. lighthouses.*

1852-1909

♦ *Each year during this period, the Annual Report of the Lighthouse Board was published.*

1858

♦ *The first three Canadian lighthouses on Georgian Bay were established at Cove Island, Griffith Island, and Nottawasaga Island.*

♦ *A revised form of "Lighthouses, Beacons, and Floating Lights of the United States" was issued by the Lighthouse Board.*

1864-1867

♦ *During this period, lard oil became the standard illuminant for use in U.S. lighthouses, replacing sperm whale oil.*

1867

♦ *The first Canadian lighthouse on Lake Superior was established at Talbot Island.*

1869

♦ *From this date on, generally, the Lighthouse Board published a "Light List" every year. The same year, the U.S. Lighthouse Service adopted a distinctive flag. It was a triangular pennant with a red border bearing a blue lighthouse on a white field.*

1870

♦ *An Act of Congress directed the Lighthouse Board to mark all pierheads belonging to the United States situated on the northern and northwestern lakes, as soon as it was notified that the construction or repair of the pierheads had been completed.*

1875

♦ *The first steam-powered fog signal on the Great Lakes was installed at South Manitou Island Light Station on Lake Michigan.*

1877

♦ *Kerosene, first refined by a Canadian, came into tentative use within the U.S. Lighthouse Service. By 1885, after the invention and proliferation of the incandescent oil vapor lamp, kerosene became the standard illuminant.*

1884

♦ *The Lighthouse Board introduced a uniform for male lighthouse keepers, as well as for masters, mates, and engineers of lightships and tenders, and made the wearing of both dress and fatigue uniforms mandatory.*

1886

♦ *The first use of electricity at a U.S. Lighthouse was in the Statue of Liberty in New York Harbor, which served as an aid to navigation until 1902.*

1891

♦ *The first U.S. lightships with self-propelling power were constructed. Prior to this, they were towed to and from their assigned stations.*

1903

♦ *By an Act of Congress, the Lighthouse Service was transferred from the Treasury Department to the newly created Department of Commerce and Labor.*

1910

♦ An Act of Congress abolished the Lighthouse Board and created the Bureau of Lighthouses to have complete control of the Lighthouse Service. The new bureau was a civilian agency overseen by a single executive officer, the Commissioner of Lighthouses. The first and longest serving Commissioner was George R. Putnam, who served in the post from July 1, 1910, until his retirement in 1935.

1925

♦ The Huron Lightship, stationed at the southern end of Lake Huron, was equipped with the first radio fog signal or radiobeacon on the Great Lakes.

1930

♦ William Livingstone Memorial Light was established on the Detroit River at the eastern end of Belle Isle. Its construction was funded by private donations and it remains the only lighthouse on the Great Lakes constructed of marble.

1939

♦ The Bureau of Lighthouses in the Department of Commerce and its functions were transferred to, consolidated with, and administered as a part of the U.S. Coast Guard in the Treasury Department. The change occurred as part of a governmental consolidation and reorganization inspired by President Roosevelt. Thus lighthouses returned to military control.

1967

♦ The U.S. Coast Guard and its functions were transferred to the newly created Department of Transportation.

1970

♦ The Huron Lightship, the last lightship in service on the Great Lakes, was decommissioned.

1983

♦ The automation of U.S. lighthouses on the Great Lakes was completed on Lake Michigan at Point Betsie, Michigan and Sherwood Point, Wisconsin.

♦ The Great Lakes Lighthouse Keepers Association (GLLKA) was incorporated as a nonprofit organization.

1991

♦ The automation of Canadian lighthouses on the Great Lakes was completed on Georgian Bay at Cove Island and on Lake Superior at Battle and Michipicoten Islands.

2000

♦ An amendment to the Historic Preservation Act called the National Historic Lighthouse Preservation Act 2000, Public Law 106-355, was enacted by Congress. The law places eligible nonprofit groups on an equal footing with other governmental agencies interested in becoming stewards of our nation's lighthouses into the new century.

The Huron Lightship Museum

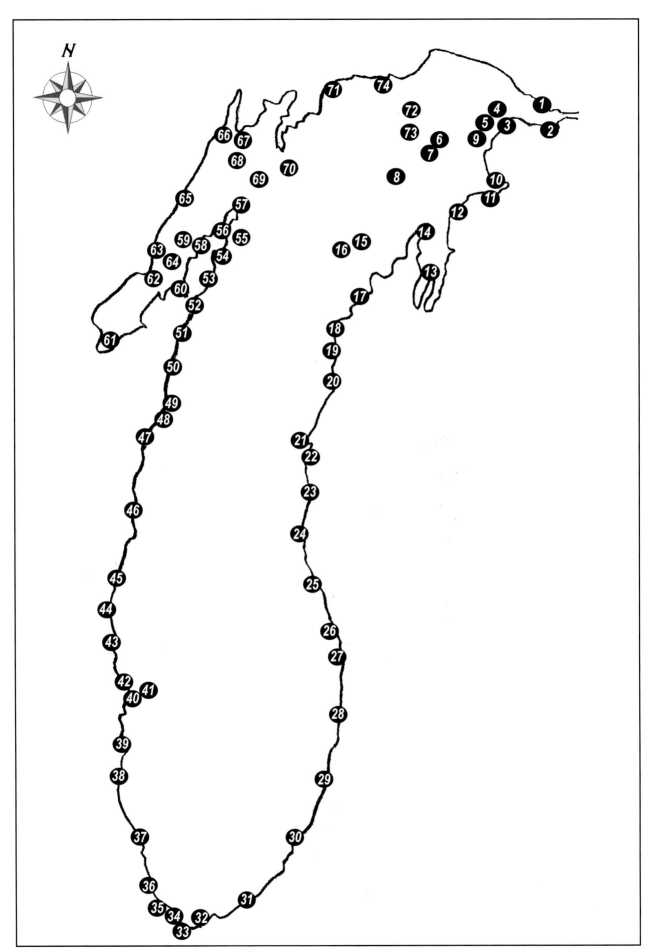

Light Stations of Lake Michigan

1 St. Helena Island

2 McGulpin Point

3 Waugoshance

4 White Shoal

5 Grays Reef

6 St. James

7 Beaver Island

8 South Fox Island

9 Ile Aux Galets

10 Little Traverse

11 Petoskey Breakwater

12 Charlevoix South Pier

13 Old Mission Point

14 Grand Traverse

15 North Manitou Shoal

16 South Manitou Island

17 Manning Memorial

18 Point Betsie

19 Frankfort North Breakwater

20 Manistee North Pierhead

21 Big Sable Point

22 Ludington North Breakwater

23 Pentwater North Pierhead

24 Little Sable

25 White River

26 Muskegon South Pierhead

27 Grand Haven South Pierhead

28 Holland Harbor South Pierhead

29 South Haven South Pierhead

30 St Joseph North Pier

31 Michigan City East Breakwater &
    Old Michigan City

32 Gary Breakwater

33 Buffington Breakwater

34 Old Indiana Harbor &
    Indiana Harbor E Breakwater

35 Calumet Harbor South End

36 Chicago Harbor &
    Southeast Guidewall

37 Grosse Point

38 Waukegan Harbor

39 Kenosha Southport &
    Kenosha Pierhead

40 Racine North Breakwater

41 Racine Reef

42 Wind Point

43 Milwaukee Harbor
    Milwaukee North Point
    Milwaukee Pierhead
    Milwaukee Breakwater

44 Kevich

45 Port Washington North Breakwater
    & Old Port Washington

46 Sheboygan North Breakwater

47 Manitowoc North Breakwater

48 Two Rivers N Pierhead

49 Rawley Point

50 Kewaunee Pierhead

51 Algoma North Pierhead

52 Sturgeon Bay Ship Canal &
    Sturgeon Bay Ship Canal N Pierhead

53 Old Baileys Harbor &
    Baileys Harbor Range

54 Cana Island

55 Pilot Island

56 Plum Island Range

57 Pottawatomie

58 Eagle Bluff

59 Chambers Island

60 Sherwood Point

61 Green Bay Harbor
    Old Long Tail Point
    Grassy Island
    Green Bay Harbor Entrance

62 Peshtigo Reef

63 Menominee N Pier

64 Green Island

65 Cedar River

66 Escanaba Harbor &
    Sand Point

67 Peninsula Point

68 Minneapolis Shoal

69 St. Martin Island

70 Poverty Island

71 Manistique E Breakwater

72 Lansing Shoals

73 Squaw Island

74 Seul Choix

Lake Michigan:

- ◆ *is the second largest Great Lake by volume with 1,180 cubic miles of water*

- ◆ *is the only Great Lake entirely within the United States*

- ◆ *is approximately 118 miles wide and 307 miles long*

- ◆ *has 1,659 miles of shoreline, including many sandy beaches and the world's largest freshwater sand dunes*

- ◆ *averages 279 feet in depth and reaches 925 feet at its deepest point*

- ◆ *has a surface area of approximately 22,300 square miles*

- ◆ *is hydrologically inseparable from Lake Huron, as the two are joined by the wide Straits of Mackinac*

- ◆ *is home to 78 fish species*

Source: *Great Lakes Atlas,* Environment Canada and U.S. Environmental Protection Agency, 1995.

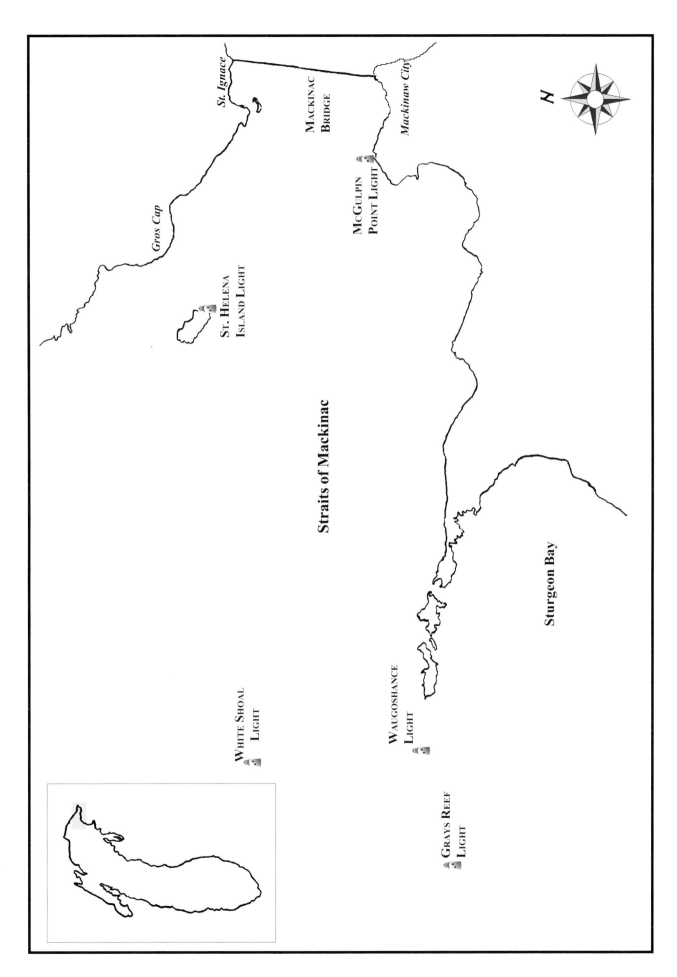

Straits of Mackinac

St. Ignace

Gros Cap

MACKINAC BRIDGE

Mackinaw City

McGULPIN POINT LIGHT

ST. HELENA ISLAND LIGHT

N

Sturgeon Bay

WHITE SHOAL LIGHT

WAUGOSHANCE LIGHT

GRAYS REEF LIGHT

St. Helena Island—A Miracle in the Straits

St. Helena Island is an uninhabited 240-acre island located six and one-half miles west of the Mackinac Bridge and two miles off the coast of Michigan's upper peninsula. A natural harbor on the north side of the island was once the site of a bustling fishing village with over two hundred residents at its peak. The harbor afforded excellent anchorage during westerly and southwesterly gales and also served as a refueling stop for early wood-burning steamers. St. Helena Island Light, located at the southeast tip of the island, marks a shoal that extends offshore in the path of vessels transiting the western Straits of Mackinac.

St. Helena Island Light was first exhibited on September 20, 1873. It consists of a conical, red-brick tower with an overall height of 71 feet. An enclosed passageway connects the tower to a one and one-half-story red-brick keeper's dwelling. The tower and the passageway are painted white. The original optic was a third and one-half order Fresnel lens that produced a fixed red light characteristic. The design of this lighthouse was repeated at three other locations on the Great Lakes. Within a few years of each other, nearly identical structures were built at Poverty Island near the tip of the Garden Peninsula in northern Lake Michigan, and on Lake Huron at Sturgeon Point and Tawas Point.

The light station contained several other structures. In 1895, a wooden boathouse, crib dock, and boatway were built. A brick oil storage house was added the next year. Although there was never a fog signal at St. Helena, an assistant keeper was assigned to the station in 1909. At that time, a one-room wood-framed cabin built behind the lighthouse close to the privy was provided as quarters. This structure proved to be inadequate in size and poorly placed (both smelly and probably unsanitary) due to its close proximity to the privy. It was replaced with a slightly larger cabin relocated north of the oil house in 1915.

St. Helena Island Light was automated with an acetylene gas lamp late in 1922 and the station va-

St. Helena Island Light

cated the following June. Although the tower and light continued to receive periodic maintenance, after automation the dwelling and other structures deteriorated from neglect, exposure to the elements, and vandalism. During a later modernization, the Coast Guard removed the Fresnel lens and lantern room from the tower, replacing them with a plastic optic mounted on a metal pole. By 1980, a Coast Guard survey recommended that all remaining buildings except the light tower be demolished as they came to be considered "attractive nuisances." Soon thereafter the boathouse and assistant keeper's cabin were razed. A similar fate awaited the brick keeper's dwelling if Mother Nature did not accomplish the task first. Then, a miracle happened.

In 1986, the Great Lakes Lighthouse Keepers Association (GLLKA) received a 30-year lease from the Coast Guard to undertake restoration of the light station. Incorporated in 1983, GLLKA is a nonprofit group composed entirely of volunteers. GLLKA had been looking for a project that would provide the

St. Helena Island Light—circa 1875

St. Helena Island Light— August 25, 1914

organization with hands-on experience and credibility in the area of historic preservation. For those readers who have never been inside an abandoned building, let alone one open to the wilds on a remote island, the devastation encountered is almost impossible to describe. The dwelling was a shambles, severely vandalized and long ago stripped of anything of value. One or more vandals started a campfire on the floor of an upstairs bedroom that burned through the floor into the kitchen below. Incredibly, the entire building did not go up in flames. With windows, doors, and a large portion of the roof missing, severe weather-related damage compounded the interior problems. The building was overrun with bats, ducks, mice, and other small creatures. Most of the first two seasons on the island were spent clearing the badly overgrown site, cleaning debris out of the building, evicting the animals, and getting the structure closed up to prevent further damage. All the work was done under the most primitive conditions—no electricity, running water, or toilet facilities. Due to the absence of a dock and shallow offshore waters, all equipment, supplies, and people taken ashore had to be shuttled in via a small motorized Zodiac watercraft. This method of transport remains the only way to get on and off the island.

St. Helena Island Light was added to the National Register of Historic Places in 1988, making it eligible for matching grants from the Bicentennial Lighthouse Fund established by Congress. The following year, GLLKA involved Boy Scout Troop 4 of Ann Arbor and Troop 200 of Calumet/Laurium in the restoration project. Since then, hundreds of Boy and Girl Scouts, adult volunteers, and local area residents have contributed to the restoration effort. Restoration of the lighthouse itself is nearly complete. The oil house and privy have been restored. A crib dock and the assistant keeper's dwelling have been reconstructed. Also, GLLKA created a visitor's display to encourage respect for the light station. Future plans call for the reconstruction of the boathouse. The project has been the recipient of two na-

Exterior view from the south—March 7, 1988

tional "Take Pride in America" awards, a "Hometown Pride Award" given by *Midwest Living Magazine*, and five top "Keep Michigan Beautiful" awards five years in a row. Dozens of articles about the restoration project have been published in newspapers and magazines. On December 9, 1997, GLLKA received a quitclaim deed for the St. Helena Island Light Station. This was accomplished via a process called legislative transfer, thus protecting an investment that would have been in jeopardy at the end of the original 30-year lease. The Coast Guard continues to maintain the light in the tower. So when will the project be done? Never. Although restoration of the lighthouse is nearly complete, emphasis must be placed on the word "nearly." There will always be something to do and there is still plenty of opportunity for anyone interested in becoming involved.

As work on the project began, it became apparent that the young people involved were coming away with an emotional ownership of the place and an awakened interest in the region's maritime history. Consistent with the goal of "developing a new

Interior view—southeast bedroom, May 1986

generation of historic preservationists," GLLKA is using the light station for educational seminars and workshops in the midst of the restoration program. Each summer, GLLKA conducts a week-long Maritime Heritage Education Workshop at St. Helena. Teachers from all around the Great Lakes stay in the old keeper's dwelling or camp in an open meadow behind the dwelling, thus experiencing living conditions that would have been familiar to the original keepers. The goal of the workshops, which began in 1989, is to share ideas and learn about ways to incorporate Great Lakes maritime heritage in primary and secondary education curricula. The workshops have led to the publication of an Education Resource Guide that is regularly updated. GLLKA also sponsors seminars at locations that are easier to reach. To date, over three thousand teachers and youth leaders and approximately forty thousand young people have been reached through GLLKA's educational programs. It is hoped these young people will become the citizens of tomorrow who will continue the work begun at St. Helena Island and other light stations on the Great Lakes.

For a group of volunteers, GLLKA's accomplishments in the areas of restoration, historic preservation, and education have been impressive, but the work continues. Those who would like to learn more about GLLKA, their educational workshops, or the restoration project at St. Helena Island are encouraged to contact:

Great Lakes Lighthouse Keepers Association
c/o Henry Ford Estate
4901 Evergreen Road
Dearborn, MI 48128-1491
Phone: 313-436-9150

Office hours are Tuesday through Friday, 9:30 a.m. to 2:30 p.m.

Status: *Active. Open to public when volunteers are present, which includes most weekends mid-May to Labor Day. Contact the GLLKA office for other potential times.*

Access: *Boat. Although there is a reconstructed dock, extremely low water levels make the approach hazardous. Only beach landings in small craft of very shallow draft should be attempted.*

St. Helena Island Light—viewed from the shoal just offshore

The Mackinac Bridge

The Mackinac Bridge spans the Straits of Mackinac between Mackinaw City and St. Ignace to connect the upper and lower peninsulas of Michigan. Constructed by the State of Michigan, the bridge opened to traffic on November 1, 1957, and replaced a car ferry service operated by the state since 1923. An engineering marvel, the Mighty

The Mackinac Bridge

Mack is the largest suspension bridge in the western hemisphere and the third largest such bridge in the world. For this discussion, it forms the boundary between Lakes Michigan and Huron.

Extremely well lit at night, the bridge was never intended as an aid to navigation but has served this additional function since its completion. Lake sailors could not be happier with this landmark. The main towers of the bridge rise 552 feet above water level. The length of the main span between the towers is 3800 feet with a vertical clearance of 155 feet at the center decreasing to 135 feet at each end—plenty of room for the largest freighters on the Great Lakes. The bridge rendered obsolete Old Mackinac Point Light (1892-1957) in Mackinaw City on Lake Huron.

The lake approaches to the 3000-foot wide shipping channel, which passes directly under the center span, are marked by lighted and unlighted buoys. A racon and fog signal located on the center span are maintained as private aids to navigation by the Mackinac Bridge Authority, the agency responsible for the bridge's operation and maintenance. The bridge and the straits are one of the most impressive sights on the Great Lakes.

The Mackinac Bridge

McGulpin Point Light

McGulpin Point lies about three miles west of Mackinaw City and is the northernmost point of Michigan's lower peninsula. McGulpin Point Light was established in 1869 as a coastal light marking the western approach to the Straits of Mackinac. It consists of a one and one-half-story, rectangular dwelling constructed of cream-colored brick with an attached octagonal brick tower at its northwest corner. The basic design of McGulpin Point Light was repeated at several locations on the Great Lakes, especially on lakes Michigan and Superior. All within a few years of each other, nearly identical structures, varied only by tower placement and shape, were built on Lake Michigan at Chambers Island, Eagle Bluff, and White River.

Almost from the beginning, mariners complained that the light was too far west to be of much use in lining up their approach to the narrowest part of the Straits between Michigan's upper and lower peninsulas. Eventually the light was supplanted by Mackinac Point Light in Mackinaw City and Round Island Light, established, respectively, in 1892 and 1896. McGulpin Point Light was discontinued on December 15, 1906. Shortly thereafter, as was common practice, the lighting apparatus and lantern room were removed from the tower for possible use else-

McGulpin Point Light—circa 1925

where. Removing the lantern room also prevented the structure from being mistaken as an active aid to navigation during daylight hours. The old lighthouse stood vacant and vandalized until it was sold off at public auction between 1912 and 1913. It has remained a private residence ever since.

Status: *Inactive. Private residence. **Please respect the privacy of the owners.***

Access: *McGulpin Point Light cannot be seen from the water as tall trees have grown in front of it. From Mackinaw City, head west on Central Ave. all the way to its end. Turn north (right) at the "T" intersection with CR-81, which is then named Lakehead St. (the same road is called Headlands if you turn left to go south). The lighthouse is on the east (right) side of the road about ¼ mile up just before it begins a descent to the rocky beach. The property is fenced and gated, but a glimpse of the old light is possible through the trees or near the gate.*

McGulpin Point Light

Waugoshance Light

On the northwestern tip of Michigan's lower peninsula, a narrow strip of land called Waugoshance Point juts two miles west from the mainland. The point is further extended almost another six miles by numerous small islands and an extensive bank of shoals. At the end of this shoal bank is the abandoned Waugoshance Light. During the latter half of the nineteenth century and into the first decade of the twentieth, the lighthouse marked the turning point for ships traveling between the Straits of Mackinac and the ports along the eastern shore of Lake Michigan. As ships grew larger, the need for a deeper channel through the shoals resulted in the blasting of Grays Reef Passage about two and one-half miles to the northwest. Grays Reef Passage remains the route in use today.

With water depth of twelve feet or less in this busy area, the shoals were a serious hazard to shipping. In 1832, the first lightship on the Great Lakes was stationed at Waugoshance and remained there during the next 19 shipping seasons. Lightships, however, were expensive to maintain, often dangerous to operate, and easily blown off-station by storms. Lightships were also difficult to get into position at the start of navigation each spring due to ice. A more permanent solution was needed.

Completed in 1851, Waugoshance Light (often referred to locally as Wobbleshanks) became the first offshore lighthouse on the Great Lakes built on a timber crib foundation. The technique had been around for decades but had been used only close to shore for piers and breakwaters, not at exposed sites in open water. The light station consisted of a 76-foot conical, cream-colored brick tower topped by a "bird-cage" style lantern room, built-in living quarters, and a manually operated fog signal bell. Some records indicate that Waugoshance may have housed the first Fresnel lens installed on the Great Lakes.

After the Lighthouse Board came into existence in 1852, they ordered the superior Fresnel lenses for all U.S. lighthouses. The conversion from Argand lamps and silvered reflectors was carried out between 1852 and 1859. At most sites, the change in lighting apparatus meant the old style bird-cage lantern room was removed. With roofs of hammered copper and many small panes of inferior glass, the lantern rooms were often too small to accommo-

Waugoshance Light

date the new lenses. Water leakage around the glass panes was a common problem and the metal sashes supporting the panes interfered with light transmission. Instead, an improved style of multisided or polygonal lantern room was substituted. These only had eight to twelve large panes of glass secured in a strong cast-iron frame-

Waugoshance Light—circa 1910

work topped by a solid cast-iron roof. Somehow, Waugoshance kept its bird-cage lantern room and it remains one of only three such specimens left on the Great Lakes. The other two are at Baileys Harbor, Wisconsin (a ruin) and Selkirk, New York (miraculously, completely intact and in excellent condition).

At its exposed location, the elements took their toll on Waugoshance Light. By 1865, wear and tear from wave action and ice fields necessitated a major renovation of the crib foundation. Originally 32 by 60 feet in size, concrete and large limestone blocks were used to enlarge the protective cribwork to 48 by 66 feet. The process was repeated in 1896, resulting in a final size of 80 by 90 feet. In 1883, the tower and attached keeper's dwelling were encased in a skin of ⅜" thick cast-iron plate to protect spalling brick from further crumbling. At the same time, the fog bell was replaced with a steam-powered fog signal consisting of two 10" whistles. A curved cast-iron building that wrapped around the base of the tower housed the equipment.

Waugoshance Light was discontinued in 1912, made redundant by the establishment in 1910 of White Shoal Light a little farther to the northwest. The deeper water near White Shoal Light afforded mariners a safer approach to Grays Reef Passage. Waugoshance fell into ruin…picked clean of anything worth salvaging, vandalized, and eventually burned out. Waves and ice carried away the improved crib works around the base of the tower. Adding insult to injury, naval aviators in training during the early years of World War II used the station as a target for strafing practice. By 1983, the cast-iron plating on the tower began to peel off and hung there precariously for many years. The plating has since dropped into the lake, leaving the failing brick tower fully exposed to the elements again.

Although Waugoshance Light was placed on the National Register of Historic Places, preservation is unlikely. Eventually the tower will collapse. The threat posed to public safety may someday prompt the Coast Guard to demolish the structure. If and when that happens, the Great Lakes Lighthouse Keepers Association (GLLKA) has requested permission to remove the historical bird-cage lantern room. Meanwhile, Waugoshance remains little more than an empty shell.

Status: *Inactive. In ruins.*

Access: *Boat.*

National Archives

White Shoal Light

White Shoal Light is one of the tallest and most visually stunning lighthouses on the Great Lakes. Located twenty miles due west of the Mackinac Bridge, it sits on the eastern edge of a gravel reef of whitish formation, hence the name. White Shoal extends west from the lighthouse almost two miles and is awash at its western end, which is marked by a buoy. A significant hazard to shipping in the Straits of Mackinac, the shoal was first marked by a lightship in 1891.

A more permanent solution was desired. Lightships were expensive to maintain, frequently blown off station by storms, and difficult to move into position at the start of navigation each spring due to ice. Building a lighthouse in such an exposed location, in this case 25 miles from the nearest protected harbor, was a major engineering feat.

Construction on the massive timber crib and concrete pier to support the

White Shoal Light

White Shoal Light—August 25, 1914

lighthouse began in 1908 and the new light was first displayed on September 1, 1910. The conical tower has a steel skeletal frame, is lined with brick, and faced with dark terra cotta blocks. Eight interior floors were divided into living quarters, storage, work areas, and machinery spaces for equipment to power the fog signal, boat hoist, and other station necessities. Two large doors on the first level opened to accept the station boat when it was lifted out of the water. The tower is 121 feet tall, but add in the height of the crib pier and (depending on the water level) the overall height becomes 140 feet.

White Shoal Light was one of only five U.S. lighthouses on the Great Lakes equipped with a second order Fresnel lens. The other four lighthouses were Grosse Point near Chicago, Spectacle Reef on Lake

Huron, and on Lake Superior, Stannard Rock and Rock of Ages. None of the largest first order lenses was ever used on the Great Lakes. The lens was a "bivalve" or clam shell design. With a diameter over nine feet, the lens floated on a bed of mercury to reduce friction. A weighted clockwork mechanism turned the lens at a speed that produced a flash every eight seconds. The focal plane of the lens was 125 feet above the lake, which gave the light produced a nominal range of 28 miles.

White Shoal Light received its distinctive red and white stripes in 1954. Automation came in 1976. In September 1983, the lens was removed from the tower with great difficulty and replaced with a modern plastic optic. Since 1987 the lens has been on display as the centerpiece of the Great Lakes Shipwreck Museum located next to Whitefish Point Lighthouse on Lake Superior. The lens display, museum, and the restored lighthouse there should *not be missed.*

Status: *Active. Not open to public.*

Access: *Boat.*

Grays Reef Light

Grays Reef is an extensive area of shallow water that extends from Grays Reef Passage west eight and one-half miles to Hog Island. Hog Island is five and one-half miles northeast of Beaver Island. The reef has depths of water ranging from rocks awash to 18 feet. Located just over 20 miles west of the Straits of Mackinac, the reef presented such a serious threat to navigation that it was first marked by a lightship in October 1891. The smaller vessels of that era used what was known as the old West Channel, which lies between the outer eastern end of the reef and the west side of Middle Shoal. That channel has a width of about 1600 feet of deep water but is now unmarked as modern vessels use the improved East Channel.

The East Channel through Grays Reef Passage is the main route for vessels drawing less than 25 feet of water traveling between the Straits of Mackinac and harbors to the south on Lake Michigan. The Passage cuts between Vienna Shoal and East Shoal on the east and Grays Reef and Middle Shoal on the west. Blasted out by the

Grays Reef Light

Federal government in the early 1930s, the improved channel is 3000 feet wide and some 9500 feet long. The channel is marked by lighted and unlighted buoys on both sides and by Grays Reef Light at its southwestern edge.

As the new channel neared completion, a more permanent solution to the lightship was desired. Lightships were dangerous to operate, expensive to maintain, and frequently blown off-station by storms—just when they were needed most. They were also difficult to get into position at the start of navigation in spring due to ice.

Grays Reef Light was far from being the first lighthouse constructed on a timber crib in an exposed offshore location. The process, however, was beset by severe weather and logistical problems in getting work crews and materials out to the site. One workman drowned during construction. Chester Greiling, the engineer and builder, nicknamed it "Gray's Grief." The lighthouse was completed and entered service in 1936.

Grays Reef Light rests on a concrete pier 64 feet square. The entire structure is steel-framed and encased in steel plates. The base of the light tower measures 30 feet square and tapers upward to support a cylindrical lantern room. The original optic was a fourth order Fresnel lens, since replaced with a modern plastic optic. The focal plane of the light produced is 82 feet above water level. A racon and foghorn signal are also kept in service.

Interior spaces were divided into living quarters, storage, work areas, and machinery spaces. Two main diesel generators and one backup provided power to the station. Typically, a five-man crew was in residence that worked four weeks on and two off and a four-hour duty watch with eight hours off. Crew members took turns cooking. The station was resupplied every two weeks during the shipping season, and at that

time crews were exchanged. Grays Reef Light was fully automated late in 1976.

Grays Reef Light has an identical twin at Minneapolis Shoal on the western side of the lake. These towers are Art Deco in style, reflecting the design preferences of the mid-1930s.

Status: *Active. Not open to public.*

Access: *Boat.*

Lifeboats at Great Lakes Maritime Academy—Traverse City, Michigan

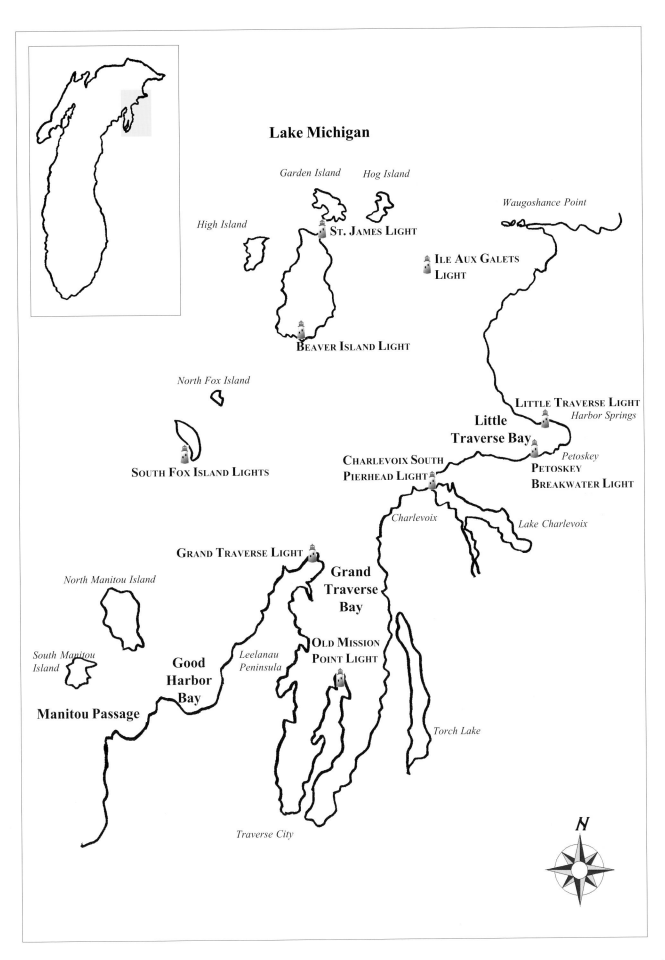

Lake Michigan

Garden Island   *Hog Island*

Waugoshance Point

High Island

ST. JAMES LIGHT

ILE AUX GALETS LIGHT

BEAVER ISLAND LIGHT

North Fox Island

LITTLE TRAVERSE LIGHT
Harbor Springs

Little Traverse Bay

CHARLEVOIX SOUTH PIERHEAD LIGHT

Petoskey
PETOSKEY BREAKWATER LIGHT

SOUTH FOX ISLAND LIGHTS

Charlevoix

Lake Charlevoix

GRAND TRAVERSE LIGHT

Grand Traverse Bay

North Manitou Island

South Manitou Island

Good Harbor Bay

Leelanau Peninsula

OLD MISSION POINT LIGHT

Torch Lake

Manitou Passage

Traverse City

N

Beaver Island

About 30 miles offshore from the Michigan mainland, Beaver Island is the largest island in the Beaver Archipelago west of Grays Reef Passage and the largest island in Lake Michigan. Thirteen miles long north and south with a maximum width of six miles, the heavily wooded island has seven inland lakes and high sand bluffs along its western side.

Beaver Island has a long and interesting history. The first white men to appear were French voyageurs in the early 1600s. In the early 1800s, Irish immigrants arrived. Their settlement was interrupted in 1847 by the arrival of a colony of Mormons that eventually grew in size to twenty-five hundred people. James Jesse Strang led the colony and crowned himself king in 1850, making Beaver Island the only kingdom ever to exist in the United States. Non-Mormons were forced off the island. The "King's" tyrannical practices aroused resentment on the mainland and within the ranks of his own followers, two of whom assassinated him in 1856. Shortly thereafter, the colony was dissolved by force and Irish farmers and fishermen quickly resettled the island. The long association of the Irish with Beaver Island has led to its moniker as "America's Emerald Isle."

St. James (Beaver Island Harbor) Light

St. James Harbor is a fine natural harbor at the northeast end of Beaver Island. The village of St. James, Michigan is located on the northwest side of the harbor. The harbor quickly became appreciated as a refuge from storms as it provided protection from all but southeast winds. The harbor also served as a wood fueling station for passing steamers and a center of activity for commercial interests in timber and fishing.

St. James Light—August 18, 1914

United States Coast Guard

The first light at St. James was established on Whiskey Point at the eastern entrance to the harbor in 1856, shortly after the demise of King Strang and his Mormon colony. Little is known of this first light. The present St. James Light was built in 1870. It consisted of a rectangular, one and one-half-story brick keeper's dwelling with an attached cylindrical brick tower. Automated in 1927, only the tower remains today. The vacant dwelling was razed by the Coast Guard during the winter of 1941-42. The tower is 41 feet in overall height and topped by a ten-sided cast-iron lantern room that continues to house the original fourth order Fresnel lens. The focal plane of the light produced is 38 feet above water level. The tinted glass panes of the lantern room create the red color characteristic of the light. In October

St. James Light

2000, the historical structure and surrounding grounds were formally leased to St. James Township. The Coast Guard will continue to maintain the light in the tower as an aid to navigation.

A U.S. Life Saving Station was also established on Whiskey Point, very near the lighthouse, in 1876. The original boat/station house was later moved inland and continues to be used as a private residence. The surviving boathouse and station office are more recent remnants of the Coast Guard Station that was formerly in service at the site.

St. James Light—circa 1914

courtesy of Dave Tinder

Status: *Active. Not open to public.*

Beaver Island (Beaver Head) Light

Beaver Island Light was one of a string of lights extending north from the Manitou Passage meant to mark the western limits of the main vessel track to and from the Straits of Mackinac via Grays Reef Passage. Located on a high bluff at the southern end of the island, construction of the first light began in 1851 and completed in 1852. In less than seven years, the foundation failed and the tower toppled. Few other details regarding this light have survived.

The present conical brick tower was built in 1858 and stands 46 feet tall overall. Originally fitted with a fourth order Fresnel lens, the tower's elevation on the bluff resulted in a light with a focal plane 103 feet above water level. An enclosed passageway connects the tower to a two-story brick keeper's house that was built in 1866. Both structures are built of cream-colored brick and were painted white at one time. Currently, just the front of the house is painted a pale yellow. The house originally held quarters for the families of the keeper and first assistant. In 1915, a two-story, wood-framed, clapboard-sided addition was built to house a second assistant. The assignment of a second assistant to the station became necessary after a steam-powered fog signal plant was established in 1913. The red-brick fog signal building remains standing at the water's edge a fair distance down the hill from the lighthouse. Beaver Island Light was discontinued in 1962 and replaced by an automated radiobeacon. Modern electronic aids to navigation have rendered radiobeacons obsolete; therefore, on the Great Lakes, these devices have been discontinued in recent years.

After 1962, Beaver Island Light Station quickly began to deteriorate from neglect and the buildings were severely damaged by vandals. The light station site was declared surplus property by the General Services Administration in the late 1960s. Sev-

Beaver Island Light

eral regional organizations showed interest in obtaining the property, and it was eventually deeded to the Charlevoix Public School District in 1975. Restoration efforts began in 1978 as part of a CETA (Comprehensive Employment and Training Act) funded work-study program set up to teach teenagers environmental awareness and basic vocational skills like painting and carpentry. Restoration of the buildings is largely complete today and the former light station is known as the Beaver Island Lighthouse School. Providing alternative educational programs, the school is open to troubled students under twenty-one who have dropped out of high school or are at risk of dropping out. For more information on the school, call 231-448-2468. The lighthouse tower is open to visitors who may climb the cast-iron spiral staircase up to the lantern deck for a panoramic view of the surrounding shoreline. The original lens is on display in the passageway at the base of the tower.

Beaver Island and the village of St. James have undergone a fair amount of "gentrification" in recent years as developers have tried to soften the rough rural image of the island. The lack of accommoda-tions for large volumes of visitors coupled with limited airplane and ferry links to the mainland have saved the island from wanton resort development. St. James remains the center of most business and social activities, leaving the rest of the island secluded, quiet, and a pleasure to explore. Lake Michigan is rimmed with highly populated cities. Beaver Island remains a place where one is able to get far, far away from the maddening crowd.

Beaver Island Light

Status: *Inactive. Tower only open to public.*

Access: *Beaver Island is reached by car ferry or airplane, both out of Charlevoix. Beaver Island Boat Company operates a ferry from a dock at 103 Bridge Park Dr. on the east side of US-31 just south of the drawbridge in downtown Charlevoix. Reservations are necessary if you are taking a vehicle to the island. For details, call 231-547-2311 or visit their website: www.bibco.com. Island Airways schedules regular flights to the island from Charlevoix Air-port on US-31 just south of the M-66 junction. For current rates and schedules call 231- 547-2141. No matter how you arrive on the island, a vehicle will be necessary to get around. A number of vendors offer cars, bicycles, and mopeds for rent. For extended distances, however, a vehicle with windows that roll up is the wisest choice as most of the roads on the island are gravel and can be very dusty. For more information, call the Beaver Island Chamber of Commerce at 231-448-2505 or check the website: www.beaverisland.net.*

Ile Aux Galets (Skillagalee) Light

Skillagalee Island—circa 1960

In French the name means "Island of Pebbles," but locally this island has virtually always been known as Skillagalee (pronounced: skill-ä-gal-lee). The island is very small and its size has varied considerably depending on the water level of Lake Michigan. A little over six miles from the mainland shore near Cross Village, the island is extremely flat and would be easy to miss in the dark. Its location out where a mariner would expect to find deep water made it all the more insidious as a hazard to navigation. The light is a guide to and from the Straits of Mackinac by way of Grays Reef Passage.

Skillagalee Light—August 16, 1914

The first light on the island was established in 1851, probably a simple wooden tower, and completely rebuilt again in 1868 when it was fitted with a third order Fresnel lens. Little else of these two lights is known and no photographs have been found.

The current tower, completed in October 1888, is an octagonal brick structure. Originally fitted with a fourth order Fresnel lens, a modern plastic optic currently produces a light 58 feet above water level. A covered passageway connected the tower to a one

Skillagalee Light—circa 1915

and one-half-story brick keeper's house. A boathouse, oil house, privy, and fog signal building also occupied the site. All of these structures were demolished after the light was automated in 1969, as the Coast Guard considered them an "attractive nuisance." The Ile Aux Galets Light tower is nearly identical to that at Port Sanilac Light (1886) on Lake Huron.

Skillagalee is a barren site today—rocks, shattered bricks from the demolished buildings, and some scrub vegetation. The island is inhabited by several species of seagulls that do not like to be disturbed.

Status: *Active. Not open to public.*

Access: *Boat. A beach landing is necessary as there is no dock. The water close to shore is shallow and rocky.*

Skillagalee Light

South Fox Island Light

North and South Fox Islands, about four miles apart, lie to the west of the main shipping course connecting the Manitou Passage and the Straits of Mackinac at Grays Reef Passage. South Fox Island is the remote location of two abandoned lighthouses. The island lies almost sixteen miles southwest of the southern tip of Beaver Island and seventeen miles northwest of Grand Traverse Light at the tip of the Leelanau Peninsula.

The first lighthouse was established at the south end of the island in 1868 to warn of an extensive bank of shoals extending over another nine miles south. This building consists of a one and one-half-story dwelling with an attached square tower, both constructed of cream-colored brick that was later painted white. It remained the main dwelling until 1905, when a large red-brick duplex was built nearby to house the assistants necessary to operate a steam-powered fog signal.

South Fox Island Light

In 1934 the light was moved to a taller skeletal cast-iron structure, eighty feet high, with an enclosed central tube containing a spiral staircase. The tower was placed a bit closer to the shoreline, just behind the fog signal building. This newer tower dates from 1905 and had originally been erected at Sapelo Island, Georgia where it remained in operation until 1933. Thereafter it was dismantled and shipped to Michigan. The light was automated in 1959. The same year, a spare lantern room from South Fox Island was transported to Old Presque Isle Light (established in 1840) on Lake Huron for installation there as part of its restoration. South Fox Island Light was discontinued in 1976.

South Fox Island Light

South Fox Island is privately owned except for the old light station. The site is poorly overseen by the Michigan Department of Natural Resources (DNR). Remaining intact are the two lighthouses, the red-brick duplex, a work shed, oil house, privy, and the fog signal building. All of the buildings are badly deteriorated and the grounds are wildly overgrown. Adding to the decay, the buildings remain open to the weather with entry barred by door and window inserts constructed of heavy wire mesh. The mesh also fails to keep out insects and small animals. A high chain-link fence topped with barbed wire blocks access to the base of the skeletal tower. In all fairness to the DNR, this would be a very difficult and expensive place to maintain due to its remote location. It remains a sad place to visit in its present state.

Status: *Inactive. Not open to public.*

Access: *Boat. A beach landing is necessary as there is no dock.*

South Fox Island Light

Little Traverse Light (Harbor Point)

Harbor Point is a narrow peninsula that extends southeast from the north shore of Little Traverse Bay to protect the harbor at Harbor Springs. This natural harbor is one of the finest on the lake for small craft, affording security in any weather. Nestled between the hillsides to the north and the water's edge, Harbor Springs is a very picturesque place. Many consider it the quintessential resort town—well-tended, tidy, and affluent.

White settlers began to move into the area around 1870 and the settlement became known as Le Petit Travers or Little Traverse. In 1880 the name of the village was changed to Harbor Springs. Logging soon became the backbone of the local economy and sawmills produced timber

Little Traverse Light—circa 1922

for schooners and small steamers waiting to carry the cargo to growing cities like Chicago and Milwaukee. The coming of the railroad in 1882 and the arrival of excursion steamboats allowed Harbor

Little Traverse Light

Springs to be discovered as a summer resort. Private resort associations sprang up at Harbor Springs, Petoskey, and numerous other places along the northeastern shores of Lake Michigan.

Little Traverse Light, at the tip of Harbor Point, was first lit on September 25, 1884. Constructed of red-brick, the structure consists

Little Traverse Light—circa 1905

of a one and one-half-story dwelling with an attached square tower. It is practically identical to Sherwood Point Light, which was established in 1883 across the lake on Green Bay. The lighthouse was deacti-

vated in 1963 and the light transferred to a taller, skeletal steel tower nearby. The lantern room still houses the original fourth order Fresnel lens. Also, a short distance in front of the lighthouse, a very

Little Traverse Light

Little Traverse Light fog signal bell tower

rare example of a wooden fog signal bell tower built in 1896 has survived into the present. The site is privately owned and maintained in pristine condition.

Status: *Inactive. Private residence.*

Access: *Little Traverse Light lies within the confines of the Harbor Point Association that encompasses the entire Harbor Point peninsula. The Association is a private and very affluent enclave of Victorian era "cottages"*

Little Traverse Light—circa 1910

(i.e. mansions) and meticulously kept grounds. The Association is gated, guarded, and regularly patrolled. Access to the lighthouse site requires the advance permission of the Association Superinten- *dent, and then only exterior photographs of the lighthouse may be taken. No landing on the beach in front of the lighthouse is permitted. The best option for a good casual look is from the water.*

Petoskey Breakwater Light

Petoskey Harbor is located on the southeast shore of Little Traverse Bay at the mouth of the Bear River. The waterfront was wholly exposed to winds from the west and northwest with a long fetch over the open water of the lake. A harbor of refuge had been considered for Petoskey, but was deemed unnecessary as the fine natural harbor of Harbor Springs lay just across the bay to the north. Instead, construction of a breakwater extending northeast from shore began in 1895. At least

Petoskey Breakwater Light—circa 1920

under moderate weather conditions, the breakwater was to provide a sheltered landing for local commercial and excursion traffic. Lumbering was a mainstay of Petoskey during the late 1800s, but it quickly became a popular resort town. Petoskey remains so today, having retained much of its Victorian era charm. A small craft harbor is maintained on the waterfront.

The first light at Petoskey was established in 1899. The design of this light was repeated on Lake Michigan in Wisconsin at Kenosha, Milwaukee, Racine, and Sheboygan and at Waukegan, Illinois. These "pagoda style" lights housed lenses of the lowest order and were hexagonal towers, fully enclosed, with steeply sloping corrugated sheet metal sides up to a small lantern deck. A projecting dormer provided an access door with a window above for interior lighting. A slightly oversized lantern room dome gave the appearance of a mushroom cap. The light at

PERCH FISHING ON THE BREAKWATER, PETOSKEY, MICH.

Petoskey Breakwater Light—circa 1915

Petoskey was washed away in a storm on December 14, 1924. Thereafter a simple metal skeleton tower held the light. Today a modern cylindrical "D9" tower of steel and concrete displays a plastic optic producing a light 44 feet above water level.

Status: *Active. Not open to public.*

Access: *From the north or south on US-31, turn north on Wachtel St. (about a block west of the Bear River) to its end near the base of the breakwater.*

Petoskey Breakwater Light

Charlevoix South Pierhead Light

Charlevoix is a name that commemorates one of the early French missionaries on the Great Lakes. Charlevoix, Michigan and its harbor lie on Round Lake, which was originally connected with Lake Michigan by a narrow stream about one-third mile long called the Pine River. Private interests undertook dredging of the river and its mouth. The Federal government took over the work in 1877. Workers ran piers out into the lake and eventually connected the eastern outlet of Round Lake via a dredged channel to Lake Charlevoix, about one mile from the Lake Michigan shoreline. Charlevoix is a flourishing city and a mecca for summer tourists.

The first pier light at Charlevoix was established at the end of the north pier in 1885. The light consisted of a simple square, wooden pyramidal tower with an open lower framework. It displayed a fifth order Fresnel lens. A raised wooden catwalk connected the structure to the shore for the safety of the keeper.

In 1911 the light was moved to the end of the south pier and the catwalk eliminated, as the light was now in the lee (i.e. protected by) of the north pier.

The current Charlevoix South Pierhead Light replaced the old wooden light structure in 1948. The light consists of a tapering square steel tower with an open

Charlevoix North Pierhead Light—circa 1908

Charlevoix North Pierhead Light—circa 1910

Charlevoix South Pierhead Light—circa 1920

lower framework. Painted red at the time of its completion, the color of the tower was changed to white in the early 1980s. Originally fitted with the fifth order Fresnel lens from the old wooden tower, the plastic optic in place today produces a light 41 feet above water level.

Status: *Active. Not open to public.*

Access: *From the north or south on US-31 (Bridge St. in downtown Charlevoix), turn west onto Park Ave., which is the first street south of the Pine River drawbridge. Continue on Park Ave. a short distance, turning north (right) onto Grant St. for one block to the beach parking area.*

Charlevoix South Pierhead Light—July 1913

Charlevoix South Pierhead Light—winter

Charlevoix South Pierhead Light—summer

Old Mission Point Light

Grand Traverse Bay is separated from Lake Michigan by the Leelanau Peninsula. The bay extends south from the lake for about 32 miles and is about 10 miles wide. The southern 17 miles of the bay are separated into East and West Arms by Old Mission Peninsula, which extends north from the mainland and ends at Old Mission Point. Traverse City, Michigan is the largest city on the bay, located at

Old Mission Point Light

the head of the West Arm. Once a major logging center, timber gave way to farming, light

Old Mission Point Light—circa 1930

manufacturing, the cultivation of cherry orchards, vineyards, and tourism. The growth of Traverse City and its environs in the last twenty years has been almost malignant in its rapidity. Old Mission Peninsula, once singular in its rural beauty, has seen some of its best farmland squandered on subdivisions.

Traverse City is home to the Great Lakes Maritime Academy, a division of Northwest Michigan College. Maritime-oriented courses, including seamanship, navigation, piloting, communication, and maritime law, prepare cadets for positions aboard Great Lakes ships.

Old Mission Lighthouse was established in 1870. It consists of a one and one-half-story wood-framed dwelling with a short square tower in line with the front wall rising above its gabled roof. Identical structures were built at Muskegon on Lake Michigan in 1870 and on Mamajuda Island in the Detroit River in 1866. Old Mission Point Light is the only one of its type remaining. The original lens was removed after deactivation in 1933, when the light was transferred to a skeletal steel tower on a detached shoal two miles northwest of the point. The State of Michigan purchased the site after World War II and created a park.

Today Peninsula Township owns the site and its use as a park continues. The lighthouse, beautifully maintained, is used as a private residence by the park manager. Surrounded by a wooden plank fence, the yard immediately around the lighthouse is not open to the public, but the rest of the grounds are accessible. A large

Old Mission Point Light—winter

Old Mission Point Light—summer

sign at the site proclaims that the lighthouse is located on the 45th parallel of latitude, which is halfway between the Equator and the North Pole. Of the many historical sites around Traverse City, this lighthouse is the most heavily visited.

Old Mission Point Light—circa 1922

Status: *Inactive. Private residence.*

Access: *Old Mission Point Light is located about 18 miles north of downtown Traverse City at the northern tip of Old Mission Peninsula. M-37 runs straight up the center of the peninsula to end at the lighthouse parking lot. From the east or west on Front St. (combined highways M-72 and US-31) turn north on Peninsula Dr. (M-37). After ½ mile, M-37 curves to the northeast and its name changes to Center Rd.*
From the south: Garfield Ave. (County Road 611) runs north past the western edge of Cherry Capital Airport. Garfield turns into Peninsula Dr. (M-37) north of Front St. Continue to go north.

Grand Traverse Light

Grand Traverse Light

Grand Traverse Light stands at Lighthouse Point at the northern tip of the Leelanau Peninsula. This coastal light marks the northeastern end of the Manitou Passage and is used by ships heading into Grand Traverse Bay.

The first light at this site was mistakenly called Cat's Head Point Light, but Cathead Point actually lies four miles to the southwest. Completed in 1852, it consisted of a rough brick tower with a detached keeper's dwelling. No photographs of it are known to exist. It stood just to the east of the present lighthouse on lower ground closer to shore. Too short and poorly placed, the tower and dwelling were razed in 1858 and replaced with the surviving structure. Grand Traverse Light consists of a two-story dwelling constructed of Milwaukee cream-colored brick painted white. A short square wooden tower emerges from the peak of the roof to support a lantern room that originally housed a fifth

Grand Traverse Light—circa 1910

order Fresnel lens. The lens was upgraded to a larger fourth order in 1870. The basic design of this lighthouse was repeated at several other locations on Lake Michigan. All within a few years of each other, very similar lights were built in Wisconsin at Port Washington, Green Island, Rock Island, and Pilot Island; at South Manitou Island in Michigan; and at Michigan City, Indiana.

In 1899 the fog signal building was constructed to house a steam-powered ten-inch whistle, which was placed in operation early in 1900. Because additional assistants were needed to operate the fog plant, in 1901 the lighthouse was divided lengthwise down the middle and converted into a duplex. It was at this time that the wings on both sides of the building were added to accommodate new entrances and stairwells. A kitchen was added to the back of the eastern apartment in 1916. The present frame back porches were built in 1953 when the house and light were electrified.

The light station was closed in 1972 when an automated light was placed at the top of the present skeletal steel tower erected nearby. Thereafter the Coast Guard leased it to the Michigan Department of Natural Resources (DNR). Boarded up, the buildings fell into disrepair. In 1985, a local group organized the Grand Traverse Lighthouse Foundation with the goal of restoring the historical buildings and creating an interesting and educational museum. The lighthouse was sublet from the DNR and reopened to the public as a museum in 1986. Restoration has progressed nicely ever since and many artifacts that were actually used at the lighthouse when it was active have been donated or recovered and placed on display. The fog signal building has been restored and once again houses a working fog signal and also serves as a gift shop. Grand Traverse Lighthouse is one of the better such museums on the Great Lakes; a visit here is highly recommended.

Grand Traverse Light

Grand Traverse Lighthouse Museum
P.O. Box 43
Northport, MI 49670
Phone: 231-386-7195

Status: *Inactive. Open to public as a museum.*

Access: *From the junction of M-22 and M-201 in Northport, continue north on M-201 through town. M-201 changes successively into County Road 640 and then County Road 629 as you continue north to Leelanau State Park. A daily or annual permit is required to enter the park. The parking lot for the lighthouse is just inside the park entrance. The total distance from Traverse City is about 40 miles.*

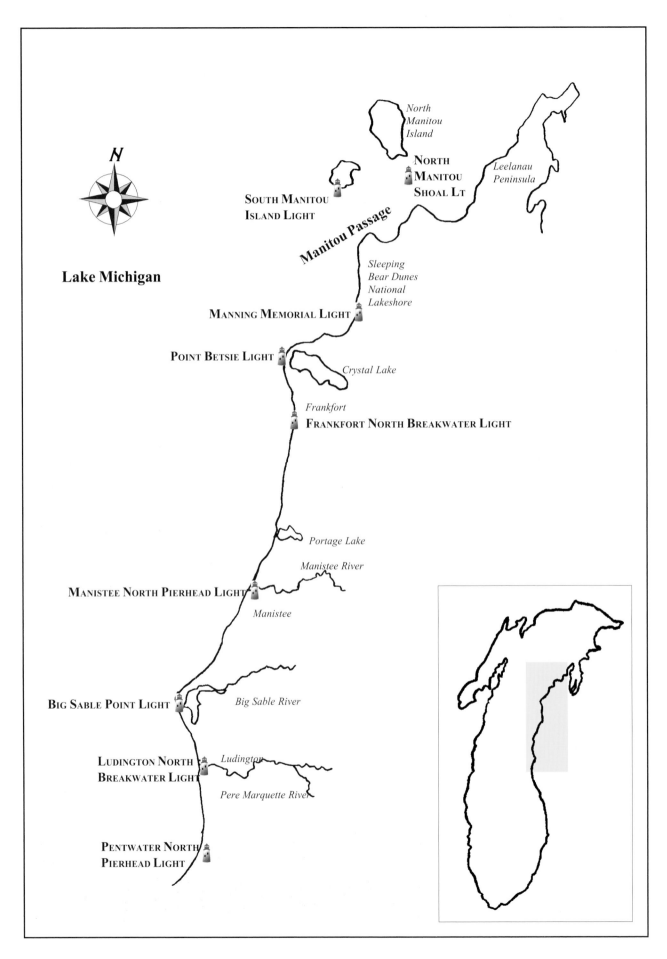

N

Lake Michigan

North Manitou Island

NORTH MANITOU SHOAL LT

Leelanau Peninsula

SOUTH MANITOU ISLAND LIGHT

Manitou Passage

Sleeping Bear Dunes National Lakeshore

MANNING MEMORIAL LIGHT

POINT BETSIE LIGHT

Crystal Lake

Frankfort

FRANKFORT NORTH BREAKWATER LIGHT

Portage Lake

Manistee River

MANISTEE NORTH PIERHEAD LIGHT

Manistee

BIG SABLE POINT LIGHT

Big Sable River

LUDINGTON NORTH BREAKWATER LIGHT

Ludington

Pere Marquette River

PENTWATER NORTH PIERHEAD LIGHT

North Manitou Island

North Manitou Island lies four miles northeast of the smaller South Manitou Island. Manitou Passage is located between the islands and the mainland to the east. By the mid-1840s, Manitou Passage was well on its way to becoming the shipping super highway of Lake Michigan. The passage is used by deep-draft vessels bound between the Straits of Mackinac via Grays Reef Passage and the south end of Lake Michigan. North Manitou Shoal extends three miles south from the southern end of the island and Pyramid Point Shoal extends north two miles from that point on the mainland. That leaves the Manitou Passage with a least width of 1.8 miles—a serious bottleneck in a congested shipping lane, especially during periods of reduced visibility. Shipping casualties in the narrow passage increased with the volume of traffic, resulting in the establishment of a U.S. Life Saving Station on the island in 1877.

North Manitou Island Light

North Manitou Island Light was established in 1898 on the southeastern tip of the island to mark North Manitou shoal. It consisted of a square, tapering, wooden tower fully enclosed and about 50 feet high. The lantern room housed a fourth order Fresnel lens. In addition to the tower, the station included a red-brick duplex keeper's dwelling, barn, oil house, and a steam-powered fog signal building. This light alone proved inadequate so a lightship was added offshore at the edge of the shoal in 1910.

Initially, Lightship No. 56 was transferred here from White Shoal in the Straits of Mackinac. Lightship No. 89 assumed the vigil in 1927 and was eventually replaced by Lightship No. 103. Lightships were expensive to maintain, dangerous to operate, and easily blown off station by storms. Lightships were also difficult to get into position at the start of navigation each spring due to ice. A permanent solution was desired.

North Manitou Island Light—August 17, 1914

North Manitou Island Light—July 2, 1930

North Manitou Shoal Light

The establishment of an offshore crib light in 1935, North Manitou Shoal Light, provided a permanent solution. The structure is steel-framed, encased in steel plates, and rests on a square concrete crib. The fourth order Fresnel lens from the old tower was placed here, but today an aeronautical style beacon produces a light 79 feet above water level. This lonely lighthouse was automated in 1980.

The new crib light made the lightship and island light redundant. North Manitou Island Light was discontinued in 1935 and collapsed in October 1942, after being undercut by waves and shoreline erosion. Nothing of the light station remains today. Lightship No. 103 moved on to become Huron Lightship at the southern end of Lake Huron. Stationed at the entrance to the Huron Cut Channel, she remained in service until 1970. Fully restored and open as a museum, Lightship No. 103 rests next to the St. Clair River at Pine Grove Park in Port Huron, Michigan.

North and South Manitou Islands are both part of the Sleeping Bear Dunes National Lakeshore administered by the National Park Service.

Status: *Active. Not open to public.*

Access:
Boat. A daily ferry service (in season) from Leland, Michigan to South Manitou Island passes close to the light on its route. For details, contact the Manitou Island Transit Company at 231-256-9061.

North Manitou Shoal Light

North Manitou Shoal Light

South Manitou Island Light

South Manitou Island lies four miles southwest of the larger North Manitou Island. Manitou Passage lies between the islands and the mainland to the east. Used by deep-draft vessels bound between the Straits of Mackinac via Grays Reef Passage and the south end of Lake Michigan, by the mid-1840s, Manitou Passage was a heavily traveled route. With a least width of 1.8 miles at its northern end, light-houses to mark the way were critical. Chicago lay 220 miles away and South Manitou Island had the only deep natural harbor between there and the Straits. The island became a haven from storms and a wood fueling station for lake steamers.

Construction of the first lighthouse at the southeast end of the island was completed in 1839. It consisted of a wooden dwelling with a short tower on the roof. The height to the base of the lantern was only 30 feet and 11 Argand lamps and 14" reflectors were used to produce the light. By 1848 the number of lamps and reflectors was reduced to eight, probably to save on fuel costs and not because the light was unimportant. No photographs of this first light are known to exist.

In 1858 the entire station was rebuilt. Set back from the beach on higher ground, the new structure was a two-story dwelling constructed of cream-colored brick. A short, square, wooden tower emerged from the roof and the lantern room now housed a much more efficient fourth order Fresnel lens. With a tower height of 35 feet, the focal plane of the light produced was 64 feet above water level. At the same time, a fog signal bell was placed in service. This proved to be a successful design. Within a few years nearly identical light-

South Manitou Island Light

houses were built in Wisconsin at Port Washington, Green Island, Rock Island, and Pilot Island; at Grand Traverse in Michigan; and Michigan City, Indiana.

Increased shipping traffic necessitated changes. The height of the light needed to be increased so it could be seen at a greater distance. In 1871, the current conical brick tower was completed and a larger third order Fresnel lens installed. The focal plane of the light produced had been raised to 100 feet and visibility increased to a nominal range of 18 miles. The light tower was removed from the roof of the previous dwelling, which was retained and connected to the new tower by an extended covered passageway. The first steam-powered fog signal on Lake Michigan was established at the station in 1875, replacing the old fog bell. Af-

South Manitou Island Light—circa 1915

South Manitou Island Light—entrance

South Manitou Island Light—view from the tower

ter more than a century of continuous service, the light station was closed in 1958. What became of the Fresnel lens remains a mystery. The only light at South Manitou Island today is a lighted gong-buoy marking a shoal off the southwest end of the island.

Development and population growth on South Manitou Island reached a peak in the late 1880s. Shipping casualties in the narrow Manitou Passage increased with the volume of traffic. A U.S. Life Saving Station had been established on North Manitou Island in 1877 to aid ships in distress. Two sites for another Life Saving Station were proposed, but a controversy ensued as to which site should be selected—South Manitou Island or the mainland. In the end, stations were placed at both sites in 1902. The mainland station was located at Sleeping Bear Point near Glen Haven. The station at South Manitou Island was placed at the south end of the harbor, just a short walk from the lighthouse.

North and South Manitou Islands are both part of the Sleeping Bear Dunes National Lakeshore administered by the National Park Service. Both 1902 Life Saving Stations survive today as museums and the lighthouse tower is open for tours. A visit to South Manitou Island is highly recommended. It is a beautiful place.

South Manitou Island Light

Status: *Inactive. Tower open to public.*

Access: *Boat. A daily ferry service (in season) to South Manitou Island from Leland, Michigan is operated by the Manitou Island Transit Company at 231-256-9061. The company also conducts an interesting open-air bus tour of the island's interior.*

Manning Memorial Light

Like the Kevich Light in Wisconsin, this is one of the newer lights on Lake Michigan. Robert H. Manning was a lifelong resident of the village of Empire who had always wished for a light to help guide him in off the lake after his fishing trips. After his death in 1989, family and friends decided to honor him by building the light he had wanted for so long. Privately funded and constructed, the simple cylindrical tower was established in 1991. Empire has no harbor. The tower stands at the north end of a public park next to the beach. A light is displayed for small craft during the boating season, but the Coast Guard has never certified the light as a private aid to navigation. On the beach near the tower is a rudimentary boat ramp, suitable for launching only the smallest of small craft.

While in Empire, be sure to visit the headquarters building for the Sleeping Bear Dunes National Lakeshore. The building is styled after an old life saving station. Besides displays on dune ecology, there is an exhibit of maritime artifacts.

Status: *Active. Not open to public.*

Access: *Empire is located at the junction of M-22 and M-72. From Traverse City take M-72 west to its end. From M-22, turn west onto Front St. in Empire and then north (right) on Lake St. Turn west (left) again at Niagra St. to the beach park. The headquarters for SBDNL is on the northeast corner of the junction of M-22 and M-72.*

Manning Memorial Light

Manning Memorial Light

Point Betsie Light

Point Betsie is a rounding sandy point a little less than four and one-half miles north of Frankfort Harbor. Originally named "Pointe Aux Bec Scies," meaning "sawed beak point," the point is located at the southern end of the Manitou Passage. Point Betsie Light was established in 1858 to mark an important turning point for vessels bound to and from the south end of Lake Michigan through the Manitou Passage.

The lighthouse consists of a two-story brick dwelling with a red gambrel roof and an attached cylindrical brick tower. The dwelling originally measured 28 feet square, but was enlarged in 1894 to its present dimensions of 28 feet by 48 feet. The 37-foot tower was fitted with a fourth order Fresnel lens with flash panels that was turned by a weighted clockwork mechanism. The focal plane of the light produced was and remains 52 feet above water level. In 1944 the clockwork mechanism was disconnected when an electric motor was installed. The turning mechanism for the lens finally failed early in February 1996. The lens was removed, transferred to the care of the National Park Service at the Sleeping Bear Dunes National Lakeshore, and placed in storage. Its final disposition has not yet been decided. A plastic optic lens takes its place in the tower today.

Point Betsie Light—circa 1915

Point Betsie Light—winter

Point Betsie Light—summer

Point Betsie was such an important coastal light that in 1880 the Lighthouse Board suggested that the original tower be replaced by a taller 100-foot structure. This was never done, although the existing tower was being seriously threatened by beach erosion. Corrective action was finally taken in April 1890, when the tower foundation was strengthened by underpinning it with a ring of concrete. At the same time a new revetment was built to reduce erosion problems. Today an apron of concrete shields the base of the tower. Erosion remains a serious, if dormant, concern at this site. As this is being written, Lake Michigan is nearing low water levels not seen since 1964. Eventually, high water levels will return and the problem of erosion will have to be solved.

Point Betsie Light

When the Coast Guard automated Point Betsie in April of 1983, it was the last manned light station on the

Point Betsie Light—circa 1908

east shore of Lake Michigan. Sherwood Point Light, also automated in 1983, was the last manned light station on the west side of the lake. Thereafter, the lighthouse continued to serve as a residence for Coast Guard personnel stationed in Frankfort. During the winter of 1996-1997, the boiler system failed. Asbestos concerns made repairs too costly and the lack of heat forced residents to vacate. The building has been empty ever since. A fog signal building, oil house, and several other outbuildings remain intact at the site.

Point Betsie Light remains an active aid to navigation and, for now, the Coast Guard continues to provide needed maintenance. The lighthouse was

reroofed in 2000. The Coast Guard, however, is trying to get out of the property management business to save money and concentrate on its core duties. The site has been "excessed." Who the new stewards will be is as yet undecided, but they will be inheriting one of the most beloved lighthouses on the Great Lakes.

Status: *Active. Not open to public.*

Access: *From M-22, turn west on Pt. Betsie Rd. (about 4½ miles north of Frankfort) and take it the short distance to its end at the beach and the lighthouse.*

Frankfort Harbor

Frankfort Harbor is located in Lake Betsie, about four and one-half miles south of Point Betsie. Once referred to as Lake Aux Bec Scies, it lies just within the shoreline of Lake Michigan and is connected to it by a dredged entrance channel. The city of Frankfort is on the north side of the lake, which extends about one and one-half miles southeast from the inner end of the entrance channel. Outside the dredged areas near its entrance, the lake is generally shallow with depths of eight feet or less. That was enough water for early vessels to use the lake as a harbor of refuge from storms on the big lake, and plenty of water for floating logs. Frankfort started as a logging port that developed a secondary resort trade. By the early 1890s, the timber was playing out.

As lucky timing would have it, the Toledo, Ann Arbor, and North Michigan Railway (later shortened to the Ann Arbor Railroad) reached the town in 1892. On November 24, 1892, that railroad initiated a cross-lake railroad car ferry service to Kewaunee, Wisconsin when it sent its new ferry, the Ann Arbor No. 1, over with a load of railcars. Manitowoc, Menominee, Escanaba, and Manistique were later added as ports of call on the opposite side of Lake Michigan. The railroads also brought more people into the resorts on the lakefront. The ferry business at Frankfort had a long run, lasting until 1982. Today, the occasional tanker delivers petroleum products to the port, but the harbor is used mainly by pleasure craft. Frankfort's maritime heritage is honored at its gateway on M-115, the main highway into the city. There two pillars shaped like Frankfort's lighthouse flank the road. A span overhead connects them and supports a model of a Lake Michigan car ferry.

Frankfort's Gateway

Frankfort South Pierhead Light

The natural outlet of Lake Betsie into Lake Michigan was a narrow channel that had been deepened somewhat by local enterprise. The Federal government became involved in 1867 and dredged a straight channel between the two lakes 750 feet south of the old outlet. A long north and even longer south pier were ex-

Frankfort South Pierhead Light—circa 1910

tended into Lake Michigan 250 feet apart. Frankfort South Pierhead Light was established in 1873 and displayed a fixed red light. Old photographs show a unique combination lighthouse and fog bell tower connected at their upper levels by an enclosed passageway. Both towers were square, wooden and pyramidal in shape. The light tower was fully enclosed and the bell tower had an open

Frankfort South Pierhead Light—circa 1910

lower framework. A raised catwalk connected the two structures along the pier to shore. The South Pierhead Light and fog signal bell towers remained in service until 1914, when the main light for the harbor was transferred to a new structure on the north pier. No reason for this change in lighting has been found.

Frankfort North Pierhead Light

Frankfort North Pierhead Light appears in a number of old photographs. It consisted of a square, pyramidal, fully enclosed tower constructed of riveted steel plates. Painted white, it was connected to shore along the pier by a raised catwalk. Except for the white paint job, this tower was identical to the present light at Manistique. The North Pierhead Light remained in service until the present

Frankfort North Pierhead Light—August 13, 1914

"arrowhead" breakwaters were completed. Thereafter, it became the upper portion of the present light tower on the north breakwater marking the harbor entrance.

Frankfort North Breakwater Light

After 1905, an "arrowhead" harbor design was introduced on the Great Lakes. Two breakwaters connected to shore north and south of the original piers converged at a 90-degree angle offshore to form a new harbor entrance and a protected outer harbor or stilling basin. The stilling basin greatly reduced the chop caused by wave action at the entrance to the piers and the channel leading into the inner harbor. Where necessary, the original piers were then shortened to clear the area comprising the outer harbor. The project that resulted in the construction of these breakwaters at Frankfort was completed around 1930-31.

In 1932, the older North Pierhead Light was placed on top of a new, 25-foot tall square steel base to create the present North Breakwater Light. The addition raised the tower height to its present 67 feet, giving the lens a focal plane 72 feet above water level. The original fourth order Fresnel lens remains in use. The upper portion of this tower is virtually identical to the Manistique East Breakwater Light. The outlines of two current and two former access doors are visible up the east side of the tower. Contrary to common belief, Frankfort North Breakwater Light was never connected to shore by a catwalk.

Frankfort North Breakwater Light

Status: *Active. Not open to public.*

Access: *From the junction of M-115 and M-22, go south one block on M-22 and turn west on Main St. Follow Main St. to its end at the beach and parking area. Access to the base of the north breakwater is reached from the beach area.*

Frankfort North Pierhead Light—circa 1930

Portage Lake North Pier Light

Portage Lake is located 23 miles south of Point Betsie and 8 miles north of Manistee. As early as 1878, the lake was considered a possible site for a harbor of refuge into which ships could safely attempt an entrance for shelter from gales on Lake Michigan. Upon survey, Portage Lake was found to contain plenty of deep water but it was completely landlocked. However, the distance between the 18-foot depths in the two lakes was only 2000 feet.

A channel was dredged, revetments placed, and piers run out into the lake. The north pier extended 560 feet into Lake Michigan and the south pier, 350 feet. A range light system was established on the end of the north pier in April 1891. The front light was a simple lantern suspended from a wooden pole. The rear light, rebuilt in 1901, was a square, wooden pyramidal tower with an open lower framework connected to the shore by a raised catwalk. The height of the rear light above the water was 40 feet. The final disposition of these old lights remains unknown.

The harbor at Portage Lake never achieved much commercial importance as it was dwarfed by the much larger ports of Frankfort to the north and Manistee to the south. Continued harbor improvements were not carried out and shoaling eventually prevented entry by the largest vessels. A booming excursion and tourist trade did develop, giving rise to the resort village of Onekama on the northeastern shore of the lake.

Today modern pole lights mark the pier at Portage Lake, which remains a harbor of refuge for small craft.

Portage Lake North Pier Light—August 12, 1914

United States Coast Guard

Manistee Harbor

Manistee Harbor is located 31 miles south of Point Betsie and 16 miles north of Big Sable Point. The harbor formed at the mouth of the Manistee River, which flows from the north end of Manistee Lake for 1.5 miles to Lake Michigan. Manistee Lake is about four miles long and up to one-half mile wide. It has depths of up to 50 feet…plenty of water for refuge from storms on Lake Michigan and the development of commercial docking facilities. First settled about 1846, Manistee started as a logging port. Incorporated in 1869, the city today straddles the river west of Manistee Lake. Once the timber played out, the shipment of agricultural products, especially fruit, became important. So did the production of salt, as there were large brine deposits in the area. Brine is still shipped from the port for processing elsewhere. Modern freighters also regularly deliver coal.

Harbor improvements at the river's mouth were initiated by local business interests. The Federal government took up the work in 1867 and began constructing two parallel piers extending about 960 feet into Lake Michigan. In 1890, the scope of the project was expanded to include deepening the entire river channel from Lake Michigan to Manistee Lake. Today, the entrance to the Manistee River is protected by an outer harbor basin (or stilling basin) formed by a long north pier and a breakwater to the south.

Old Manistee River Light

Details regarding the early lighting of Manistee Harbor remain very sketchy. Conflicting and missing information cloud the sequence of events. The first lighthouse at Manistee was built on the north side of the river near its mouth. Completed in 1870, it consisted of a wood-framed dwelling with a short square light tower on the roof. This structure likely resembled the lighthouses built the same year at Muskegon and Old Mission Point. The first lighthouse was destroyed by fire in October 1871. Unfortunately, no photographs of it are known to exist. Its replacement was completed in 1873 and remains intact today, minus the light tower, as a private residence. As originally built, it consisted of a two-story wood-framed dwelling with a short square tower in line with the front wall rising above its gabled roof. The focal plane of the light produced was about 43 feet above water level and the characteristic displayed was a fixed white light varied by a red flash. No mention of the original optic has been found.

In 1873, as rebuilding of the main lighthouse continued, a beacon light was established on the south pier. The design was typical of that era. Old photographs show a square, wooden, pyramidal structure with an open lower framework connected to shore

Old Manistee River Light—August 12, 1914

by a raised catwalk. In order to service this light, the keeper had to cross the river in a small boat…not very convenient, especially in bad weather. No reason for placing a light on the south pier instead of the north one has been found. A likely explanation, however, is that construction of the south pier was further along than its northern counterpart at the time. The immediate need for a light to mark the harbor entrance dictated that it be placed on the south pier. The light on the south pier was moved to the gable end of a fog signal building on the north pier in 1894.

Old Manistee River Light—circa 1900

Adding more confusion surrounding Manistee is an entry in the records announcing the discontinuance of the main light on October 15, 1875. Instead, a light was to be displayed on the south pier. No reason for this action is given. Perhaps it was felt the south pier light was sufficient to mark the harbor entrance. In any event, the old Manistee River Lighthouse was relit at some point and remained in service for several years.

Old Manistee River Light—during conversion into a private residence

Although there are photographs that show the light still in service well after the 1875 date, there are serious gaps in the records that might help solve the mystery. At some point, the lantern room and light tower were removed from the building and it was sold into private ownership. Originally located near the beach at the west end of 5th Avenue, the building was moved a couple of blocks to the northeast and eventually converted into rental housing. It was moved again to its current location in 1993 to make room for a large marina and condominium development on the beachfront. The current owners converted the building into a single family residence and have substantially altered its exterior appearance. The highly disguised old Manistee River Lighthouse is located on a lot between the west ends of 2nd and 3rd Avenues, west of Melitzer Street.

Manistee North Pierhead Light

The south pier light tower was discontinued in 1894 and its light moved to a new fog signal building at the end of the north pier. The building was wood-framed and sheathed in cast-iron plates for durability. It housed the equipment for a steam-powered 10" whistle. A raised catwalk connected the structure to shore. A lantern room for the lighting apparatus was placed on the gable end of the building facing the lake. This structure remained in service until the present light was established.

The present Manistee North Pierhead Light was established in 1927. It consists of a conical cast-iron tower with an overall height of 39 feet. The original optic was a fifth order Fresnel lens. A modern plastic optic is in use today with a focal plane 55 feet above water level. The raised catwalk remains intact in excellent condition.

Victorian architectural styles predominate in Manistee, which rightfully bills itself as "The Victorian Port City" of Lake Michigan. The old lumber barons spent lavishly on their homes and downtown storefronts, many of which have been refurbished.

Manistee North Pierhead Light—circa 1910

Manistee North Pierhead Light—August 1913

Manistee's entire central business district is listed on the National Register of Historic places and it is a charming place to visit. The beaches at Manistee are among the finest on the lake. While in town, be sure to visit the former carferry *S.S. City of Milwaukee*, which is berthed on the west shore of Manistee Lake at the east end of 9th Street. The ship is a nautical time capsule of the 1930s. The carferry was moved to Manistee in January 2000 from Elberta, Michigan on Lake Betsie where she sat in limbo for many years. Fund raising efforts are underway to finance restoration. The ship is staffed by volunteers and open for tours on weekends. For more information call 231-398-0328 or 231-352-6101 or visit the website: www.carferry.com.

Status: *Active. Not open to public.*

Access: *Access to the base of the north pier is reached from the 5th Avenue Beach on the north side of the Manistee River. From US-31, turn west on Monroe St. and west (right) again on Lakeshore. Drive through the Harbor Village Marina and Condominium development to the parking lot behind the Coast Guard Station.*

Manistee North Pierhead Light

S.S. City of Milwaukee *on Manistee Lake*

Big Sable Point Light

The location of a major coastal light, Big Sable Point lies 16 miles south-southwest of Manistee and about 8 miles north-northwest of Ludington. One of the most prominent points of land on the eastern shore of Lake Michigan, the original French name of "Grande Pointe au Sable" meaning "great point of sand" remains an apt description. By the mid-1850s, vessel traffic and the number of shipwrecks in the vicinity had grown enough to prompt local business interests to request the establishment of a lighthouse on the point.

Construction began in 1866 and was completed in 1867. Given the French name of the place, the new light was appropriately named the "Grande Pointe au Sable Lighthouse." Everyone knew what the French name meant and all was well until 1874 when a lighthouse named "Big Sable" was established on Lake Superior 12 miles west of Grand Marais, Michigan. Having two lighthouses on the Great Lakes with similar names led to much confusion. As a remedy, in 1910 the name of the light on Lake Superior was changed from "Big Sable" to "Au Sable" and the name of the light on Lake Michigan was changed from "Grande Pointe au Sable" to "Big Sable." Many years later, researchers inherited the confusion. Because of the name changes, historical records regarding the two lighthouses are often found mixed.

Big Sable Point Light was first lit on November 1, 1867. The lighthouse originally consisted of a tall, conical, cream-colored brick tower with an overall height of 112 feet. An enclosed passageway connected the tower to a one and one-half story, cream-colored brick keeper's dwelling that contained quarters for the families of the keeper and his assistant. The original optic was a third order Fresnel lens that produced a light with a focal plane 106 feet above water level. Construction of a fog signal building commenced in 1908. The steam-powered fog signal, which necessitated the assignment of additional personnel for its operation, was placed in service in 1909. Later the same year, the dwelling was enlarged via a two-story addition to create three apartments for the families of the keeper and two assistants.

The soft-faced Milwaukee brick used in the construction of the tower proved to be no match for the elements and wind-driven sand at Big Sable Point. In 1880, the entire tower needed to be repointed, but the deterioration continued. By 1898, the brick was in bad condition. In order to save the tower, in 1900 it was encased in cast-iron plates up to the bottom of the windows in the service room. The space between the plates and the brick wall of the tower was filled with concrete. Viewed from a ship in the daytime, the cream-colored brick tower had always been difficult

Big Sable Point Light—June 1900

United States Coast Guard

to spot against its background of sand dunes. After the plates were installed, the tower was painted white with a broad black band in the middle to make it more effective as a daymark.

Surprisingly, no photographs have ever been found of the brick tower before the cast-iron plates were added. The photograph provided was taken in 1900 and it is one of the oldest photographs of Big Sable Point Light known to exist. It shows the work of painting the newly installed plates nearing completion. Note that the service room windows are still visible at the top of the tower just below the watch room deck. In 1905, this upper portion of the tower enclosing the service room was also encased in cast iron to bring the metal cladding up to the watch room deck. Despite the new black and white color scheme, the top of the tower remained difficult to see as the white paint blended in with the sky and clouds. In order to provide a better daymark, in 1916 the lantern room, watch room, and watch room deck were painted black. The resulting paint scheme is still in use on the tower today.

The structural integrity of the tower had been saved from the effects of crumbling bricks. Beach erosion, however, was to become a more formidable problem. Old photographs viewed sequentially show that a large amount of real estate in front of the lighthouse has been lost. When Big Sable Point Light was completed in 1867, it was more than 500 feet from the shoreline. By 1909 when the fog signal building was completed, the distance from the tower to the water had decreased to 385 feet. A severe winter storm early in 1942 destroyed the fog signal building and a replacement diaphone fog signal tower erected in 1941 was almost lost to erosion one year later. In 1943, the Coast Guard built a steel seawall in front of the lighthouse to control the erosion. Additional reinforcement work was required in 1952 and 1953.

While the battle with erosion continued, other changes were underway. A rough service road from Ludington State Park through the dunes to the sta-

Big Sable Point Light

tion was constructed in 1933. The light itself was electrified in 1948. The keeper's dwelling did not receive electricity until 1953. Full automation came in 1968 and the station was vacated. Use of the fog signal was discontinued in 1970. With no one in residence, the buildings deteriorated from neglect and severe damage was done by vandals. The Fresnel lens was removed due to vandalism in 1985 and replaced with the present modern plastic optic. The old lens was restored and in a November 1, 1987 ceremony marking the 120th anniversary of its original lighting, it was rededicated and put on display at the Rose Hawley Museum in Ludington. The museum and the lens have since relocated to the White Pine Village Museum just south of Ludington. The museum is operated by the Mason County Histori-

Big Sable Point Light—circa 1911. Note entire top of tower is painted white.

Big Sable Point Light

Modern "D9" replacement with old tower in background

was not necessary and it was removed from the site in June 1996. The Coast Guard continues to maintain the light in the old tower. Restoration of the lighthouse itself is nearly complete and has been beautifully executed.

Big Sable Point Lighthouse stands within Ludington State Park. Nestled in the sand dunes along miles of undeveloped shoreline, it is very easy to get a sense of the isolation the old lightkeepers experienced. The dunes themselves present a fascinating ecological environment. The lighthouse is open to visitors 10 a.m. to 6 p.m. daily from May 1 through October 31. Once inside the park, visitors must hike the last 1.5 miles to the lighthouse either along the beach or along the service road beginning at the Pines Campground. Entry to the lighthouse is free, but there is a small fee to climb the tower. The view from the top is magnificent. During the months it is open, volunteers live at the lighthouse for two-week stints to staff the gift shop and provide upkeep. For visitors unable to make the hike, the Lighthouse Keepers Association provides bus transportation directly to the lighthouse three times a year for a modest fee. Contact them for the specific dates.

Big Sable Point Lighthouse Keepers Association
P.O. Box 673
Ludington, MI 49431
Phone: 231-845-7343

Status: *Active. Open to public as a museum.*

Access: *From the junction of US-31 and US-10 just east of Ludington, go west on US-10, which turns into Ludington Ave. Take Ludington Ave. almost to its end at the lakefront and turn north (right) onto Lakeshore Rd., which is M-116. Follow M-116 north to its end at Ludington State Park. A daily or annual permit is necessary to enter the park. Use the parking lot at the State Park bathhouse/concession stand along the beach or the lot at the fish cleaning station just inside the park entrance. The hike along the beach to the lighthouse (hiking in sand is strenuous) or along the access road from the Pines Campground (recommended) is about 1.5 miles long. Only official vehicles are permitted on the access road. Parking is not allowed in the Pines Campground.*

cal Society. The fourth order Fresnel lens from Ludington North Breakwater Light is on display in the same room. For more information on the White Pine Village Museum call 231-843-4808.

Early in 1977 a severe storm destroyed a large section of the seawall and water was soon lapping within four feet of the tower. The shoreline received additional reinforcement work, but repeated storms coupled with high water levels continued to hasten the erosion. The Coast Guard was so convinced the old lighthouse was doomed that they constructed a replacement tower up on the dune just to the south. The new "D9" tower was completed in December 1985 and consisted of little more than a 60-foot tall steel cylinder. Fortunately, it was never needed.

A local group called the Big Sable Point Lighthouse Keepers Association formed in 1987 and assumed the work necessary to stabilize the site. Seawall reconstruction and other anti-erosion measures were a top priority. Their efforts were so successful that the Coast Guard decided the replacement tower

Ludington Harbor

Ludington is located 7.5 miles south of Big Sable Point and 12 miles north of Pentwater. Ludington was incorporated as the city of Pere Marquette in 1867. In 1874, the city was renamed after James Ludington, a prominent local lumber baron. The harbor is in Pere Marquette Lake and the city is on the north side of the lake. The lake is about two miles long, averages one-half mile in width, and has water depths up to 43 feet. The lake made a good refuge from storms on Lake Michigan and deep-draft facilities for lake shipping were easily developed. Logging, timber, and sawmills comprised the early economy. The railroad soon arrived. On June 25, 1874, the Flint and Pere Marquette Railroad initiated cross-lake railroad car ferry service from Ludington to Sheboygan, Wisconsin. Milwaukee, Manitowoc, Manistique, and Kewaunee were later added as ports of call on the opposite side of Lake Michigan.

The transport of railroad cars ended in November 1990, but the tradition of cross-lake passenger travel continues today. The *S.S. Badger*, operated by the Lake Michigan Carferry Company, links Ludington and Manitowoc, Wisconsin. In service every year from mid-May through mid-October, the *Badger* is the last of its kind. The four-hour crossing in either direction is a unique experience and highly recommended. For additional information call 800-841-4243 or 888-947-3377, or visit the website: www.ssbadger.com.

Early Lights in Ludington

Private business interests connected with the many sawmills that once bordered the city initiated harbor improvements in the 1850s. After the Civil War, the Federal government assumed the work in 1867. Within a few years, the channel connecting Pere Marquette Lake to Lake Michigan had been deepened and protected by piers extending out into the deeper water of the big lake. Details regarding the early lighting of Ludington Harbor remain very sketchy. The first pier light was established in 1871, probably on the south pier as it was the longer of the two piers. By the middle of 1898, after several extensions, the south pier was 929 feet longer than the north pier and projected 620 feet farther beyond the shoreline. Around 1877, this pier light was rebuilt, probably moved to the gable end of a fog signal building housing the equipment for a steam-powered 10" whistle. A system of range lights was established on the north pier around 1890. All of these structures were likely connected to shore by raised catwalks.

Ludington North Breakwater Light

After 1905, an "arrowhead" harbor design was introduced on the Great Lakes. Two breakwaters connected to shore north and south of the original piers converged at a 90° angle offshore to form a new harbor entrance and a protected outer harbor or stilling basin. The stilling basin greatly reduced the chop caused by wave action at the entrance to the piers and the channel leading into the inner harbor. Where necessary, the original piers were then shortened to clear the area comprising the outer harbor. The project

Ludington North Breakwater Light—circa 1950s

Ludington North Breakwater Light

on the White Pine Village Museum, call 231-843-4808.

Status: *Active. Not open to public.*

Access: *From the junction of US-31 and US-10 just east of Ludington, go west on US-10, which turns into Ludington Ave. Take Ludington Ave. to its end at the lakefront and Stearns Park just to the north, from where the base of the north breakwater may be accessed.*

that resulted in the construction of these breakwaters at Ludington was largely complete by 1914. A light on the end of the south breakwater was established to mark the new harbor entrance. In 1914, the light marking the harbor was moved across the entrance to the end of the north breakwater. It is unclear whether the south light was picked up and moved over to the north breakwater or a new light was constructed there. Surprisingly, no details about these relatively recent lights have been found.

The present Ludington North Breakwater Light was built in 1924 and automated in 1972. It consists of a fully enclosed, square, pyramidal steel tower supporting a polygonal lantern room that originally housed a fourth order Fresnel lens. The front and rear bases of the 57-foot tower are shaped like the prow of a ship to break incoming waves and divert rafting ice. In 1994, the concrete superstructure upon which the lighthouse rests was squared-off and slightly enlarged. The added weight caused the underlying timber-crib foundation to settle and shift. As a result, the light tower leans approximately 3-4° to the north-northeast. On October 17, 1995, the Fresnel lens was removed and replaced by a modern plastic optic that produces a light with a focal plane 55 feet above water level. The old lens was put on display in the maritime building of the White Pine Village Museum, operated just south of town by the Mason County Historical Society. The third order Fresnel lens from Big Sable Point Lighthouse is on display in the same room. For more information

Fourth order Fresnel lens from the Ludington North Breakwater Light, now in the White Pine Village Museum

Pentwater Pierhead Lights

The harbor of Pentwater, Michigan is in Pentwater Lake, 20 miles south of Big Sable Point. Early commercial activity around Pentwater consisted chiefly of lumbering and later the shipment of agricultural produce. Pentwater today is a pleasant place to visit and a bustling resort during the summer season.

Pentwater South Pierhead Light—August 11, 1914

courtesy of Dave Tinder

Originally there was an unnavigable connection between Lake Michigan and Pentwater Lake. Work on a dredged channel, revetments, and piers began in 1867. In time, both the north and south piers extended 610 feet past the shoreline into Lake Michigan.

The South Pierhead Light was established in 1873. It consisted of a square, wooden, pyramidal tower with an open lower framework connected to shore by a raised catwalk. In contrast to later designs, the lantern room was supported by the sharply tapering upper walls of the structure and not by a lantern deck. In 1890 a front range light consisting of a lantern suspended on a wooden pole was added but later discontinued as unnecessary. The 1873 light remained in service until 1937 when it was replaced by the current skeletal steel structure (not pictured).

The modern cylindrical steel tower presently at the end of the north pier entered service on October 8, 1987. Weighing 12,000 pounds and 30 feet high, the tower supports a solar powered plastic optic and an automated fog signal horn. The tower also housed a radio beacon transmitter, since discontinued. The prototype of this design is credited to Jon Kiernan of the Coast Guard's Ninth District Shore Maintenance Detachment in Cleveland. It is modeled after the "D9" tower of which there are now many on the Great Lakes. The "D9" tower, however, is somewhat smaller in diameter and can only house a light, not the other navigational aids. No matter how functional these new lights may be, they will never be very attractive.

Status: *Active. Not open to public.*

Access: *Best access to the pier lights is at the south end of the beach area in Charles Mears State Park. A daily or annual permit is required for entrance. From US-31, follow Business Route 31 into town until it turns into Hancock St. Turn west on Lowell St. to the park entrance.*

Pentwater North Pierhead Light

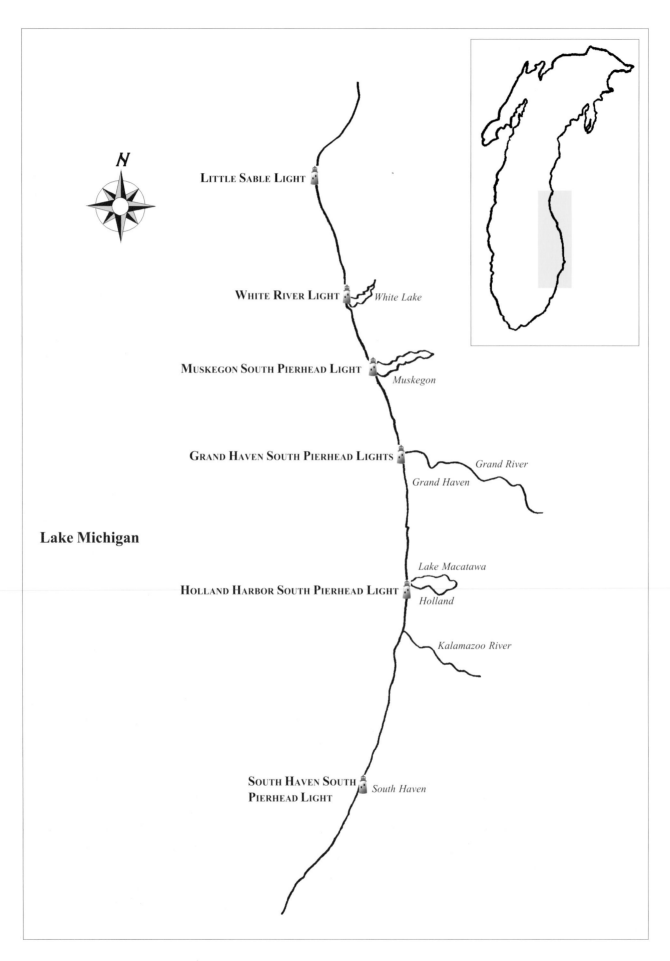

N

LITTLE SABLE LIGHT

WHITE RIVER LIGHT — *White Lake*

MUSKEGON SOUTH PIERHEAD LIGHT — *Muskegon*

GRAND HAVEN SOUTH PIERHEAD LIGHTS — *Grand River*

Grand Haven

Lake Michigan

Lake Macatawa

HOLLAND HARBOR SOUTH PIERHEAD LIGHT — *Holland*

Kalamazoo River

SOUTH HAVEN SOUTH PIERHEAD LIGHT — *South Haven*

Little Sable Light

Broad and rounding, Little Sable Point is one of the most prominent points of land on the eastern shore of Lake Michigan. The original French name of "Petite Pointe au Sable" meaning "small point of sand" remains an apt description. In reality, however, Big Sable Point 28 miles to the north is not that much larger. Beginning in 1870, the Lighthouse Board urged the construction of a coastal light in this area because of the long stretch of shoreline that was unlighted and the increased volume of vessel traffic in the vicinity.

Given the French name of the place, the new light was appropriately named "Petite Pointe au Sable Lighthouse." Construction was completed in 1873 and the new light was first exhibited at the start of navigation in the spring of 1874. Nearly identical lighthouses were also established in 1874 on Lake Superior at Au Sable Point and Outer Island. The long name proved cumbersome and was officially changed to "Little Sable Point" in 1910. Currently, the surviving tower is simply referred to as Little Sable Light.

The lighthouse originally consisted of a tall, conical, red-brick tower with an overall height of 115 feet. An enclosed passageway connected the tower to a two and one-half-story red-brick

Little Sable Light

keeper's dwelling that contained quarters for the families of the keeper and his assistant. The original optic, which remains in place, is a third order Fresnel lens that produces a light with a focal plane 108 feet above water level. Viewed from a ship in the daytime, the brick tower was difficult to spot against its background of sand dunes. As a remedy, the tower was painted white in 1900 to make it a more effective daymark. In 1911, the dwelling was essentially converted into a three-story building by the addition of a large roof dormer built to enlarge the living space. A fog signal was never established at Little Sable Point.

Little Sable Light was elec-

Little Sable Light—August 11, 1914

United States Coast Guard

trified in 1954 and fully automated in 1955. The Coast Guard demolished the keeper's dwelling and all of the other outbuildings that were no longer needed to save on maintenance costs in 1955. At the same time, a concrete containment wall was built and buried in the sand about ten feet in front of the tower for erosion protection. Maintenance costs associated with keeping the tower painted were also eliminated around 1974 when the tower was sandblasted to reveal the underlying red-brick. Modern freighters no longer needed the tower as a daymark.

Old photographs viewed sequentially show that a large amount of real estate in front of Little Sable Light has been lost to erosion. Heavy storms coupled with high water levels in 1986 and 1987 necessitated additional anti-erosion measures in 1988 as a safeguard. The large riprap stones at the base of the tower are evidence of that work. However, this light has never been as seriously threatened as the tower at Big Sable Point.

Today, Little Sable Light lies within Silver Lake State Park. The state added a parking lot to allow visitors to view the light tower and to use the beach frontage for swimming and recreation. Shifting sands have severely encroached upon the tower and it is difficult to envision the large house and other buildings that once made up this light station. The surroundings, however, are beautiful and a visit is highly recommended.

Status: *Active. Not open to public.*

Access: *From US-31, take the exit for Shelby Rd. and go west on Shelby for a little over six miles to Scenic Dr. Turn north (right) onto Scenic and follow the paved road, which jogs to the east on Buchanan for a short distance and then north again as 18th Ave. Continue north on 18th Ave. about three and one-half miles to its end at Silver Lake Rd. Turn west (left) onto Silver Lake Rd. and follow the signs for a little over one mile to the parking lot operated by the state park. A daily or annual permit is necessary to use the lot.*

Little Sable Light—circa 1905

Little Sable Light—circa 1920

Little Sable Light—circa 1910

White Lake Harbor

White Lake Harbor is located 20 miles south-southeast of Little Sable Point and a little over 11 miles north of Muskegon. The towns of Montague and Whitehall, Michigan are at the northeast end of White Lake, about four miles from the connecting channel with Lake Michigan. Logging, timber, and sawmills were the main commercial concerns on White Lake for many years. The first sawmill was established by Charles Mears in 1838 and the last one closed in 1907. Passenger traffic to local resorts and shipping of agricultural products, especially fruit, also became important. The lake is relegated to small craft use today.

The White River formed the original connection between White Lake and Lake Michigan. The river was narrow and crooked, but private business interests attempted to improve its depth. The Federal government abandoned this channel and a straight cut was dredged from lake to lake south of the natural river mouth. The work was completed late in 1870. Construction of parallel piers into the deep water of Lake Michigan began shortly thereafter.

White River South Pierhead Light

The first light at White River was established on the outer end of the south pier in 1871. It consisted of a square, wooden, pyramidal tower with an open lower framework and an overall height of 27 feet. White in color when built, the tower was painted red in 1917. The original optic was a fifth order Fresnel lens with a focal plane 33 feet above water level. The light was downgraded to a sixth order lens in 1902. The structure was connected to shore along the pier by a raised catwalk. Ongoing harbor improvements resulted in the south pier being lengthened a total of four times between 1871 and September 1901, finally projecting 650 feet beyond the shoreline. Each time, the pier light was moved out to the new end and the catwalk extended to close the gap.

Over the years, the pier and catwalk were repaired numerous times after being damaged by storms, ice,

White River South Pierhead Light—circa 1911

fires, and collisions with ships attempting to enter the harbor. Dilapidated beyond repair, the catwalk was demolished in May 1925. At the same time, the pierhead light was automated with an acetylene gas lamp controlled by a sun valve. Both piers were substantially rebuilt with concrete in 1930. On August 9, 1930, the acetylene light was transferred to an open steel skeletal tower erected on the end of the south pier. The old tower was razed. The acetylene light was finally electrified in 1949. A modern pole light with a plastic optic dating from the late 1980s marks the pierhead today.

White River Light—circa 1907

White River Light

Construction of the main lighthouse to mark the harbor entrance began in September 1875 and was completed three months later in December, some four years after the establishment of the south pierhead light. The surviving lighthouse consists of a one and one-half-story rectangular dwelling constructed of cream-colored brick with an attached octagonal brick tower on the northwest corner. A fourth order Fresnel lens was installed late in April 1876. The light was first exhibited on May 13, 1876. The light was electrified in 1918 but the kerosene lamp was retained for use as an emergency backup as power outages were common. The dwelling itself was not electrified until May 1924. The light was automated in 1945 and eventually discontinued in 1960.

The basic design of White River Light was repeated at several locations on the Great Lakes, especially on Lakes Michigan and Superior. All within a few years of each other, nearly identical structures, varied only by tower placement and shape, were built on Lake Michigan at Chambers Island, Eagle Bluff, and McGulpin Point.

The light station site was purchased by Fruitland Township in

White River Light

White River Light—circa 1913

1966 for use as a museum and public park. The refurbished lighthouse opened to the public as a museum late in the summer of 1970. The original lens makes up one of the ground floor exhibits. The museum is open Memorial Day through Labor Day, Tuesday through Friday from 11 a.m. to 5 p.m. and noon to 6 p.m. on Saturday and Sunday. The museum is open only on weekends through the end of September.

No discussion of White River Light would be complete without mentioning its longest serving keeper, Captain William Robinson. Captain Robinson's association with the site began with his assignment as keeper of the South Pierhead Light in 1871. Four years later he assisted with the construction of the main lighthouse. Responsible for both lights, he served a total of 47 years at the station and raised a very large family there. Both his eldest son and grandson began their lightkeeping careers at White River. A couple of other sons also took up lightkeeping. Forced to retire due to old age, Captain Robinson was 87 years old when he died in the lighthouse on April 2, 1919. He was the oldest keeper on active duty at the time of his retirement just two weeks earlier. His grandson succeeded him as keeper. To say that Captain Robinson was strongly attached to the place is putting it mildly. His vigilant spirit is said to still be keeping watch over the station.

White River Light—February 1952

Status: *Inactive. Open to public as a museum.*

White River Light Station Museum
6199 Murray Rd.
Whitehall, MI 49461
Phone: 231-894-8265

Access: *From US-31, exit onto White Lake Dr. and go west to South Shore Dr. Turn south (left) on South Shore Dr. and continue to follow museum signs to the end of Murray Rd. (South Shore turns into Murray Rd. after it crosses Scenic Dr.). At the end of Murray Rd. look for a driveway and sign on the left that leads up to the museum parking lot.*

White River Light

Muskegon Harbor

Muskegon Harbor is at the outlet of Muskegon Lake into Lake Michigan. The harbor is located just over 11 miles south of the harbor at White Lake and 12.5 miles north of Grand Haven. Muskegon Lake is about four miles long and up to two miles wide at its western end with plenty of deep water throughout. It provided a fine harbor for commerce and refuge from storms. After its early years as a logging port, Muskegon de-

Muskegon Harbor and South Pierhead Light—circa 1914

veloped an industrial base and remains a large manufacturing center. For many years, Muskegon was linked with Milwaukee, 80 miles to the west, by a cross-lake ferry service. There are numerous deep-draft facilities along the south shore of Muskegon Lake. Large lake freighters still handle bulk commodities at the port, especially coal, cement, and limestone.

The first lighthouse at Muskegon was established in 1852 on the southern edge of the harbor entrance.

Little is known of this first light. Some sources indicate it may have consisted of a short light tower on the roof of a wood-framed keeper's dwelling. The harbor entrance remained in its natural condition until 1863 when private interests organized as the Muskegon Harbor Company began improvements. The Federal government took up the work in 1867, deepening the entrance channel, remodeling the piers that had been started, and extending them into deeper water in Lake Michigan.

Muskegon Light

As harbor improvements progressed, the lighthouse at Muskegon was rebuilt in 1870. It consisted of a one and one-half-story wood-framed dwelling with a short square tower in line with the front wall rising above its gabled roof. Identical structures were built at Old Mission Point on Grand Traverse Bay (also in 1870) and on Mamajuda Island in the Detroit River (1866). Muskegon Lighthouse was discontinued in 1903 when a system of range lights went into operation on the south pier. Its fourth order Fresnel lens was

Muskegon Light—circa 1902

transferred to the rear range tower, which later became the present South Pierhead Light. A U.S. Lifesaving Station was established on the entrance chan- nel a short distance behind the main lighthouse in 1880. That building survives and remains a part of the Muskegon Coast Guard Station.

Muskegon South Pierhead Light

Muskegon received its first pier light in 1871. However, no record has been found that indicates whether it was located on the north or south pier. Nor does it appear in any photographs from that era.

A steam-powered fog signal and light were established at the end of the south pier in 1899. The building was wood-framed and sheathed in cast-iron plates for durability. A lantern room was placed on the gable end of the building facing the lake. A raised catwalk connected the structure to shore.

In 1903, the present conical cast-iron tower was erected several hundred feet behind the fog signal building. The catwalk connecting both structures to shore was retained. This tower has an overall height of 53 feet and was originally fitted with the fourth order Fresnel lens taken from the 1870 main light. Today, a modern plastic optic produces a light with a focal plane 50 feet above water level. The tower and fog signal building, each with its own light, created a range useful to ships approaching the harbor. The north and south piers were much longer at the time the range light system was implemented than they are today. Both piers were substantially shortened to their present lengths as part of a later harbor expansion project, leaving the South Pierhead Light where it is today. The catwalk no longer exists.

Muskegon South Pierhead Light—circa 1912

Muskegon South Breakwater Light

A new type of harbor design called the "arrowhead" was introduced on the Great Lakes after 1905. Two breakwaters connected to shore north and south of the original piers converged at a 90° angle offshore to form a new harbor entrance and a protected outer harbor or stilling basin. The stilling basin greatly reduced the chop caused by wave action at the entrance to the piers and the channel leading into the inner harbor. Where necessary, the original piers were then shortened to clear the area comprising the outer harbor.

Construction of arrowhead breakwaters at Muskegon began around 1916 and was largely complete by the early 1920s. Muskegon South

Muskegon South Pierhead Light with the breakwater light in the background—1940s

Breakwater Light dates from the end of the project and remains the main light marking the harbor entrance. It consists of a slender, steel, pyramidal tower that is fully enclosed and rests on a rectangular steel base. The modern plastic optic in use produces a light with a focal plane 70 feet above water level. The project also created the present stilling basin (outer harbor) that had to be cleared of the long north and south piers extending out into it. Both piers were shortened back to their present lengths. This resulted in the demolition of the original fog signal building and the catwalk back to the rear range tower, which then became the present South Pierhead Light.

There are two additional nautical attractions worth visiting in Muskegon. Not far from the base of the south pier, just inside the channel at 1346 Bluff Street, is the *U.S.S. Silversides*, a restored and much decorated World War II submarine. A smaller former Coast Guard cutter and a beach landing craft of World War II vintage are also part of the display there. For hours and information phone 231-755-1230 or log on to website www.silversides.org. Late in 2000, the former passenger ferry *S.S. Milwaukee Clipper* opened for weekend tours at a slip along the southeastern edge of Muskegon Lake. Originally named the *Juaniata* when she was built in 1905, the *Milwaukee Clipper* carried thousands of passengers and automobiles between Muskegon and Milwaukee from 1941 until 1970. For more information on the ship and its restoration log on to website: www.milwaukeeclipper.com.

Muskegon South Pierhead Light with the South Breakwater Light in the background

Status: *Active. Not open to public.*

Access: *From US-31, take the Sherman Blvd. exit. Go west on Sherman Blvd. about 5¾ miles to Beach St., just past the Muskegon Country Club. Turn north (right) on Beach St. Beach angles to the northwest and makes a sharp turn to the left but continues north. Follow Beach St. to its end near the Coast Guard Station and the Pere Marquette Park parking area. Both the south pier and south breakwater may be accessed from this area.*

Muskegon South Pierhead Light looking east toward shore—circa 1910

Grand Haven Harbor

The harbor at Grand Haven consists of the mouth and lower portion of the Grand River. Commerce here began in 1825 when Rix Robinson, an agent of the American Fur Company, established a trading post at the mouth of the river. Originally called Ottawa, the name was changed to Grand Haven in 1863. Development here was rapid, as the mouth of the Grand River provided one of the widest and deepest natural harbors on Lake Michigan. Large freighters still visit the port, and the main commodities handled today are coal and sand.

Grand River Light

The first lighthouse at Grand Haven was built in 1839. Called the Grand River Light, it was located on the south side of the river's mouth under the bluff. The height of the tower from its base to the lantern deck was only 30 feet. Eleven Argand lamps and 14" reflectors produced the light, reduced to four in number by 1848 as a fuel saving measure. Little else of this first light is known. In 1855, it was replaced by a brick tower with an attached dwelling perched on a high bluff behind the original site. This light, 150 feet above lake level, was visible from a much greater distance.

Grand Haven South Pier Lights

The harbor at Grand Haven was easy to improve and the Federal government undertook the work in 1867. The entrance channel was dredged and parallel piers run out into the lake. Large volumes of water from the Grand River kept the system flushed so only minor dredging was necessary to keep the entrance free of any sand bars that developed. This was one of the few sites on Lake Michigan where offshore breakwaters were never needed to ensure an easily entered harbor of refuge.

In 1875, a wood-framed building to house steam-powered fog sig-

Grand River Light viewed from the north side of the river—circa 1894

nal equipment was built at the end of the south pier. A light was added to its lakeward face in 1895 and the light on the bluff was discontinued. The south pier was extended several times so that by 1905 the fog signal building was 600 feet from the end. At that time, the building was moved to the outer end of the pier and a new, taller, conical cast-iron tower was erected in its place. The tower and fog signal building, each with its own light, created a range useful for approaching the harbor. A raised catwalk connected both structures along the pier and to shore. The catwalk was an important safety feature in the days when keepers had to make their way be-

Grand Haven South Pier Lights from atop the catwalk—circa 1915

tween the two structures despite crashing waves that often swept over the piers.

Grand Haven South Pierhead Entrance and Inner Lights

Grand Haven South Pierhead Entrance Light (the old fog signal building) rests on an elevated base of reinforced concrete dating from 1921, when the first work to cap the pier with concrete was completed. The side facing the lake is shaped like the prow of a ship to break incoming waves and rafting ice. In 1922 the building was sheathed with corrugated steel to prevent deterioration of its wooden sides. The focal plane of the light produced is 42 feet above water level. Grand Haven South Pierhead Inner Light (the conical cast-iron tower) supports a light with a focal plane 52 feet above water level. Sixth order Fresnel lenses were the original optics for both lights, since replaced with modern plastic lenses. Both were automated in 1969. One of the Fresnel lenses is on display in Grand Haven at the Tri-Cities Historical Museum located along the river front at Harbor and Washington Streets.

By the end of 1983, automation of all U.S. lighthouses on the Great Lakes had been completed. Thereafter the Coast Guard looked for ways to reduce maintenance costs. Early in 1987, bids were taken for the demolition of the catwalk at Grand Haven. Although nostalgic, the structure was not nec-

Grand Haven South Pierhead Entrance Light—circa 1917

essary in an era of unmanned lights. The catwalk was scheduled for demolition on June 2, 1987. Before that could happen, however, local resident Edward J. Zenko lead an effort to save the catwalk. Mr. Zenko and his supporters were successful and made plans to electrically light the catwalk at night. The catwalk was first lit on November 25, 1988, and has been lit every night since. Unfortunately, Mr. Zenko died at the end of December 1987 and never saw his plans come to fruition.

Winter sunset at Grand Haven South Pier

Grand Haven and St. Joseph are the only two places on the Great Lakes having pier range light systems with both towers and catwalks intact. The lights at Grand Haven are perhaps the most recognizable of all Michigan lights. Grand Haven is home to a modern Coast Guard base, and the city hosts a Coast Guard Festival the first weekend of August every year. Grand Haven has retained much of its ambiance despite tremendous growth, not only as a summer destination, but as a place to reside year-round. The Harbor Walk along the Grand River from downtown out to the end of the south pier is one of the most pleasant paths available anywhere.

Status: *Active. Not open to public.*

Access: *From US-31, turn west on Jackson St., which is about ¼ mile south of the bridge on US-31 that spans the Grand River. In town, Jackson St. turns into Harbor Dr. Harbor Dr. hugs the river right out to the south pier and the adjacent Grand Haven State Park. A parking lot off Harbor Dr. near the base of the pier is operated by the state park. A daily or annual permit is required for its use.*

Grand Haven South Pierhead Entrance Light

Holland Harbor

Holland Harbor is formed by Lake Macatawa (formerly known as Black Lake) and the mouth of the Macatawa River, which flows into its eastern end. The western end of Lake Macatawa is connected to Lake Michigan by an improved entrance channel. Large freighters call at the port, handling such commodities as coal, salt, cement, stone, and agricultural chemicals.

Holland was first settled in 1847 by a band of religious pilgrims from the Netherlands. One year after arriving, the Dutch settlers applied for Federal assistance to create a connecting channel between Lakes Michigan and Macatawa. When the help wanted did not materialize, they took matters into their own hands by digging a shallow but navigable channel and protecting it with piers and revetments made of timber and stone. In 1867, the same year the village was incorporated, the Federal government assumed the work. By 1899 the project was largely complete.

Holland Harbor South Pierhead Light (Big Red)

The first light at the end of the south pier was established in 1872. Little is known of this first light. Typical of the period, it most likely consisted of a small, square, wooden pyramidal structure with an open lower framework. The Lighthouse Board installed a new light atop a metal pole in a protective cage in 1880. An oil lantern was lowered by pulleys for service. One source indicates that this light dated from 1890 and infers that it may have served as a front range light with the older structure serving as the rear light of the range. Perhaps a range light system was necessary to help the increased traffic at the port. As the harbor neared completion, a flourishing resort trade sprang up with various hotels competing to provide the best attractions. The Graham and Morton shipping line made two trips daily from Chicago, bringing droves of summer visitors. It was at the height of the resort era traffic that better lighting of the harbor entrance became necessary.

Holland Harbor South Pier—July 30, 1906

Holland Harbor South Pierhead—circa 1912

The third light at Holland Harbor was established sometime prior to the commonly accepted date of 1907. An old picture postcard dated July 30, 1906 clearly shows a square, tapering, cast-iron tower with an open lower framework standing alone at the end of the pier, connected to the shore by a raised catwalk. Another old photograph (not shown) depicts the same structure tilted to one side after being damaged in a winter storm. In 1907, the fog signal building that would later become Big Red was built immediately behind the taller light tower at the end of the pier. The raised catwalk connecting both to shore was retained. Both structures were painted white.

The fog signal building was wood-framed but sheathed in

Holland South Pierhead Light—circa 1912

cast-iron plates for durability. There were living quarters for the keeper on the second floor. It has been said that the building's gabled roof is reminiscent of traditional Dutch styles and reflects the in-fluence of the settlers in the area. This observation, however, may be discounted as nearly identical structures were built within a few years of each other at Waukegan, Illinois and Kewaunee, Wisconsin.

Holland Harbor South Pierhead Light

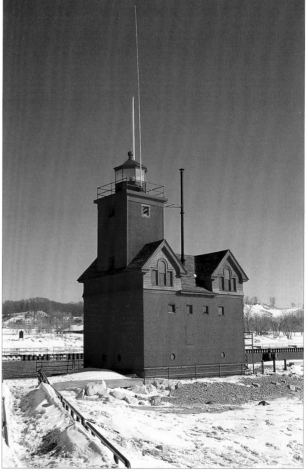

... or "Big Red"

Holland Harbor Light Station was automated in 1932. In 1936, the freestanding light tower in front of the fog signal building was discontinued. Its lantern room and sixth order Fresnel lens were transferred to the top of a square tower that was built through the gabled roof at the western end of the fog signal building. It is probably around this time that the catwalk was also eliminated. The lighthouse received its distinctive red paint job in 1956. The Fresnel lens was later removed and donated to the Netherlands Museum in town. Today a modern plastic optic produces a light with a focal plane 52 feet above water level. When the Coast Guard recommended that the lighthouse be abandoned in 1970, citizens circulated petitions to save it. The Holland Harbor Lighthouse Historical Commission was then organized to preserve and restore this landmark. Big Red remains one of the most visually distinctive lighthouses on the Great Lakes and certainly one of the most instantly recognizable in Michigan.

Status: *Active. Not open to public.*

Access: *Direct access to the south pier entails crossing privately owned property that is part of the Macatawa Association at the southwestern corner of Lake Macatawa. This route has been blocked in recent years. A very good view is available from the north pier that adjoins Holland State Park. From US-31, exit at Lakewood Ave. and proceed west to the branching with Douglas Ave. Continue west on Douglas Ave., which turns into Ottawa Beach Rd. and ends at the entrance to the state park. A daily or annual permit is required for entry.*

Holland Harbor South Pierhead Light

Kalamazoo River Light

The present entrance to the Kalamazoo River and the harbor of Saugatuck lies just seven miles south of Holland Harbor. One of the earliest lights on Lake Michigan was built on the north side of the river's mouth in 1839. Little is known of the first Kalamazoo River Light. The height of the tower from its base to the lantern deck was only 30 feet. Eleven Argand lamps and 14" reflectors were the light source, reduced to six in number by 1848 as a fuel saving measure. In 1859, a new light was constructed on higher ground in the dunes nearby as erosion had washed out the first light.

Kalamazoo River Light—circa 1912

The 1859 light consisted of a two-story wood-framed dwelling with a square wooden light tower emerging from the roof peak. This was a design repeated at several locations around the lakes and especially on Lake Michigan. Within a few years of each other, nearly identical lighthouses were built at Cheboygan Point on Lake Huron and on Lake Michigan at Sheboygan, Tail Point, and St. Joseph. The lighthouse remained in service through the close of navigation in 1914. The abandoned structure was finally toppled by a tornado in 1956. Supposedly, some of the lumber was salvaged and used to build a summer cottage nearby.

The original distance from the mouth of the river to the twin villages of Saugatuck and Douglas on Kalamazoo Lake, which is little more than a wide spot in the river, was three miles. Shoaling was a constant problem as the river twisted and turned through this distance. Such a channel was sufficient for logging, but not for shipping.

Private business interests initiated harbor improvements that the Federal government took over

Abandoned Kalamazoo River Light—circa 1940

in 1869. Revetments were placed, piers extended to the lake, and the channel dredged. As soon as a navigable channel was established, it quickly filled in again after the dredge departed. Finally, a new entrance from Lake Michigan was cut seven-tenths of a mile north of the natural river mouth. It bypassed a mile of the natural river, leaving an L-shaped pond not connected with the lake or the river and known locally as Ox Bow Lake. Kalamazoo River Light, now in the wrong place, was discontinued as the improvements neared completion. By this time, only small excursion boats serving the resort trade used the harbor.

Small modern pole lights mark the entrance to the Kalamazoo River and Saugatuck Harbor today. Saugatuck has built its reputation as an artist community and remains a popular tourist destination. While in the area, drive around Kalamazoo Lake to the village of Douglas and tour the museum ship *S.S. Keewatin*. The *Keewatin* is a former passenger steamship of the Canadian-Pacific Railway that operated on the Great Lakes from 1907 to 1965. The ship has been berthed in Douglas since June 1967 and is open for tours daily from Memorial Day weekend through Labor Day. For information call 616-857-2464.

*Museum ship **S.S. Keewatin***

South Haven Harbor

The harbor at South Haven is located at the mouth of the Black River, 19 miles south of Saugatuck and 22 miles north-northeast of St. Joseph. Local citizens began harbor improvements that were assumed by the Federal government in 1869. A dredged entrance channel leads from the deep water in Lake Michigan between parallel piers through the mouth of the river upstream to the Dyckman Avenue bridge. Timber and fishing gave way over time to the shipment of agricultural products, especially fruit. Early in its history, South Haven became a well-known summer resort and was linked by daily steamship service to Chicago. Pleasure craft ply the harbor today and the city's status as a resort continues. South Haven deservedly remains one of the most popular tourist destinations in southwest Michigan.

South Haven Harbor—circa 1916

South Haven South Pierhead Light

South Haven has had a lighthouse on the south pier since 1872. Common to the era, the design consisted of a square, wooden, pyramidal tower with an open lower framework. It was connected to shore by a wooden catwalk. This lighthouse remained in service until the present light was established on November 13, 1903. It consists of a conical cast-iron tower with an overall height of 36 feet. The original optic was a sixth order Fresnel lens, since replaced by a modern plastic optic with a focal plane 37 feet above water level. In June 1913, a mechanically operated fog bell was mounted from a bracket on the lakeward face of the tower. The fog bell was replaced by an air-powered fog horn in 1937. A modern fog signal remains in use yearly from May 1 to November 1. The raised iron catwalk has survived into the present. The old keeper's house remains near the base of the south pier. Currently it is used for administrative offices by the Michigan Maritime Museum.

While in South Haven, *do not miss* the Michigan Maritime Museum located in town on Dyckman Avenue just before the bridge. The museum is dedicated to "interpreting, preserving and presenting the story of the people who built ships and traveled the Great

The first South Haven South Pierhead Light—circa 1900

Both piers and South Haven South Pierhead Light—circa 1902

Fishing, South Haven, Mich.

South Haven South Pier—circa 1908

Passenger steamer bound for Chicago passes the South Haven Pierhead—circa 1908

Lakes and its waterways." The museum has the only known collection of restored, vintage U.S. Coast Guard rescue boats, including a 36-foot motor lifeboat.

The boats are displayed in a modern boathouse built to resemble those used by the U.S. Lifesaving Service in the late 1870s. Hours are from 10 a.m. to 5 p.m. Tuesday through Saturday and noon to 5 p.m. on Sunday.

Michigan Maritime
Museum
260 Dyckman Avenue,
At the Bridge
South Haven, MI 49090
Phone: 800-747-3810

Status: *Active. Not open to public.*

Access: *From I-196, take exit 20 and go west on BR-196, which becomes Phoenix St. Continue west on Phoenix through town, which eventually turns into Water St. after it crosses Kalamazoo St. Continue west on Water St. to its end at the South Beach parking lot. The base of the south pier is just to the north of the parking lot.*

South Haven South Pierhead Light viewed from the opposite pier

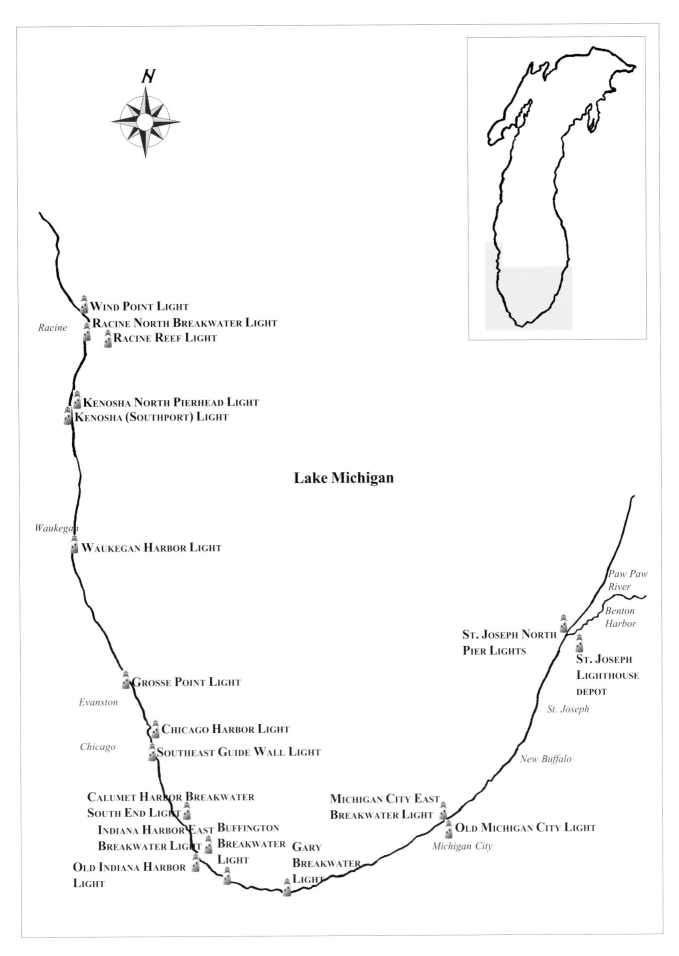

N

Lake Michigan

Racine

WIND POINT LIGHT
RACINE NORTH BREAKWATER LIGHT
RACINE REEF LIGHT

KENOSHA NORTH PIERHEAD LIGHT
KENOSHA (SOUTHPORT) LIGHT

Waukegan

WAUKEGAN HARBOR LIGHT

Paw Paw River

Benton Harbor

ST. JOSEPH NORTH PIER LIGHTS

ST. JOSEPH LIGHTHOUSE DEPOT

GROSSE POINT LIGHT

Evanston

St. Joseph

CHICAGO HARBOR LIGHT

Chicago

SOUTHEAST GUIDE WALL LIGHT

New Buffalo

CALUMET HARBOR BREAKWATER SOUTH END LIGHT

MICHIGAN CITY EAST BREAKWATER LIGHT

INDIANA HARBOR EAST BREAKWATER LIGHT

BUFFINGTON BREAKWATER LIGHT

GARY BREAKWATER LIGHT

OLD MICHIGAN CITY LIGHT

Michigan City

OLD INDIANA HARBOR LIGHT

St. Joseph Harbor

St. Joseph Harbor is located about 22 miles south-southwest of South Haven, 35 miles northeast of Michigan City, and 60 miles northeasterly across Lake Michigan from Chicago. The harbor is at the mouth of the St. Joseph River. St. Joseph was first permanently settled in 1830. It lies near the center of Michigan's famed fruit-growing belt, so the shipment of fruit and other agricultural products was very important to the port. The town also developed into a popular summer resort, especially among Chicago and Milwaukee residents. For many years, St. Joseph was linked to those cities by daily passenger steamers. Although gravel and cement are still handled at the harbor, today it is used mainly by pleasure craft.

The outlet of the St. Joseph River was originally a shifting channel with a depth fluctuating between three and seven feet. Work to improve the harbor began in 1836 and the project called for a dredged entrance channel 16 feet deep protected by parallel piers 270 feet apart. By 1898, the north and south piers extended 1,300 feet and 550 feet, respectively, past the shoreline. The entrance was dredged upstream for about one mile to the junction with the Paw Paw River. Above the dredged channel, the St. Joseph River turns south and flows between St. Joseph on the west bank and the city of Benton Harbor on the east bank.

North Pier Lights at St. Joseph

St. Joseph River Light

St. Joseph vies with Chicago as the site of the first lighthouse established on Lake Michigan. Both were established in 1832, but the one at Chicago was built earlier in the year. The first lighthouse at St. Joseph was a landfall light constructed on high ground near the mouth of the river on its southern bank. In a design common to the early pioneer period, it consisted of a conical, rubble-stone tower with a detached single-story stone keeper's dwelling. The tower was 30 feet tall from its base to the lantern deck. Eleven Argand lamps and 14" reflectors housed in a bird-cage style lantern room provided the light source, reduced to four in number by 1848 as a fuel saving measure. No photographs of the lighthouse are known to exist. This early lighthouse was replaced in 1859 by another built on shore.

St. Joseph South Pier with the north pier lights to the right—circa 1909

Old St. Joseph Light

The second lighthouse at St. Joseph was also a land-fall light, but on even higher ground in town on Lake Boulevard. Established in 1859, it consisted of a two-story, wood-framed dwelling with a square wooden light tower emerging from the roof peak. This was a design that was to be repeated with minor variations at several locations around the lakes, and especially on Lake Michigan. Within a couple of years, nearly identical structures were built at Cheboygan Point on Lake Huron and on Lake Michigan at Sheboygan, Tail Point, and the Kalamazoo River (Saugatuck). The keepers living in the dwelling were also responsible for maintenance of the pier lights. The light on the dwelling was made redundant in 1907 when the present system of range lights was established on the north pier. However, local politicians were able to put enough pressure on the Lighthouse Establishment to keep the light in operation until 1924. Eventually declared surplus property, the old lighthouse was made available to and purchased by the City of St. Joseph. Thereafter the building was used to house a number of different charitable organizations such as the American Red Cross, the American Cancer Society, and the Society for Crippled Chil-

Old St. Joseph Light—circa 1918

dren. Local preservationists lost their battle to save the historic landmark, which was finally razed in September 1955 to make room for a parking lot.

Pier Lights at St. Joseph

The first pier light at St. Joseph was established in 1846 and most likely consisted of a simple, wooden pyramidal structure common to the period. Both the north and south pierheads were lit at one time or another, but lighting of the north pier predominated as it was always the longer of the two piers. The north pierhead light was moved and/or rebuilt frequently in the 1880s as the pier was extended farther and farther out into the lake. The old photograph shown dates from around 1895 and shows the north pierhead light as rebuilt in 1890 joined to a fog signal building. The light tower consisted of a square, tapering, wooden structure with the upper two-thirds enclosed and an open lower framework. The fog signal building was wood-framed and encased in cast-iron plates for durability. It housed the steam-powered equipment for a 10" whistle. Both structures were connected to shore by a raised catwalk. In 1898, an inner light (rear range light) was established on the north pier, thus creating a range light system useful to vessels approaching the harbor entrance. These range lights remained in service until 1907 when they were replaced with the present towers.

St. Joseph North Pierhead Light—circa 1895

St. Joseph North Pierhead and North Pier Inner Lights

The final 1000-foot extension of the north pier was completed in 1906, necessitating the rebuilding of the range light system marking the harbor entrance. Work on the present range lights, which are 315 feet apart, was completed in 1907. St. Joseph North Pierhead Light (the front range light) consists of a conical cast-iron tower with an overall height of just under 36 feet. The original fifth order Fresnel lens remains in place and has a focal plane 31 feet above water level.

St. Joseph North Pier Inner Light (the rear range light) is a combination fog signal/light tower nearly identical to the Michigan City East Pierhead Light. Resting on a raised concrete foundation, the structure is steel-framed, encased in cast-iron plates, and lined with brick. It has a hipped roof topped by an octagonal tower supporting a round cast-iron lantern room. The overall height of the structure is about 57 feet. The original optic was a fourth order Fresnel lens, later reduced to the fifth order lens that remains in place. It has a focal plane 53 feet above water level. Both structures remain connected to each other and along the pier to shore by a raised catwalk.

St. Joseph and Grand Haven are the only two places on the Great Lakes having pier range light systems with both towers and catwalk intact. They remain among the most recognizable of all Michigan lights.

United States Coast Guard

St. Joseph Pierhead Light in ice—1947

Status: *Active. Not open to public.*

Access: *Take I-94 to exit 27 (Niles Rd./M-63). Turn north (right) and continue 5 miles through downtown St. Joseph. Once over the river, turn right onto Upton Dr. Follow Upton to Mariner Dr. (a brick road). Turn left onto Mariner Dr. and follow it to the entrance of Tiscornia Park, from where the beach and the base of the north pier may be accessed.*

St. Joseph North Pierhead Light (front range)

St. Joseph North Pier Inner Light (rear range)

St. Joseph Lighthouse Depot

The Federal government began construction of this depot, which included a main storehouse and keeper's dwelling, in 1891. It was completed on January 7, 1893, at a cost of $35,000. Located on the north bank of the river just inside the piers, the site was readily accessible to supply boats and tenders.

Until 1917, the depot served as the primary supply and buoy repair station for the Lighthouse Establishment's Ninth District (Lake Michigan), which by 1900 included 114 lighthouses. It was used for receiving, overhauling, and storing buoys for the various lighthouse stations. All concrete sinkers for anchoring buoys used in the district were also made there. Late in 1904, construction of another depot in Milwaukee began. The Milwaukee depot would later surpass the one at St. Joseph in importance.

In 1918, the depot was transferred to the Navy Department, housing some naval militia and naval reserve functions until about 1950, when the government discontinued funding. By 1952 the depot was home to the Army Reserves. From 1956 to 1993, it housed the Michigan Army National Guard. Soon after being vacated, the site was placed on the National Register of Historic Places.

St. Joseph Lighthouse Depot Brewpub and Restaurant

Practicing Life Saving Crew and St. Joseph Depot— circa 1907

Status: *Open as a restaurant and brewery/pub.*

Access: *Take I-94 to exit 27 (Niles Rd/ M-63). Turn north (right) and continue five miles through downtown St. Joseph. Once over the river, turn right onto Upton Dr. Turn left onto Mariner Dr. then left onto Lighthouse Lane.*

Three local businessmen eventually purchased the property in February 1996. This is a prime waterfront site and it was initially feared a condominium development lay in the future. The new owners, however, converted the historic storehouse into a brewery and restaurant. The Lighthouse Depot Brewpub and Restaurant opened for business in September 1997. The new owners have displayed great taste and sensitivity in the conversion of this historic site to its new use.

St. Joseph Depot—circa 1930

New Buffalo Light

New Buffalo is a small craft harbor and resort town about 25 miles southwest of St. Joseph and about 10 miles northeast of Michigan City. The site for New Buffalo was chosen in 1834 by Captain Wessel Whittaker of Hamburg, New York (near Buffalo, hence the name). He turned land speculator after suffering a shipwreck nearby. Whittaker thought a harbor could be promoted and developed where the shallow Galien River, flowing through Pottowattamie Lake, entered Lake Michigan. Unfortunately the site was unstable, as the actions of the lake and river currents frequently changed the shape of the entrance to the river.

Whittaker and his partners pushed the Federal government for harbor improvements starting with a lighthouse as a draw for lake shipping. Construction of a lighthouse commenced in 1839 on a raised dune site about one-quarter of a mile south of the river mouth. The tower consisted of a conical rough brick tower 25 feet in height from its base to the lantern deck and topped with a bird-cage style lantern room. A detached house and kitchen stood nearby. No photographs of the lighthouse are known to exist.

Quality control problems plagued the construction process and delayed completion of the station. Originally to have been completed in October 1839, the light was not first displayed until June 20, 1840. This was the era of "the lowest bidder" in lighthouse construction (before the establishment of the Lighthouse Board in 1852) and the New Buffalo Light was in need of constant repairs for the first several years of its existence. Finding competent, conscientious individuals to serve as keepers also proved problematic.

Despite the efforts of the promoters, little was done to improve the harbor and few ships called at New Buffalo. The importance of the light diminished. The original illumination system consisted of eleven Argand lamps and 14" reflectors. By 1848, only four lamps and reflectors were in use. The lamps and reflectors were replaced with a sixth order Fresnel lens, the lowest order available in 1857.

A spurt in lakefront activity occurred in 1847 when the Michigan Central Railroad completed its line to New Buffalo on June 5 of that year, making the town its western terminus. Two long piers were built into the lake north of the river mouth to make the rail line accessible to steamboats. The year 1849 saw a beacon placed on the end of one of the piers. Shipping activity spurred by the railroad was short-lived, however. The line was extended to Michigan City in 1850 and on to Chicago shortly thereafter, thus ending the need for steamer traffic as goods could be shipped directly through by rail.

The port of New Buffalo lingered on for a few more years, but it was dwarfed in importance by the larger ports of St. Joseph to the north and Michigan City to the south. New Buffalo Light was not relit after the close of navigation in 1858 and the light was officially discontinued on August 1, 1859. Erosion was also seriously threatening the safety of the site as natural river and lake currents kept moving the river channel farther and farther south. What materials were salvageable at the site were sold at public auction in 1861 and 1862. Erosion finally claimed the little that remained. The land that had been the site of the light station remained the property of the Federal government for many more years. It too was finally sold at public auction on December 16, 1902 for a paltry $75, $125 less than it had cost the government 64 years earlier. By then, few people remembered there had ever been a lighthouse at New Buffalo.

*Launched in 1972, the motor vessel **Stewart J. Cort** was the first 1000-foot freighter to enter service on the Great Lakes*

Michigan City Harbor

The harbor at Michigan City is located at the mouth of Trail Creek, 35 miles south-southwest of St. Joseph and 38 miles southeast of the mouth of the Chicago River. The town site was laid out late in 1832 as developers believed a good harbor could be made there for the State

Lighthouse and foghorn on piers, Outer Harbor, Michigan City

of Indiana. The first settlers arrived in 1833. Trail Creek, however, was very shallow where it entered the lake. The sand bar at its mouth could be crossed at times by foot without difficulty. Arriving schooners would anchor offshore and transport cargo and passengers ashore via scows, small boats, and barges called "lighters." The process was called "lightering" and it was a dangerous undertaking, even in calm weather. Nevertheless, a prosperous trade in lumber and grain developed and grew rapidly.

The Federal government began harbor improvements in 1836. An entrance channel was dredged and parallel piers run out into the lake. Proposed improvements were not completed due to a lack of appropriations and the work that had been finished prior to the Civil War fell into decay. In 1865, the citizens organized the Michigan Harbor Company to resume harbor improvements and the Federal government took over the work shortly thereafter. By 1885, a well-protected inner harbor basin had been dredged well up into the creek and an outer harbor of refuge partially created behind a detached breakwater. Today the harbor entrance is protected on the west by a long detached breakwater and on the east by a greatly extended east pier that angles to the northwest at its outer end. The remaining west pier now ends only a short distance from shore.

By the turn of the last century, the booming grain trade at the port had been taken over largely by the railroads. Michigan City never developed large manufacturing industries that would have benefited from the delivery of raw materials by water. The harbor today is used mainly by pleasure craft.

Old Michigan City Light

The first light at Michigan City to guide approaching vessels was little more than a lantern on a post. It was maintained by private interests. This post-light was replaced by the first Federal lighthouse in 1837. Located on the east bank at the mouth of Trail Creek, it consisted of a conical rubble-stone tower with a detached one and one-half-story stone house. Both structures were whitewashed. The tower was 40 feet tall from its base to the lantern room deck. The light source consisted of 11 Argand lamps and 14" reflectors reduced to four in number by 1848 as a fuel saving measure. As shipping traffic increased at the port, a better light was needed to guide the ships.

In 1858, a new lighthouse was built about 100 feet east of the previous tower, but still very near the lakeshore. As originally built, it consisted of a two-story dwelling of cream-colored brick on a foundation of Joliet stone. A short, square, wooden tower painted white emerged from the peak of the roof at the northern end of the building to support a lantern room. The original optic was a fifth order Fresnel lens. The design of this lighthouse was repeated at several locations on Lake Michigan. All within a few years of each other, nearly identical structures were built in Wisconsin at Port Washington, Pilot Island, Rock Island, and Green Island; and in Michigan at Grand Traverse and South Manitou Island. Starting in 1887, the light was kept lit year-round rather than only during the normal shipping season from April to November. Improved kerosene lamps were installed in 1902.

The 1858 lighthouse was extensively rebuilt in 1904 and continues to form the core of the present museum building. The 1858 date is still visible on the south wall. An assistant keeper was assigned to the station in November 1874 but lived off-site. In 1904, the dwelling was enlarged by adding two rooms to each floor on the north side. The building was then divided lengthwise down the middle and converted into a duplex with east and west apartments for the families of the keeper and the assistant. Both families had separate entrances. A semi-circular porch and balcony went on the east side and a rectangular porch on the west, both supported by graceful Greek columns.

Other renovations included a gable rising from the east roof to shelter an arched door recess above the balcony. Window tops on the lower story were arched and in keeping with the Greek theme, doors and windows were decorated with pillars and classic motifs. The upper story was shingled with cedar shakes. On October 20, 1904, the light tower was removed from the roof and the lens transferred to the present iron tower above the fog signal building on the east pier.

Michigan City Pier Lights

On November 20, 1871, the first beacon light was established on the east pier, which extended 1500 feet into the lake. The design, common to the era, consisted of a square, wooden pyramidal tower with an open lower framework. It was connected to shore by a long, raised wooden catwalk. This light also had to be maintained by the keeper.

In the fall of 1874, the Lighthouse Board decided to move the east pier light over to the west pier, which extended 500 feet farther into the lake. The move meant the keeper would have to cross the creek in a small boat to access the west pier…not a user-friendly procedure, especially in bad weather. The keeper at the time, Miss Harriet Colfax, requested the assignment of an assistant to the station in October 1874 to help with this added burden and finally got one in November. Harriet Colfax was one of the early female lightkeepers on the Great Lakes. She served as keeper for 43 years at Michigan City between 1861 and her retirement in 1904. The timing in getting an assistant proved to be excellent. Weather related problems delayed the completion of a catwalk on the west pier and the establishment of a light there until November 16, 1874. The assistant actually lived on the west side of Trail Creek,

Michigan City East Pierhead Light—circa 1908

United States Coast Guard

greatly reducing the number of boat crossings needed to transport supplies from the main light.

The keeping of a light on the west pier was beset by weather related problems. Damage to the pier, catwalk, light, or all three was recorded almost every year thereafter. For example, severe storm dam-

Michigan City East Pierhead Light—circa 1910

age to the pier and catwalk on December 6, 1885 made it impossible to reach the light except in the calmest weather. Fearing for the safety of the tower itself, the lens and lighting apparatus were removed, placed in storage, and the light officially discontinued until repairs could be made in the spring. The light was not reestablished until the following June, but the same thing happened after an early fall storm in 1886. The tower was empty when, just a few weeks later, it was carried away by a severe gale on October 14, 1886. Starting in 1887, the light atop the 1858 dwelling was lit year-round. The inability to keep a consistent light

Michigan City Harbor Scene—circa 1910

on the west pier was undoubtedly a contributing factor.

Michigan City East Pierhead Light

A fog signal had been recommended for Michigan City as early as 1894. Work on the new combination fog signal/light tower was not begun until June 1904, after the extension of the east pier was completed. Resting on a raised concrete foundation, the structure is steel-framed, encased in cast-iron plates, and lined with brick. It has a hipped roof topped by an octagonal tower supporting a round cast-iron lantern room. The structure is connected to shore by a very long raised catwalk. On October 20, 1904, the light on top of the 1858 dwelling was discontinued and the fifth order Fresnel lens moved to the new tower. The keepers continued to service the light and the fog signal that was finally installed in 1905. In 1933, the light was electrified and operated from shore. At the same time, the fog signal was converted to an electrically powered air compressor. Full automation arrived in 1960. Today a modern plastic optic produces a light with a focal plane 55 feet above water level. The original lens is on display in the Old Lighthouse Museum.

Michigan City East Pierhead Light with the 1911 Michigan City Breakwater Light in the background

By 1983, the 1904 catwalk was in bad shape. In order to eliminate maintenance costs, the Coast Guard scheduled it for demolition. That action was opposed by city officials and concerned citizens who organized a grassroots campaign to save the historic landmark. The successful effort to "Save the Michigan City Catwalk" took almost 14 years. By the end of 1996, restoration and preservation of not only the catwalk, but also the east pierhead light and the pier itself was complete. Two local women, Patricia Gruse Harris and Betty Moore Rinehart, were key players throughout this process. They were joint winners of the 1997 Servaas Memorial Award presented by the Historic Landmarks Foundation of Indiana.

United States Coast Guard

Michigan City West Pierhead Light—circa 1914

Entrance to Michigan City Harbor in winter—circa 1916

Michigan City Breakwater Lights

New west pierhead and breakwater beacons were also established on October 20, 1904. They consisted of short conical cast-iron towers. A modern pole light marks the end of the short west pier today. The breakwater light was twice destroyed and reestablished after storms in 1906 and 1910. The present Michigan City Breakwater Light dates from 1911 and consists of a slender pyramid of reinforced concrete. A modern plastic optic is displayed 36 feet above the water.

Looking toward Michigan City from outer breakwater—circa 1919

Old Michigan City Lighthouse Museum

The dwelling remodeled in 1904 was vacated by the last civilian keepers in 1940. Thereafter it was used briefly as a private residence and headquarters for the local Coast Guard Auxiliary. The elements and vandals both took their toll on the vacant building. The old lighthouse was declared government surplus in 1960 and sold to Michigan City to be used for historical purposes. On March 9, 1965, the Michigan City Historical Society entered into a lease agreement with the city to restore it and establish a museum. The Historical Society restored the building according to the 1904 plan minus the kitchen and bath facilities. A replica of the original light tower was placed on the roof early in 1973. The museum was officially dedicated and opened to the public on June 9, 1973. The building was listed on the National Register of Historic Places in November 1974. This is a great museum and well worth a visit. Hours are from 1 to 4 p.m. Tuesday through Sunday all year.

Old Lighthouse Museum
Heisman Harbor Road—
Washington Park
P.O. Box 512
Michigan City, IN 46360-0512
Phone: 219-872-6133

Status: *1858 lighthouse: Inactive. Open to public as museum.*
East Pierhead Light: Active. Not open to public.

Access: *From I-94, take exit 34 and go north on US-421, which is also called Franklin St. Continue north on Franklin to 9th St. Turn east (right) onto 9th St. for one block and then north (left) again onto Pine St. As it crosses US-12 (Michigan Blvd.), Pine St. curves left and rejoins Franklin St. Turn north (right) onto Franklin St. and cross the bridge into Washington Park. The Old Lighthouse Museum is just to the left across the bridge. However, due to traffic routing, a left turn into the museum parking lot is prohibited. Instead, bear right for about a block on Lake Shore Dr. and make a U-turn at the turnaround. Then go west on Lake Shore Dr. back to the museum. Once in Washington Park, follow the roads north around the marina to the parking area adjacent to the beach. The east pier is accessed from this location.*

Old Michigan City Lighthouse Museum

The Underbelly of the Beast

Indiana Dunes National Lakeshore is at the south end of Lake Michigan, between Michigan City and Gary, Indiana. The Lakeshore was authorized in 1966 and formally established within the National Park Service in 1972. From this point westward all the way to the Chicago Lakefront expect to see very little open green space. This stretch of shoreline is the industrial underbelly of Lake Michigan—back-to-back steel mills, cement plants, chemical refineries, public utilities, and other commercial concerns. Except for a few marinas and casino ships sandwiched between industrial plants, there is no public access to the shoreline.

The first large facility encountered past Indiana Dunes is Burns International Harbor, also known as the Port of Indiana. Lying 14 miles southwest of Michigan City, it is a modern but completely artificial creation formed by extensive dredging, landfill, and a large breakwater extending into the lake. Opened in 1970, it contains no lights of photographic or historic interest.

Gary Breakwater Light

Gary Harbor is a private harbor at the southern extremity of Lake Michigan, about 8 miles past Burns Harbor and 14 miles southeast of Calumet. The United States Steel Corporation developed and owns this entirely artificial harbor. The harbor consists of a channel extending south into the shoreline for about one mile between parallel piers to a turning basin. A breakwater extending generally northeast from the west side of the entrance protects the entrance to the channel. The harbor was developed after the turn of the last century and Gary Breakwater Light was established in 1911 at the east end of the breakwater. The tower is a unique design of conical cast iron that tapers sharply in its upper portion. Resting on a concrete base, the 30-foot tower supports a light with a focal plane 40 feet above water level. Originally fitted with a sixth order Fresnel lens, the light was automated to acetylene gas lamp early on and today is electrically operated. The actual light in use rests on a metal framework atop the lantern room. The lantern room houses a standby (or backup) light.

Status: *Active. Not open to public.*

Access: *Boat.*

Gary Breakwater Light

Buffington Breakwater Light

Buffington Harbor is a private harbor owned by the Universal Atlas Cement Division of the United States Steel Corporation. It lies about three miles southeast of Indiana Harbor and four and one-half miles northwest of Gary. The harbor is an entirely artificial creation that was built into the lake in front of the company's plant on bulkheaded and filled land that extends 2,400 to 2,900 feet beyond the natural shoreline. At the time of this writing, Buffington Harbor is home to two casino ships. Buffington Breakwater Light was established in 1926 and is a slender conical tower built of reinforced concrete that is poorly maintained. The lantern room houses a plastic optic that produces a light with a focal plane 48 feet above water level.

Status: *Active. Not open to public.*

Access: *Boat.*

Buffington Breakwater Light

The Lighthouses of Indiana Harbor

Indiana Harbor is a large artificial harbor at East Chicago, Indiana, about three miles northwest of Buffington Harbor and six miles southeast of Calumet Harbor. Private interests constructed piers into the lake, dredged the area between them to a depth of 21 feet, and began to construct what would become the Indiana Harbor Canal to connect the harbor with the Little Calumet River. In 1910 the Federal government took over the improvement of the canal by constructing two rubble mound breakwaters to protect the harbor entrance. Today Indiana Harbor consists of an outer and inner basin. Flanked by huge industrial plants occupying vast areas of bulkheaded landfill, the harbor extends into the lake over two and one-half miles northeast of the natural shoreline. Sharing the growth of the Chicago area, Indiana Harbor received such bulk commodities as oil, iron, coal, and lumber. Just a few of the companies present today include LTV Steel, Inland Steel, Amoco Oil, Mobil Oil, and United States Gypsum.

Old Indiana Harbor Light

Old Indiana Harbor Light—circa 1940

The first lighthouse established at Indiana Harbor was completed in 1923 at the inner base of the then relatively short east breakwater. It was a substantial, steel-framed, three-story building with walls of reinforced concrete and red-brick topped by a circular lantern room. The entire structure rested on a concrete crib containing additional storage and machinery spaces. An elevated steel catwalk connected the crib to the shore. The light was downgraded in 1935 after a new light went into service at the end of the extended east breakwater, but the Coast Guard maintained a residential presence at the site through 1969.

Indiana Harbor Light No. 5—note present East Breakwater Light in the distance

Thereafter both lights were fully automated. Photographers John and Ann Mahan captured on film what may be one of the last photographs taken of this light in 1983 while it was still intact. Their photograph appears on page 47 of the book *Northern Lights* by Charles K. Hyde. Within two years the light was demolished down to the level of the crib deck. Today the crib supports a modern white cylinder light simply named Indiana Harbor Light No. 5.

Status: *Active. Not open to public.*

Access: *Boat.*

Indiana Harbor East Breakwater Light

As Indiana Harbor expanded into the lake, the east breakwater was extended more than one-half mile. The Old Harbor Light was now too far inland to be of use to vessels approaching the port, so a new one was built and went into service in 1935. Constructed atop an arched concrete base, the square steel tower tapers upward to support a light with a focal plane 78 feet above water level. A very long raised steel catwalk, now in poor condition, connects the light to the shore near the crib of the Old Harbor Light. As mentioned earlier, this was a manned station through 1969 and Coast Guard personnel lived in the Old Harbor Light.

A light identical to this one at Indiana Harbor was built the same year at Port Washington, Wisconsin. Except for the concrete base, and within a few years of one another, identical steel towers were built at Conneaut and Huron,

Indiana Harbor East Breakwater Light

Ohio and at Gravelly Shoal in Saginaw Bay on Lake Huron. Design similarities are apparent in the Lake Michigan crib lights at Grays Reef and Minneapolis Shoal. These towers are considered Art Deco in style, reflecting the design preferences of the mid-1930s. All were originally fitted with fourth or fifth order Fresnel lenses housed in a circular lantern room. All were remotely operated and later automated. Today, none of these towers retains their original optics or lantern rooms, having been replaced by plastic optics mounted on metal poles.

Status: *Active. Not open to public.*

Access: *Boat.*

Calumet Harbor (South Chicago)

Calumet Harbor is 14 miles northwest of Gary Harbor and about 333 miles by water from the Straits of Mackinac. The harbor is in the south part of the city of Chicago, Illinois and consists of an outer harbor protected by breakwaters and the Calumet River. The combined harbors of Chicago and Calumet form one of the largest inland ports in the world. Deep-draft traffic enters the harbor from Lake Michigan, and barge traffic enters from the Mississippi River via the Illinois Waterway. Early harbor improvements at Calumet were intended to relieve congestion at Chicago Harbor a few miles to the north. The port facilities developed quickly came to specialize in handling bulky commodities such as iron ore, coal and limestone, whereas lighter packaged freight, merchandise, passenger, and excursion traffic continued to go to the Chicago River.

Trade and industrialization brought not only prosperity, but also pollution. As noted in the following discussion of Chicago Harbor, repeated contamination of the city's drinking water supply forced the Chicago Sanitary District to reverse the flow of the Chicago River away from Lake Michigan. The flow was first reversed in 1871 and made more efficient and permanent through the construction of the Sanitary and Ship Canal between 1892 and 1899. In like manner, the flow of the Calumet River was also reversed via the Cal-Sag Channel. Built between 1911 and 1922, the channel connected the Calumet River on the south side of Chicago to the Sanitary and Ship Canal at a point just north of Lockport, Illinois. Designed to carry sewage away from Lake Michigan, the Cal-Sag Channel also became an important component of the Illinois Waterway for commercial barge traffic.

As lake ships grew larger, their ability to maneuver within the congested confines of the Chicago River was impaired. Despite the development of an enlarged outer harbor basin at Chicago, trade at the lakefront began a slow decline after 1916. By 1930, Calumet Harbor had virtually supplanted the mouth of the Chicago River as the city's main port.

Calumet River Light

Calumet River Light was established in 1852 at the mouth of the Calumet River on the north bank. It consisted of a rubble-stone tower typical of the period. John Wentworth, an early land speculator in the area, was instrumental in getting the lighthouse established. The effort, however, was premature as a sandbar with only four feet of water over it prevented ships from entering the river. Mariners complained that the light, frequently mistaken for the light at Chicago, greatly endangered both property and life because there was no harbor at the mouth of the Calumet River. As a result, the lighthouse was discontinued in 1853 and sold. The new owner rented it for $50 per year to the Oehmichs, a family of fishermen, as housing until 1870.

Calumet Pierhead Light

The Federal Government began harbor improvements in 1870. The river mouth was deepened, the sand bar cut across, and parallel piers 300 feet apart extended repeatedly into the deep waters of the lake. By 1896, the south

Calumet Pierhead Light—circa 1910

National Archives

pier had been extended to 2,020 feet and the north pier 3,640 feet. The old stone lighthouse was reacquired by the Lighthouse Board and relit on September 7, 1873. It was discontinued for good on August 15, 1876, when the lens and lighting apparatus were transferred to a newer wooden structure, Calumet Pierhead Light, at the end

Calumet Pierhead Light—June 1933

of the north pier. No photos of either the original stone tower or the first wooden pierhead light are known to exist.

Calumet Pierhead Light was connected to shore by an elevated catwalk that had been extended along with the pier. In 1898, a cylindrical cast-iron tower replaced the wooden light. An identical tower was completed at Waukegan, Illinois less than one year later. Close behind the tower a fog signal building was added in 1899 to house the equipment for a 10" steam whistle. Discontinued on July 20, 1907, the steam-powered fog signal was replaced by a fog bell struck by machinery every twenty seconds. Also at this time, the light was downgraded from a fourth to a sixth order Fresnel lens. These changes reflected the diminished importance of the pierhead light to

ships approaching the harbor. Just one year earlier, on July 20, 1906, Calumet Harbor Light, sitting on the end of the new breakwater offshore, had become the main leading light for Calumet Harbor.

Calumet Pierhead Light continued in service until August 1976, when it was razed after being struck by a ship that lost its steering. Old photographs viewed sequentially show the pierhead light getting closer and closer to shore, and by 1933 it was listed as being on the "outer stub end of north pier." What had once been a very long pier running out into deep water became shorter and shorter as the area behind it was backfilled and the shoreline artificially advanced into the lake. In 1977, a modern light on a short steel tower replaced the old pierhead light. Today even that light is gone as the old north pier is completely confluent with the shoreline.

Calumet Harbor Light

Congress authorized a breakwater for Calumet Harbor in 1896 and by 1915 the projected outer harbor work was complete. The protective breakwater provided a safe, 300-foot wide entrance to the Calumet River and an outer harbor of refuge about one-half square mile in area. By 1906, work on the

first phase of the new breakwater had progressed to the point where a new light could be built at the end, 7000 feet from shore, technically placing it in Indiana. Calumet Harbor Light was displayed for the first time on July 20, 1906.

The light station consisted of a conical cast-iron tower rising from the peaked roof of an attached dwelling and fog signal building. The building was wood-framed and sheathed in cast-iron plates for durability. The original optic was a fourth order Fresnel lens producing a light 51 feet above lake level. A small shed behind the main building provided cover for the station's boat.

Calumet Harbor Light—circa 1914

As the old photographs suggest, the height of the breakwater did not provide much freeboard and the building suffered frequent damage from high waves and rafting ice. In August 1923, the entire structure was jacked up and a new base of reinforced concrete constructed beneath it.

Calumet Harbor Light—August 1923

The lighthouse thus gained an additional 13 feet of height, but it proved not to be enough. Pounding waves from a great storm on October 22, 1929 succeeded in shifting the entire superstructure 18 inches out of alignment with the concrete base.

Calumet Harbor Light—July 5, 1924

There was no choice but to rebuild the entire station and the work was completed early in 1930. The new style was "steamboat modern." The cast-iron tower was retained but now it emerged from the upper deck of a superstructure with walls of concrete framed in steel and sheathed with steel plate.

Calumet Harbor Light—July 1931

As ships continued to grow in size, a long breakwater extension was constructed to double the size of the outer harbor of refuge. Calumet Harbor Light came to mark only a gap in the breakwater, a gap too narrow for the larger freighters to safely use.

Calumet Harbor Light—June 1933

Eventually only small craft came to use the gap and Calumet Harbor Light, no longer needed, deteriorated from neglect. Apparently not considered eligible for the National Register, the Coast Guard awarded a contract to a company in Gary, Indiana to raze the structure. Demolition took place over a 22-day period in May and June of 1995.

Thereafter, a temporary light on an open metal mast was displayed. A modern "D9" cylinder light was put in place late in 1998.

Calumet Harbor Light—May 1999

Calumet Harbor Breakwater South End Light

Today a dredged approach channel from Lake Michigan leads southwest around the south end of the breakwater extension to the outer harbor. Calumet Harbor Breakwater South End Light, 50 feet above the water, is shown from a tapering steel tower with a lower open framework. Dating from 1935, it lost its lantern room in a later modernization.

Status: *Active. Not open to public.*

Access: *Boat.*

Calumet Harbor Breakwater South End Light—circa 1945

United States Coast Guard—9th District

Calumet Harbor Breakwater South End Light

Chicagoland

Chicago Harbor lies on the southwest shore of Lake Michigan. It is 11 miles north of Calumet Harbor (South Chicago), and along with Calumet Harbor forms one of the largest inland ports in the world. The harbor consists of an outer harbor of refuge protected by extensive offshore breakwaters and an inner harbor formed by the Chicago River and its branches. While there is some deep-draft traffic, barge traffic from the Mississippi River via the Illinois Waterway constitutes the major commercial use of the harbor. Pleasure craft, tour boats, restaurant ships, and, in recent years, foreign cruise ships now dominate the use of Chicago Harbor. From the open waters of the lake, whether by day or even better by night, the Chicago skyline is a spectacular sight that should not be missed by anyone visiting the area.

Chicago owes its greatness to its strategic location on Lake Michigan as the point of greatest distance for lake traffic heading toward the growing West. Chicago had become an important link in a transportation route that connected by portage the Chicago River with the Illinois River, and from there the Mississippi River and the Gulf of Mexico. The portage later became unnecessary with the completion of the Illinois and Michigan Canal in 1848. Begun in 1836, the 97-mile long canal connected Chicago with the Illinois River at the town of LaSalle. The canal formed a link with the Mississippi River system, bringing trade and prosperity. The canal came to Chicago because of its harbor on the lake. The Great Lakes could be used to ship goods farther yet. The canal made it possible for Chicago to outstrip St. Louis as the dominant commercial center of the Midwest.

Railroads, like canals, contributed to the growth of lake transportation. They did so by opening up areas in the hinterlands from which agricultural surplus was shipped to lake ports and to which manufactured items were shipped in return. The first railroad reached Chicago in 1848. Chicago's first locomotive, the "Pioneer" (for use on the Galena and Chicago line, later part of the Chicago and Northwestern system), arrived at the city by ship in October of the same year. Railroads spread out from Chicago in all directions. Trade mustered the merchants, bankers, brokers, and shippers who would form the city's commercial foundation.

By the end of the Civil War, Chicago emerged as the rail center of the United States and as the giant of lake shipping. Trade in lumber and grain were joined by meat packing, iron and steel production, and heavy manufacturing. Three-quarters of all waterborne exports from Lake Michigan were carried in lake ships loaded at one of the busy docks crowded along the Chicago River. Old photographs from this era show the river choked with schooners and small steamers, a veritable forest of masts and exhaust smoke, all competing for limited dock facilities. The scene must have been a spectacle, and it is certainly one the author wishes he could have seen in person.

Chicago Lighthouse

The first lighthouse on Lake Michigan was placed at the mouth of the Chicago River in 1832, located on the south bank just northwest of the Fort Dearborn military outpost. The rubble-stone tower was 40 feet high from its base to the lantern deck. Originally fitted with 13 Argand lamps and 14" reflectors

Chicago Light with Fort Dearborn to the right—from an old lithograph circa 1863

in a bird-cage style lantern room, the number of lamps and reflectors was reduced to five by 1848 to save fuel. No photographs of the 1832 tower are known to exist, although it does appear in a number of later engravings and lithographs of the period. The 1832 tower was actually the second tower attempted at the site. In 1831, another builder started a tower 50 feet high. Due to a poor foundation and/or the use of inferior materials, it collapsed under its own weight in October 1831 just before completion. The 1832 tower remained in service until 1858, when it was finally darkened. It was razed in 1860.

At the time the lighthouse was completed, the Chicago River made a sharp bend southward only 70 yards or so before reaching the lake. The river then traveled south fully one-half mile before emptying into the lake, leaving between the river and the lake a large sand bar that grew with each northeasterly gale. As early as 1817, the garrison at Fort Dearborn tried to cut a river outlet straight across the bar, only to have it quickly refill with sand.

First Pierhead Lights

The Federal government finally became involved in 1833 and by 1835, two piers extended into the lake flanking a channel 200 feet wide. The sand bar reformed and the piers were further extended in 1837 and 1840. By 1847 the north pier extended 3900 feet into the lake with the last portion constructed in an arc extending north so as to form a crescent. The shape of the pier, it was hoped, would stem the formation of another sand bar across the entrance channel. A small wooden lighthouse was placed at the end of the pier to serve the new harbor entrance. In 1852, a more permanent light, still of wood, was built on timber piles about 50 feet north of the end of the pier. No photographs of either of these lights are known to exist.

A new Chicago Light went into service at the end of the long north pier on July 9, 1859. The tower consisted of prefabricated parts assembled on site and made from cast iron, which was just becoming a popular building material. The lighthouse was a taller tower with an open skeletal framework and a central enclosed tube in its upper portion that contained a spiral staircase. A wood-framed, two-story keeper's dwelling was located near the base of the tower. By 1870, smoke from belching factories and numerous steamships virtually obscured the light from view. The Lighthouse Board responded in 1873 by moving the main leading light for Chicago Harbor to a prominent bluff north of the city in Evanston, Illinois. Grosse Point Light, with its huge second order Fresnel lens, became the major landfall for mariners on their approach to Chicago.

Although its function was impaired, Chicago Light remained in service. It was finally discontinued on November 15, 1893, by which time the present Chicago Harbor Light had been completed back at the mouth of the Chicago River. Dismantled shortly thereafter, the tower was heightened, renovated, and re-erected for service at Rawley Point (Twin River Point) to the north in Wisconsin.

The 1880s saw continued growth as Chicago became one of the busiest ports in the United States.

Chicago Light—circa 1885

In 1882 alone, the port registered over 26,000 ship arrivals and departures, substantially more than at the salt water ports of New York, New Orleans, and San Francisco combined. Tonnage moved peaked at eleven million tons in 1889. Its slow but steady decline thereafter was largely due to congestion at the harbor and along the river. Docked, dredged, bridged and tunneled under, the Chicago River had been developed to the point where it resembled an artificial waterway, without public landings or access. Little room for expansion remained. As office buildings, hotels, theaters, and department stores of Chicago's business center encroached on industrial sites along the river, land became more valuable. Industries relocated, many of them to the south along the Calumet River.

Chicago Harbor Light

In 1893 Chicago received its last lighthouse near the mouth of the river at the base of the very long north pier. However, it was not destined to remain there. Ships on the Great Lakes were getting larger in size and the Chicago River could not accommodate them. By 1900 the practical limits for a vessel attempting to navigate the river were a length of 325 feet, a beam of 42 feet, and a draft of 16 feet. A harbor commission appointed by the city council in 1909 recommended the development of an outer harbor just north of the entrance to the Chicago River. The new harbor would handle freight and passengers and replace wharves no longer in use on the river. Two years later the city decided to proceed with the establishment of an outer harbor on the lakefront and asked the Federal government to assist by constructing a protective breakwater for the new facility.

Chicago Harbor Light—circa 1925

Chicago began construction of the municipal pier, later named Navy Pier, in April 1914 and completed it in July 1916. The construction of detached breakwaters to protect the lakefront had begun in the 1870s and continued at intervals since then. The ends of existing breakwaters had been lit as early as 1876. Work on the Federal project to extend the existing north breakwater began in 1916 and was largely complete by 1918. In 1919, Chicago Harbor Light was moved from the mouth of the river to a concrete foundation at the newly built south end of the north arm of the outer breakwater. There it remains.

Chicago Harbor Light is the landmark so commonly associated with the lakefront today. More than six stories high, the cast-iron tower is lined with brick for stability and insulation. At the base of the tower is an attached fog signal building on one side and a rectangular boathouse on the other side, both with hipped roofs. The structure supports a light with a focal plane 82 feet above water level. The original optic was a third order Fresnel lens consisting of red and white panels. The lens had been on display earlier in 1893 at the Columbian Exposition held in Chicago, after which it was placed in the new tower. The tower accommodated up to four keepers, whose duties then included servicing the harbor's minor beacons as well. The lighthouse was electrified in 1935 and finally automated in 1979.

Chicago Harbor Light

Later Pierhead Lights

Chicago North Pier Light—circa 1910

Chicago Pierhead Lights with Navy Pier under construction in the background— September 17, 1914

United States Coast Guard

As work on offshore breakwaters progressed, the north pier was shortened in order to clear what was to become the outer harbor area. A system of range lights was established on the pierhead in 1906. The rear range light consisted of a conical cast-iron tower that supported a mechanically struck fog bell and a light with a focal plane 48 feet above water level. A locomotive headlamp served as the front light. It was supported 30 feet above water level in a slender cast-iron cylinder. The front light remained in use until the early 1930s. Then it became apparent a range was not necessary as the Army Corps of Engineers was building a lock at the mouth of the Chicago River just a short distance to the south. The rear tower became a vestigial light as the end of what had been the north pier was connected to the base of the northern lock wall by a new breakwall running north and south. The north pier light was finally discontinued in the 1950s.

Water, Water Everywhere, but Dare to Hazard a Drink

Few people realize there is a lock at the mouth of the Chicago River, and fewer probably understand why it was built. Chicago has always taken its drinking water from Lake Michigan. Trade and industrialization brought prosperity and along with it, pollution. Sewers emptied into the Chicago River, which itself became an open sewer for every type of industrial and domestic refuse. As long as the river emptied into Lake Michigan, the assurance of a safe supply of drinking water was threatened. As early as 1854, Chicago experienced a cholera epidemic in which 5% of the population died. The city responded in 1871 by reversing the flow of the river away from

the lake through an enlarged Illinois and Michigan Canal. A lasting solution, however, proved to be more complex.

Late spring thaws, heavy rains, and increasing discharges of industrial waste into the river overwhelmed the system designed to reverse the river's flow, causing sewage to spill into the lake and taint the water supply. A severe storm in 1885 caused sewage discharge to reach the city's only water intake crib. Approximately 12% of the people in the city died from disease carried in the contaminated water. By the end of the 1880s, mounting typhoid death rates resulted in widespread public panic. Smallpox, dysentery, and cholera also struck the population at alarming rates. By 1891, the death rate due to typhoid fever had reached a high of 124 per 100,000 population. The building of another canal was the first major step taken to attempt to protect Chicago's water supply.

Construction of the Sanitary and Ship Canal began in September 1892 and was completed at the end of 1899. The main channel was flooded for the first time on January 2, 1900. The new canal ran parallel to the old Illinois and Michigan Canal, but was of much larger dimensions, having a navigable depth of 25 feet and a width varying from 160 to 306 feet. Like the 1871 canal, the 28-mile canal reversed the flow of the Chicago River away from the lake. The increased water flow helped break down sewage flowing through the canal. Connecting the South Branch of the Chicago River with the Des Plaines River at Lockport, the canal also became an important component of the Illinois Waterway for commercial barge traffic.

This eliminated the danger of contamination to Chicago's water supply, but controlling the flow of water through the system proved difficult. High lake water levels and periodic heavy rains caused flooding downstream that wreaked havoc in the affected communities. Surrounding states objected to the diversion of Lake Michigan water. In 1930, the U.S. Supreme Court ordered the Chicago Sanitary District to decrease its diversion of lake water. To implement this order, in 1934, the District and the Army Corps of Engineers constructed the Chicago Lock (600 feet long and 80 feet wide) at the mouth of the Chicago River to control forever the flow of water between the river and lake. Thus was created Chicago's inner harbor, completely walled off from the fluctuations of the Lake Michigan waterfront.

Southeast Guide Wall Light

In 1938, the appropriately named Southeast Guide Wall Light was placed at the eastern end of the south lock wall. It consists of a square, tapering steel tower with an open lower framework. The focal plane of the light produced is 48 feet above water level. Since the photograph shown was taken, a horizontal green band was painted around the middle of the tower to serve as a daymark.

Status: *Active*

Access: *There are many possible approaches to the Chicago lakefront. Make sure to obtain a detailed city street map for travel around Chicago. Find your way down to Navy Pier and park wherever you are legally able to do so. The walk out to the end of Navy Pier is a long but pleasant one. From there, both the Harbor Light and the Southeast Guide Wall Light may be viewed from a distance. Another option is to take one of the many harbor tour boats that regularly depart from the south side of Navy Pier and other locations on the river during the tourist season. These tour boats usually pass very close to Chicago Harbor Light.*

The Army Corps of Engineers operates the Chicago Lock and there is no public access. Prior arrangements must be made and a waiver signed before access from shore is permitted.

Southeast Guide Wall Light

Grosse Point Light

As the French name implies, Grosse Point is the largest prominent point of land north of Chicago, which lies 13 miles to the south. By the end of the Civil War, Chicago had evolved into a major railway transportation hub and the dominant player in Lake Michigan shipping. Chicago's lake trade had grown to such an extent that, in 1870, the Lighthouse Board recommended that the leading light for Chicago be moved to a more "eligible site." Smoke from belching factories and numerous steamships virtually obscured Chicago Light, rendering it useless. In 1874 the light was moved to Grosse Point in Evanston. Grosse Point Light, with its huge second order Fresnel lens, became the dominant landfall for mariners on their approach to Chicago Harbor.

Construction was completed in June 1873 and Grosse Point Light became operational on March 1, 1874. The conical brick tower is constructed of cream-colored brick and rises to a height of 113 feet from its base to the ventilator ball at the top of the lantern room roof. The tower has always been painted

Grosse Point Light—circa 1910

pale yellow. Located on a low bluff, the lens focal plane is 119 feet above water level.

Grosse Point was one of only five U.S. lighthouses on the Great Lakes equipped with a second order Fresnel lens and is the only one to retain its original lens atop the tower. The other four lighthouses were Spectacle Reef on Lake Huron, White Shoal in northern Lake Michigan, and on Lake Superior, Stannard Rock and Rock of Ages. None of the largest first order lenses was ever used on the Great Lakes. Although denied by the lampist who installed the lens in 1873, a legend persists that the lens, manufactured in Paris in 1850, was destined for a Florida lighthouse. Supposedly it had been buried in the coastal sands at the onset of the Civil War to keep it from falling into Confederate hands. After the war it was recovered, sent to Washington, D.C., and finally delivered to Evanston.

An enclosed passageway connects the tower to a large two and one-half-story keeper's duplex, also

Grosse Point Light viewed from the beach

Grosse Point Light viewed from the street

constructed of cream-colored brick and painted pale yellow. In 1880, two houses for duplicate steam sirens were built on the bluff just behind the tower. Only one of the fog signals was used, the other serving as a backup in case of equipment failure. The steam sirens were switched to 10" steam whistles in 1892. By 1914, the brick walls of the tower had deteriorated and the entire tower was encased in four inches of concrete.

Grosse Point Light was electrified in 1923 and automated in 1932 shortly after the use of the fog signals was discontinued. The position of keeper at the station was formally eliminated on March 31, 1934. In 1935 the City of Evanston was granted a revocable license for use of the light station property, except for the tower. On May 1, 1941, the light was extinguished as a war measure called for by the National Air Raid Protection Plan. Control over the tower was transferred to the city in July 1942. The entire station was turned over to the Evanston Historical Society to be preserved as a landmark in 1946. It was formally relit as a private aid to navigation on February 9, 1946.

Grosse Point Light—circa 1910

Since then, preservation and restoration have been ongoing processes. In its day, the light station was a showplace for the Lighthouse Establishment and represented a choice assignment for any keeper. So close to a major metropolitan center, there was none of the isolation that plagued personnel at remote locations. Grosse Point Light blends in well with its surrounding affluent neighborhood. It is possible to drive by and not even realize the structure is a lighthouse as the view of the tower from the street is blocked by trees at various angles. Still maintained as a private aid to navigation certified by the Coast Guard, the lighthouse is primarily used as a historical museum. The only negative aspect remains access to the museum inside. Unfortunately, extremely rigid and limited hours of operation restrict entry, and this is a shame given its location in a large urban setting. At least from the outside, Grosse Point Light remains one of the most impressive and beautiful lighthouses on the Great Lakes.

Grosse Point Light Station
2601 Sheridan Road
Evanston, IL 60201

Only guided tours are offered at 2, 3, and 4 p.m. on Saturday and Sunday afternoons, June through September. There is an admission fee. For additional information call 847-328-6961.

Status: *Active. Open to public as a museum.*

Access: *The lighthouse is located at the intersection of Central St. and Sheridan Rd. at the north end of Evanston, Illinois. From I-94, take exit 35A and proceed east on East Lake Ave. Turn south (right) onto Green Bay Rd. for a short distance and then east (left) onto Central St. to its end. Free parking is available at the Evanston Art Center, which is next door to the lighthouse. Many other approaches are possible. As always, a detailed city street map of the area is highly recommended.*

The Port Clinton and Taylorsport Lighthouses

Port Clinton and Taylorsport were small towns located along the Illinois shoreline between Evanston and Waukegan. The sites today are contained by the cities of, respectively, Highland Park and Glencoe.

Taylorsport was established in 1836 and Port Clinton in 1850. Entrepreneurs and land speculators founded both, hoping to capitalize on the boom in lake shipping by serving the needs of local commerce. Timber was still plentiful and sawmills were the main industry. Piers were run out into the lake to serve this local trade and to provide cordwood as fuel for passing steamers. Neither town developed a protected harbor.

*Some old lakeboats never die. The **J.B. Ford**, launched in 1904, remained in active service through 1985. This old-timer served as a cement storage barge on the Calumet River in South Chicago (shown above) from 1989 until June 2001. It has since been moved to Superior, Wisconsin for similar duty.*

Lighthouses at both towns were established in 1855 and were nearly identical in every respect. Set on low bluffs along the shoreline, the lighthouses consisted of a 21-foot brick tower with an attached one and one-half-story brick keeper's dwelling containing six rooms and outside dimensions of about 22 feet square. Both towns thrived for a while but were bypassed by the railroads. Dwarfed by the larger ports of Waukegan to the north and the colossus of Chicago to the south, trade in both towns quickly dwindled and they were abandoned. Both lighthouses were discontinued in 1859.

Waukegan Harbor (Little Fort)

Waukegan is a manufacturing city with a small commercial harbor on the west side of Lake Michigan, 35 miles north of Chicago Harbor. The primary cargoes handled presently are bulk cement and gypsum rock. Except for a large, modern marina, Waukegan Harbor has seen better days. Rundown buildings, weedy fields, and debris-strewn lots create a sense of post-industrial abandonment.

Waukegan Harbor grew to meet the demands of local trade near the mouth of a little stream that was of no importance for harbor purposes. Lacking a natural harbor, early lake vessels loaded and unloaded at unprotected docks on the lakefront. The plan for constructing an artificial harbor consisted of digging an interior basin into the low ground be-

tween the lakeshore and a bluff and running two piers and a breakwater into the lake. This would enclose as much water surface area as possible to create a stilling basin.

Private business interests began the improvement work assumed by the Federal government in 1880. Waukegan's prospects brightened in 1889 when it became the terminus of the Elgin, Joliet, and Western Railroad, which connected with more than 30 railroads running to all parts of the country. Due to the rail connection, Waukegan, like South Chicago, grew rapidly as an alternative harbor serving shipping interests wanting to avoid the congestion of Chicago Harbor.

Waukegan Light

Congress authorized the first lighthouse for Little Fort, as the town was then known, in 1847. Completed in 1849, it consisted of a round brick tower that emerged from the roof of a two-room brick house with a full basement. The lighthouse stood on a bluff near the south bank of the Waukegan Stream close to the intersection of present day Lake Street and Sheridan Road (then called State Street). No photographs of this first light are known to exist. In 1860,

a completely new lighthouse, wood-framed and clapboard-sided, was built 50 feet north of the first light on the same piece of property. Like its predecessor, a wooden addition comprising a kitchen and storeroom soon proved necessary, giving the building a unique "L" shape. The first lighthouse was subsequently razed. The second light saw service through the end of the 1898 shipping season.

Waukegan Light—circa 1898

Great Lakes Historical Society

Waukegan Harbor Light

On January 1, 1899, Waukegan Harbor Light was completed at the entrance to the harbor on the end of the recently extended south pier. Consisting of a cylindrical cast-iron tower equipped with a fourth order Fresnel lens, the new tower was identical to the one at Calumet Pierhead placed in service just a few months before. In 1905, a fog signal building sheathed in iron plates was attached close behind the tower. Both were connected to the shore by a raised catwalk for the safety of the keeper. Living quarters for the keeper were located on the second floor. The design of the fog signal building

Waukegan Harbor Light—circa 1904

appeared again on the lake at Kewaunee, Wisconsin and Holland, Michigan. After the new harbor light went into service, the tower of the 1860 lighthouse

Waukegan Harbor Light—June 1933

was removed and the property sold to the City of Waukegan. Supposedly, the old building was incorporated into the fabric of the present structure at the site that houses the Puerto Rican Society at 150 South Sheridan Road.

In May 1967, a fire sparked by an electrical short circuit destroyed the fog signal building and severely damaged the light tower. The fog signal building was razed and the light tower restored, but the lantern room was removed in a later modernization. Without the lantern room, the cylindrical tower took on the appearance of a tall drum...not much to look at, and hence its nickname as the "drum light." Like so many other sites on the west side of Lake Michigan, the catwalk has not survived into the present, although remnants of it remained close to the tower as late as 1995.

Waukegan Harbor Light after the fire—May 1967

Waukegan Harbor Light after the fire—May 1967

Status: *Active. Not open to public.*

Access: *From the Amstutz Freeway that runs along the Waukegan lakefront, exit on State Route 132 (Grand Ave.) and head east on Grand Ave. Turn south (right) on Pershing Rd. and east (left) on Madison St. The south pier is accessed from the parking lot of the marina.*

Waukegan Breakwater Light

Waukegan Breakwater Light, a minor light at the harbor, deserves mention. Placed at the end of the north breakwater early in 1899, it was a design that would be repeated on Lake Michigan at Kenosha, Milwaukee, Racine, and Sheboygan in Wisconsin and Petoskey, Michigan just before the turn of the century. These "pagoda style" lights housed lenses of the lowest order and were hexagonal towers with steeply sloping corrugated sheet metal sides up to a small lantern deck. All enclosed, a projecting dormer provided an access door with a window above for interior lighting. A slightly oversized lantern room dome gave the appearance of a mushroom cap. When this light at Waukegan was removed from service remains unknown. At other sites, lighthouses of this design were washed off their foundations by severe storms or struck by ships trying to enter port. None of these structures has survived to the present.

Waukegan Harbor Light

Waukegan Breakwater Light—circa 1905

Kenosha Harbor

Kenosha Harbor formed at the mouth of Pike Creek, about 50 miles north of Chicago Harbor and 35 miles south of Milwaukee. The village of Pike Creek was established in 1835. In 1837 the name of the settlement was changed to Southport, as this was the southernmost port in Wisconsin. The final name change to Kenosha occurred in 1850. Kenosha Harbor serves as a base for commercial fishermen and pleasure craft.

The mouth of Pike Creek was barely navigable and often closed off completely by sand bars before the implementation of harbor improvements in the mid-1840s. Arriving schooners would anchor offshore and transport cargo and passengers ashore via scows, small boats, and barges called "lighters." The process, called "lightering," was a dangerous undertaking even in calm weather. The first crude beacon located on shore south of the creek's mouth was a large oak tree cut down, leaving a stump ten feet high. The top of the stump was fireproofed and volunteers took turns keeping a fire kindled nightly during the navigation season. Supposedly, this beacon lasted until 1840. Another early beacon, established around 1846, consisted of an open timber framework 24 feet high. On top of this sat a three-foot-square sash lantern, which was a box with a window on one side. Its $60 cost was funded by a private individual and it also was tended by volunteers.

Kenosha (Southport) Light

Simmons Island (originally called Washington Island) lies on the north side of the mouth of Pike Creek. In August 1848, the first lighthouse at Southport was established on a site 22 feet above lake level at the southern edge of the island. At this location, it marked the northern side of the harbor entrance. The lighthouse consisted of a rubble-stone tower with an overall height of 80 feet and a detached keeper's house. Five Argand lamps and 14" reflectors were the light source, replaced in 1857 by a fifth order Fresnel lens. Failure of the foundation and other structural defects led to the demolition of the tower in 1858. It was completely rebuilt the same year. The second tower only lasted eight years before it too had to be razed because of structural problems. No photographs of these first two towers have been found.

The third and surviving Southport Lighthouse was built in 1866. Constructed of cream-colored brick, the conical tower stands 55 feet tall with a detached brick keeper's dwelling completed nearby in 1867. First lit at the start of navigation in 1867, the original optic was a larger fourth order Fresnel lens. The lighthouse remained in service until May 23, 1906, when the lens and lighting equipment

Kenosha (Southport) Light

were trans-ferred to a new tower at the end of the north pier. The lantern room was also removed for possible use elsewhere and to eliminate any confusion for approaching mariners.

Around 1913, the decapitated tower became a Weather Bureau Station. A 25-foot tall steel tripod mast was erected on top of the tower for the display of weather and storm warning signals. The mast was removed around 1960, leaving more than a generation of Kenosha residents with no memory of anything other than a lanternless tower. The Old Southport Light and keeper's

Kenosha (Southport) Light

Kenosha (Southport) Light—circa 1908

dwelling are owned by the City of Kenosha. The Kenosha County Historical Society, with the help of the State Historical Society of Wisconsin, began restoration efforts in 1991. On May 7, 1994, a replica lantern room was placed back on the tower. During Fourth of July celebrations in 1996, Old Southport Lighthouse was ceremoniously relit. The light does not function as an aid to navigation, and is lit only for special occasions. Currently the old keeper's house is used as rental housing. Someday, the Kenosha County Historical Society hopes to see it converted into a museum.

Status: *Inactive. Not open to public.*

Access: *From I-94/US-41 west of Kenosha, take exit 342 and go east on Hwy. 158 to Sheridan Rd. (as you enter the city limits, Hwy. 158 changes names to 52nd St.). Turn north (left) on Sheridan Rd. for a short distance and then east (right) onto 50th St. (also called Lighthouse Dr.) for another short distance onto Simmons Island. Turn right at the first opportunity and Old Southport Lighthouse will soon be on your left.*

Kenosha North Pierhead Light

By 1899, harbor improvements at Kenosha were nearing completion. North and south piers had been run out into the deep water of the lake. A detached breakwater had been built on the north side of the entrance channel to protect the harbor entrance from northeast seas. By the mid-1880s it became apparent that the Southport Light's days as a landfall light were numbered. Kenosha Harbor would best be served by improved lighting at its entrance.

Typical for the period, a short, square, wooden, pyramidal tower with an open lower framework marked the end of the north pier as early as 1856. The surviving Kenosha North Pierhead Light went into service on May 23, 1906. In consists of a conical cast-iron tower with an overall height of 50 feet. The original optic was the fourth order Fresnel lens from the Southport Light in town, which was discontinued. The modern plastic optic in place today produces a light with a focal plane 50 feet above water level. The light was tended by the keeper of the old Southport Light, who continued to reside with his family in the house next to that tower.

A square, tapering, wood-framed fog signal building once stood on the end of the north pier in front of the new tower and was connected to it by an enclosed passageway. A raised catwalk connected both structures to shore. The light was automated in the early 1940s. Neither the

Kenosha North Pierhead Light—circa 1908

Kenosha North Pierhead Light—September 22, 1914

United States Coast Guard

Kenosha North Pierhead with Kenosha Breakwater in background—circa 1914

fog signal building nor the catwalk has survived into the present. Kenosha Light, as it is properly known today, stands alone at the end of the north pier.

Status: *Active. Not open to public.*

Access: *From I-94/US-41 west of Kenosha, take exit 342 and go east on Hwy. 158 to Sheridan*

Kenosha North Pierhead Light

Rd. (as you enter the city limits, Hwy. 158 changes names to 52nd St.). Turn north (left) on Sheridan Rd. for a short distance and then east (right) onto 50th St. (also called Lighthouse Dr.) for another short distance onto Simmons Island. Turn right at the first opportunity and Old Southport Lighthouse will soon be on your left. For the Kenosha Light, continue ahead as the street curves to the left and ends at a public parking lot near the base of the north pier.

Kenosha Breakwater Light

Kenosha Breakwater Light, when lined up with the North Pierhead Light, formed a range useful to mariners approaching the harbor entrance. The first Kenosha Breakwater Light was established at the southeast end of the detached breakwater between 1898 and 1900. It was a "pagoda style" light, a design repeated on Lake Michigan at Milwaukee, Racine, and Sheboygan in Wisconsin, Waukegan, Illinois, and Petoskey, Michigan. These lights housed lenses of the lowest order and were hexagonal towers, fully enclosed, with steeply sloping corrugated sheet metal sides up to a small lantern deck. A projecting dormer provided an access door with a window above for interior lighting. A slightly oversized lantern room dome gave the appearance of a mushroom cap. None of these structures has survived into the present and when the one at Kenosha was removed from service remains unknown. Today a modern cylinder light marks the end of the breakwater.

Kenosha Breakwater Light—circa 1905

144

Racine Harbor

Racine Harbor lies at the mouth of the Root River, 60 miles north of Chicago and 21 miles south of Milwaukee. Founded in 1834 as Port Gilbert, the village was settled by land and grew slowly. Residents began building piers into the lake in 1842. Prior to that, "lightering" of passengers and cargo to shore from ships anchored offshore was common. In the early years of its history, Racine was an important point for receiving immigrants and shipping grain and flour. Today the harbor is used mainly by pleasure craft.

Root River Light

The first lighthouse at Racine was established in 1839 on a bluff overlooking the mouth of the Root River. The Root River Lighthouse was located near the present site of the Racine Public Library at Lake Avenue and 7th Street. At the time the lighthouse was built, the Root River made a sharp bend to the south before reaching Lake Michigan. The river then traveled south fully one-half mile before emptying into the lake. The lighthouse consisted of a conical brick tower 34 feet tall with a detached one-story brick keeper's dwelling. Both buildings were kept whitewashed. Eleven Argand lamps and 14" reflectors were the light source, reduced in number to nine by 1848 as a fuel saving measure. In 1858, the tower was raised 6 feet to a height of 40 feet and the old lighting equipment was replaced by a more effective fourth order Fresnel lens. The end for the Root River Lighthouse

Racine Harbor Light

came after a new river mouth was dredged straight into the lake one-half mile to the north. The lighthouse was discontinued on September 10, 1865. The property and buildings were sold at public auction in 1870 to two partners for $1625. Subsequently one partner became the sole owner and the buildings were demolished in 1876. Salvaged materials were used in the foundations of new structures on the property. No photographs of the Root River Lighthouse are known to exist.

A year passed before Racine had another lighthouse to mark its harbor. In the meantime, a pier light served the purpose. A simple wooden light structure had been erected at the end of the north pier in 1849. It remained in service until the stormy night of December 3, 1859, when the schooner *Newman* collided with the pier and carried the light away. A replacement was quickly erected.

Racine Harbor Light minus its lantern room—May 1916

Racine Harbor Light

Racine Harbor Light

Construction commenced on two new piers at the mouth of the river in 1861 to coincide with the dredging of the new channel there. By 1866, the north pier extended 200 feet from shore. At its end, Racine Harbor Lighthouse was built on a stone-filled timber crib. The structure consisted of a one and one-half-story brick keeper's dwelling with an attached square brick tower. A red light was first displayed on September 10, 1866 at a height of 47 feet above water level. The optic used was the fourth order Fresnel lens from the old Root River Lighthouse.

The north pier was extended eastward into the lake another 400 feet in 1868 and a red beacon light established at the end, at a height of 28 feet above water level. The pierhead light consisted of a square, tapering wooden structure with an open lower framework. A raised catwalk that began near the front of the Harbor Light extended out to it. The north pierhead light along with Racine Harbor Light formed a range useful to vessels approaching the harbor entrance. By 1889 the north pier was 1,760 feet long and projected into the lake 1,150 feet past the shoreline; the south pier was 1,470 feet long and projected into the lake 1,350 feet. The north pierhead light was rebuilt several times and moved out to the new end of the north pier each time it was extended.

Racine Harbor Light was discontinued on November 23, 1901 when the leading light for the harbor became a new cast-iron structure at the end of the north pier. The lantern room was removed from the tower, which was then capped by a hipped roof. The keeper continued to live in the attached dwelling, which was extensively remodeled to its current appearance in 1903 when a large dormer was added to the second story. A U.S. Life Saving Station was built close behind the old lighthouse in 1883. After 1939, the two buildings formed the core of the Racine Coast Guard Station. After the Coast Guard Station was closed, the property was sold. Currently, both old buildings are privately owned by Pugh Marina.

Racine North Breakwater Light

Racine North Breakwater Light was originally located at the end of the north pier. One source suggests it may have first seen duty on the end of the south pier, but was moved by barge to the end of the opposite pier in 1901. It consists of a square, tapering cast-iron tower with an open lower framework 53 feet tall overall. Originally painted white (now red), a fog signal bell was mounted on its lakeward face. A sixth order Fresnel lens was the original optic. The raised catwalk that connected the previous wooden structure to shore was retained.

As at other ports on Lake Michigan, construction of a breakwater to enlarge the outer harbor and create a stilling basin was well underway by the late 1890s and largely complete by 1910. The outer end of the north breakwater was first marked by a "pagoda style" light structure. It was a design that would be repeated on Lake Michigan at Kenosha, Milwaukee and Sheboygan in Wisconsin, Waukegan, Illinois, and Petoskey, Michigan. These lights housed lenses of the lowest order and were hexagonal towers with steeply sloping corrugated sheet metal sides up to a small lantern deck. All enclosed, a projecting dormer provided an access door with a window above for interior lighting. A slightly oversized

Racine North Pierhead Light—September 5, 1914

Racine North Pierhead Light (later to become the North Breakwater Light)—circa 1911. Note the first North Breakwater Light at the far right.

The first Racine North Breakwater Light—circa 1911

lantern room dome gave the appearance of a mushroom cap.

Between 1916 and 1929, Federal work on Great Lakes harbors was largely confined to completing earlier projects, replacing wooden piers and breakwater superstructures with concrete, repair, and general maintenance. It was during this period (exact date unknown) that Racine's north pierhead light was moved to the outer end of the north breakwater, displacing the earlier structure. In its new position, the breakwater light became the main light for Racine Harbor. After the move, the project to enlarge the outer harbor basin resulted in the demolition of the north pier and its catwalk all the way back to the front of the former Racine Harbor Lighthouse.

Development of Racine's waterfront has been extensive and beautifully executed…a nice mix of offices, residential apartments, open parks, and marinas. Racine North Breakwater Light was finally discontinued and moved in 1987.

Racine North Breakwater Light (previously located on the north pierhead)—January 1928

The move was prompted by an expansion of the harbor basin, when a new light at the harbor entrance was installed on a modern skeleton tower. Saved as a symbol of the city, the refurbished tower is floodlit at night.

Status: *Inactive. Not open to public.*

Access: *From I-94, take exit 333 and go east on State Hwy. 20. Hwy. 20 becomes Washington Ave. in Racine. Stay on Washington Ave. to State Hwy. 32, which is Main St. Turn north (left) on Hwy. 32 (Main St.) for a short distance to 4th St. Turn east (right) onto 4th St., which will turn into Christopher Columbus Causeway. Continue east on the causeway past Reefpoint Marina to the parking lot at its end. There is a good view of the old breakwater light from the public park.*

A good view of the old buildings at the former Coast Guard Station is possible a short distance away from Gaslight Pointe at the foot of 2nd St. east of Lake Ave.

Racine North Breakwater Light

Racine Reef Light

In the days when Racine was a busy commercial port, Racine Reef posed a very serious hazard to navigation. The reef is an irregular limestone formation three-quarters of a mile wide north to south and one and one-quarter mile long east to west with a least depth of water of around one foot near its center. The reef is located about two miles southeast of Racine Harbor, but the western end of the shoal area, presently marked by a lighted buoy, approaches to within 3000 feet of the harbor entrance. In the 1850s, the

Racine Reef Light—circa 1945

reef was first marked at its eastern edge by a large pear-shaped buoy made of riveted cast iron. Wind Point Lighthouse, about three and one-half miles to the northwest, displayed a red light from 1880 to 1906, which was intended to help mariners stay off the reef on their approach to the harbor. Nevertheless, in the 20-year period between 1875 and 1895, 11 ships sank on the reef.

In 1899, an automated red Pintsch gas light was established at the top of an iron skeletal tower on a concrete crib in 10 feet of water. Pintsch gas, manufactured from oil, was a precursor of the acetylene gas lamp that would prove to be superior as an automated light source. By the end of 1934, nearly all Pintsch gas lights were converted to acetylene. Too short and too weak, the Pintsch beacon left much to be desired and construction on a better replacement began in 1905.

Modern Racine Reef Light

Located at the northeast corner of the reef, Racine Reef Light was established on October 6, 1906. The lighthouse was built on an octagonal concrete crib that rose 17 feet out of the water. The lighthouse itself was octagonal in design and built of white and brown brick over an iron skeleton. Five interior levels were divided into living quarters, storage areas, and machinery spaces. Close to the base of the lighthouse was an iron boathouse on one side and a similar shed used for storage on the other. The original optic was a fourth order Fresnel lens with a focal plane 72 feet above water level. The structure also housed a fog signal. The lighthouse was normally manned by a crew of four men with two on duty at any given time. Racine Reef Light was one of only a few lighthouses on the Great Lakes to be manned year round, in this case, due to the presence of cross-lake railroad car ferry traffic. Almost all of the ferries had reinforced hulls capable of icebreaking.

By the late 1940s, commercial shipping activity at Racine Harbor had dwindled. The lighthouse was automated in 1954 and razed in 1961. The Fresnel lens was moved to the Racine County Historical Museum where it remains on display. In 1961, a fully automated light at the top of a skeletal steel tower was placed in service on the old crib foundation.

Judging by the old photographs, Racine Reef Lighthouse was a handsome and unique structure. No others like it were ever built on the Great Lakes.

Status (of Modern Racine Reef Light): *Active. Not open to public.*

Access: *Boat.*

*Motor vessel **Adam E. Cornelius***

courtesy of Ken and Barb Wardius

Wind Point Light

The location of a major coastal light, Wind Point lies three and one-half miles north of Racine Harbor. For ships approaching from the north, the point often blocked the view of Racine's harbor lights. For many years, passing mariners used a single, very tall, windblown tree on the point as a landmark…not much help at night. The tree supposedly remained standing until 1910. Although there are several small detached shoals within two miles of the point, the greatest danger for ships approaching Racine Harbor was Racine Reef, two miles east of the harbor entrance.

Wind Point Light was established on November 15, 1880. The lighthouse consists of a graceful conical brick tower with an overall height of 108 feet. An enclosed passageway connects the tower to a one and one-half-story brick keeper's dwelling. In 1899, the dwelling was enlarged to create three apartments for the families of the keeper and two assistants. A fog signal was added in 1900.

The tower originally housed two lights. The main coastal light consisted of a third order Fresnel lens that produced a flashing white light with a focal plane 113 feet

Wind Point Light

above water level. This lens was removed from the tower in July 1964. Today, a modern aeronautical-style beacon produces the same characteristic at 111 feet. Also exhibited from a window in the tower just below the lantern room was a red light produced by a fifth order Fresnel lens with a focal plane 105 feet above water level. The red light, aimed to the southeast, was intended to help mariners stay clear of Racine Reef, which was only marked with a buoy at the time. This smaller lens was replaced with a locomotive headlight in 1897. The red light was discontinued in 1906 after Racine Reef Light was established. Wind Point Light was electrified in 1924.

Final automation came in 1964 after use of the fog signal was discontinued. Thereafter, except for the tower, the Coast Guard leased the grounds and other buildings at the site to the Village of Wind Point. The lighthouse complex serves as a police station and village hall with a caretaker living on the premises. Formal ownership of the complex was transferred to the village in 1997. The Coast Guard continues to maintain the light.

Wind Point Light station is one of those places that has changed very little in appearance over the years. The setting is picturesque and the buildings are beautifully maintained. The original Fresnel lens remains at the site, on display in the village hall. Unfortunately, neither the tower nor the village hall

Wind Point Light—circa 1906

Wind Point Light

are open to the public. Visitors are welcome to explore the grounds and lakefront.

Status: *Active. Not open to public.*

Access: *From I-94, take exit 326, which is 7 Mile Rd., east to State Hwy. 32. Turn south (right) on Hwy. 32 to 4 Mile Rd. Turn east (left) on 4 Mile Rd. and continue past Charles St. and Main St. Four Mile Rd. runs into Lighthouse Dr., which will curve to the right. The driveway to Wind Point Light is on the left and leads down to a parking lot.*

Wind Point Light—circa 1909

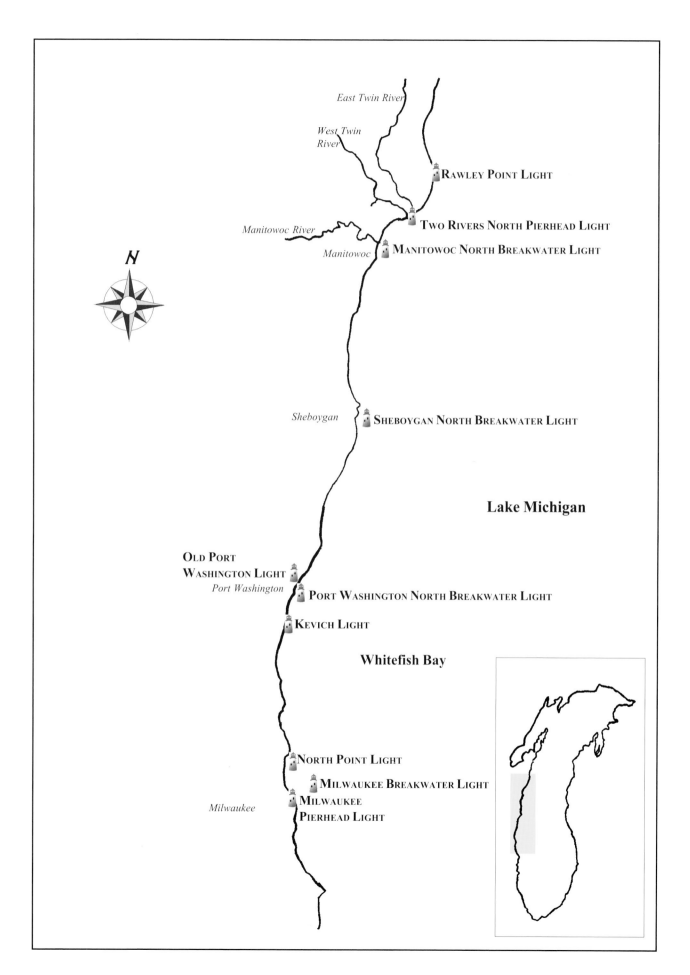

East Twin River

West Twin River

Rawley Point Light

Manitowoc River

Two Rivers North Pierhead Light

Manitowoc

Manitowoc North Breakwater Light

Sheboygan North Breakwater Light

Sheboygan

Lake Michigan

Old Port Washington Light

Port Washington

Port Washington North Breakwater Light

Kevich Light

Whitefish Bay

North Point Light

Milwaukee Breakwater Light

Milwaukee

Milwaukee Pierhead Light

Milwaukee Harbor

Milwaukee Harbor is one of the major ports on the Great Lakes and second in importance on Lake Michigan only to the combined ports of Chicago and South Chicago (Calumet Harbor). The harbor is at the mouth of the Milwaukee River, which flows into Milwaukee Bay. The bay is a broad indentation on the west side of Lake Michigan about 85 miles north of Chicago Harbor and 25 miles south of the harbor at Port Washington. The harbor consists of an extensive outer harbor of refuge formed by breakwaters paralleling the shore and an inner harbor formed by three rivers: the Milwaukee, Menominee, and Kinnickinnic. Milwaukee is a major manufacturing center. Both the inner and outer harbors have numerous deep-draft wharves, piers, and docks. Cargoes handled include every known bulk commodity as well as general cargo and petroleum products. The largest freighters on the Great Lakes continue to call at the port.

Milwaukee Harbor—circa 1908

*Canadian vessel **Algosteel** entering the Milwaukee River. Launched as a traditional straight-deck bulk freighter in 1966 named the **A.S. Glossbrenner**, she was converted to a self-unloader and renamed in 1990.*

At the time Milwaukee was incorporated in 1835, the Milwaukee River turned south just before reaching Lake Michigan and ran over one-half mile before emptying into the lake. Due to a sand bar, the depth of water available at the river's mouth was less than five feet, yet just inside the mouth the natural depth was about eleven feet. The first efforts to improve the harbor extended over a ten-year period from 1836 to 1846 and were aimed at opening the natural mouth of the river. Eventually, the mouth was dredged and the work protected by piers built on the sides of the channel.

Milwaukee Light

Milwaukee Light, established in 1838, was built on a 56-foot bluff at the eastern end of present day Wisconsin Avenue, over a mile north of the river's mouth. It consisted of a conical brick tower with a detached, single-story brick keeper's dwelling. The tower was 30 feet tall from its base to the lantern room deck. Eleven Argand lamps and 14" reflectors provided the light source, reduced to seven in number by 1848 to save on fuel costs. The lighthouse remained in service until late in 1855, when it was replaced by a taller landfall light built on the city's North Point, even farther north of the harbor entrance. Thereafter, the old tower and dwelling were razed. No photographs of the first Milwaukee Light are known to exist.

Money was appropriated and in 1852 a plan was adopted to cut a straight channel from the river at a point just before it started its bend to the south directly into Lake Michigan. The project proposed a channel 260 feet wide and 13 feet deep protected by parallel piers each 1,120 feet long. Work progressed slowly while vessel traffic at the port continued to increase. A small channel was finally opened in 1857. Further enhancements were needed as usage increased. By 1868, the project was modified to create a channel 19 feet deep by dredging and extending the piers another 600 feet. The first pier light at Milwaukee was established in 1872. The channel depths and pier lights earlier projected were not finally achieved until around 1897. For comparison, the improved entrance channel at Milwaukee today has a width of 250 feet that widens to 450 feet at its inner end and a controlling depth of 27 feet. The cutting of a new harbor entrance led to the creation of the present Jones Island. Eventually, the original river mouth was abandoned and filled in, leaving Jones Island no longer an island.

North Point Light

As the name suggests, North Point defines the northern end of Milwaukee Bay and today comprises much of the very scenic Lake Park. The site chosen for Milwaukee's landfall light was an 80-foot bluff a little over two miles farther north of the old Milwaukee Light. North Point Light was first lit on November 22, 1855. It consisted of a 28-foot tall, conical, cream-colored brick tower with a detached, wood-framed, two and one-half-story keeper's dwelling set back farther on the bluff. Information about the original optic has not been found, but a new fourth order Fresnel lens was installed in 1868. No photographs of this first North Point Light are known to exist. Threatened by erosion, the tower was razed in 1888 and the lens moved to a new structure 100 feet to the west built adjacent to the keeper's dwelling.

The new North Point Light consisted of a 39-foot tall, octagonal, cast-iron tower equipped with the

North Point Light—circa 1910

North Point Light, another view—circa 1910

fourth order Fresnel lens from the previous tower. An enclosed passageway connected it to the keeper's dwelling, which was extensively rebuilt to house two families and later, three. By 1911, the light was obscured by trees that had grown on the property next to the light station. The present tower was created in 1912 by placing the original cast-iron tower on top of a new 35-foot octagonal base constructed of riveted steel plates. The addition raised the tower height to 74 feet and gave the lens a focal plane 154 feet above

North Point Light—circa 1915

lake level. The renovation was not completed until April 1913, but the work was far enough along that the light was reestablished on December 15, 1912. The enclosed passageway between the tower and the dwelling was rebuilt after the addition, but removed

with later modernizations. North Point Light was automated in the 1960s and discontinued on March 15, 1994. The lens was removed from the tower and is on display at the Milwaukee Coast Guard Station. That the light remained in service for so long is nothing short of amazing. Its usefulness as an aid to navigation had been eclipsed decades before by the surrounding city lights and a better-placed lighthouse on the breakwater at the harbor's entrance.

North Point Lighthouse is located within beautiful Lake Park next to a very affluent neighborhood. Despite its urban location, the old light station is suffering from neglect. Surprisingly, the condition of the house interior is almost as bad as that seen at lighthouses on remote islands. The site is begging for adaptive reuse. To that end, in 1999 a group called the North Point Lighthouse Friends organized. The group works under the aegis of two other local organizations, the Water Tower Landmark Trust and Lake Park Friends. Together, it is hoped, they will find the means to restore and reopen this historical landmark.

North Point Lighthouse Friends
c/o Water Tower Preservation Fund, Inc.
P.O. Box 668
Milwaukee, WI 53201-0668
Phone: 414-961-7051

Status: *Inactive. Not open to public.*

Access: *There are many possible approaches to the Milwaukee Lakefront. It is best to obtain a detailed city street map for travel around Milwaukee. From*

North Point Light

I-43 north of the downtown area, exit at North Ave. and go east until North Ave. intersects Lake Dr. Turn north (left) onto Lake Dr. for a few blocks and then east (right) onto Bradford for two blocks. Turn north (left) onto N. Wahl. Less than two blocks ahead the lighthouse will be on your right, set back off the road in the park. You may park in the street or drive up the gravel driveway and park in the small area immediately behind the lighthouse.

North Point Light

Milwaukee Pierhead Light

Milwaukee Pierhead Light was first established on the north pier in 1872. In a design common to that era, it consisted of a square, wooden, pyramidal tower with an open lower framework. Over the years, a system of range lights has come and gone there as well as a steam-powered fog signal plant equipped with a 10" whistle. Likewise, the once long piers have changed drastically due to the backfilling of adjacent low-lying areas and other structural alterations. The south pier has been completely absorbed into the present waterfront and only a short remnant of the north pier extends beyond the shoreline.

The present Milwaukee Pierhead Light was established in 1906. It consists of a conical cast-iron tower with an overall height of 41 feet. The original optic was a fourth order Fresnel lens housed in a round lantern room with helical bars. This lens was moved to the breakwater lighthouse in 1926 and replaced with one of the fifth order. At the same time,

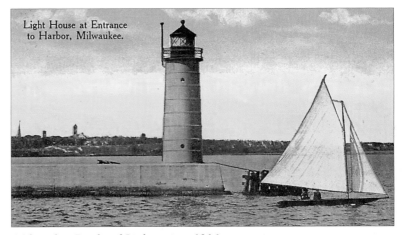

Milwaukee Pierhead Light—circa 1916

Milwaukee Pierhead Light—circa 1920

the present ten-sided lantern room with flat planes of glass was substituted. Thereafter, the light was powered and remotely operated from the breakwater light station. Automation came in 1966. Presently, a solar-powered plastic optic produces a light with a focal plane 42 feet above water level.

Status: *Active. Not open to public.*

Access: *The pierhead light can be tricky to find as it is tucked in behind the Henry Maier Festival Park and Marcus Amphitheater, part of the Summerfest grounds on the lakefront. A little hunting may be necessary if you become disoriented, as there are several short one-way streets in this area. From the I-94/I-43 interchange in downtown, exit east onto I-794 and continue east to the exit for Lincoln Memorial Dr. Turn north (left) onto Lincoln Memorial Dr., go one block, and turn east (right) onto Michigan St. Turn south (right) at the next street, which is Harbor Dr. Continue south on Harbor Dr. to Polk St. Turn west (right) onto Polk for two blocks to its end at East Erie St. Turn south (left) onto East Erie St. and follow it to its end at the parking lot near the base of the north pier. In this process you will pass under the elevated Hoan Bridge.*

Milwaukee Pierhead Light

Milwaukee Breakwater Light

Long breakwaters paralleling the shore form the outer harbor of refuge at Milwaukee. Construction began in 1881. Gaps were left in the breakwater at specific points so small craft would not have to travel all the way north or south to the main harbor entrance in order to escape a storm or to get out onto the lake on a nice day. As construction on different segments of the breakwater progressed, minor lights, usually automated, were established at the gaps. In the mid- to late 1890s, a design emerged that would be repeated on Lake Michigan at Kenosha, Racine, and Sheboygan in Wisconsin, Waukegan, Illinois, and Petoskey, Michigan. These "pagoda style" lights housed lenses of the lowest order and were hexagonal towers, fully enclosed,

with steeply sloping corrugated sheet metal sides up to a small lantern deck. A projecting dormer provided an access door with a window above for interior lighting. A slightly oversized lantern room dome gave the appearance of a mushroom cap. All of these structures were eventually replaced. None has survived into the present.

The present Milwaukee Breakwater Light was established in 1926 on the south end of the north breakwater to serve as the main light for the harbor entrance. Its completion eventually eliminated the need for the Milwaukee Lightship (Lightship No. 95), which was stationed three miles offshore from 1912 through 1932. The lighthouse rests on a timber crib foundation topped by a concrete pier measuring 54 feet by 60 feet and 23 feet high. The entire structure is steel-framed, encased in steel plates, and has an overall height of 53 feet. The cylindrical lantern room originally housed the fourth order Fresnel lens taken from the Milwaukee Pierhead Light. The modern plastic optic in place today has a focal plane 61 feet above water level.

Interior spaces were divided into living quarters, a boathouse, storage and work areas, and machinery spaces for fog signal equipment and the diesel generators that powered the station. Typically, a four man crew was in residence and they were also responsible for the minor lights in the harbor. In addition, the pierhead light was remotely operated from the breakwater station. Milwaukee Breakwater Light was finally automated in 1966 and is currently powered from shore via a submarine cable. A seasonally operated foghorn continues in service. Exterior floodlights enhance the structure's visibility from sunset to sunrise.

Status: *Active. Not open to public.*

Access: *Boat, but it may be viewed offshore from the pierhead light location.*

Milwaukee Breakwater Light— circa 1911

Milwaukee Breakwater Light

Kevich Light

Many people dream of living in a lighthouse, but the supply of privately-held old lighthouses is very limited. When they infrequently come on the market, the asking price is usually exorbitant. The solution: build your own.

The Kevich Light is a private home built between 1979 and 1981 near Grafton, Wisconsin by Brana and Nena Kevich, émigrés from Yugoslavia. The light consists of a 45-foot

Kevich Light

conical, masonry tower with an attached house, both stuccoed and painted white. The light is maintained as a private aid to navigation and certified as such by the U.S. Coast Guard. This lighthouse sits on a high bluff overlooking Lake Michigan (between Milwaukee and Port Washington), which places the light 163 feet above water level. Mr. Kevich's talents as a woodcarver are evident throughout the house, especially on the door to the tower. The Kevich family sold the lighthouse to its current owners several years ago.

The Kevich Light sits on the site of a former town called Port Ulao (pronounced: you-lee-o). Founded in 1847, the town was a bustling lumber stop and steamer refueling station through the Civil War years. Port Ulao boasted a wooden pier that stretched 1000 feet into the lake. Lacking an improved harbor, it provided no refuge from storms for passing ships. There is no record of a lighthouse actually being built at Port Ulao, although a parcel of land was set aside for one. Less of a port and more of an open roadstead, when the timber supply dwindled, the port quickly passed into history.

Status: *Active. Private residence.*

Access: *From the south take US-43 to exit 89. Proceed east on County Road C (Pioneer Rd.). Turn east (right) on Lake Shore Rd. The lighthouse is just south of the junction with Ulao Rd. (Extension of County Rd. Q). From the north take US-43 to exit 92. Proceed east on County Rd. Q (which turns into Ulao Rd.) to Lake Shore Rd. The lighthouse sits back from Lake Shore Rd. on a PRIVATE driveway. Please respect the privacy of the owners. A close photograph is not possible from Lake Shore Rd.*

Carved door to the tower at Kevich Light

Port Washington Harbor

Located on a beautiful little bay about 25 miles north of Milwaukee, Port Washington was called Wisconsin City when it was first settled in 1835. Early steamboats touched here regularly. Commercial fishing has long been an important part of the local economy and continues so today. Modern lake freighters still visit this port, delivering coal to an electric power public utility plant on the south edge of the harbor. Tankers also deliver gasoline and heating oil.

Port Washington Harbor grew to meet the demands of local trade near the mouth of a little stream called Sauk Creek that was of no importance for harbor purposes. Lacking a natural harbor, early lake vessels loaded and unloaded at unprotected docks on the lakefront. The project to construct an artificial harbor began in 1870. It consisted of digging an interior basin into the low ground between the lakeshore and a bluff and running two piers out into the deep water of the lake. Exposure to storms from the north through the east remained a long-standing problem. In the early 1930s, breakwaters were constructed in the lake to the north and south, creating a new harbor entrance and a protective stilling basin.

Old Port Washington Light

The first two lighthouses at Port Washington were landfall lights built on a high bluff called St. Mary's Hill located northwest of the present harbor. They were intended to help mariners find the port from out on the open waters of the lake. The first lighthouse was built in 1849 and consisted of a conical, cream-colored brick tower with a detached brick keeper's dwelling. The present structure was built in 1860 just to the west of the older tower. It consists of a two-story dwelling constructed of cream-colored brick painted white. At one time a short, square, wooden tower emerged from the peak of the roof to support a lantern room that housed a fourth order Fresnel lens. The design of this lighthouse was repeated at several locations on Lake Michigan. All within a few years of each other, nearly identical structures were built in Wisconsin at Green Island, Pilot Island and Rock Island; in Michigan at Grand Traverse and South Manitou Island; and at Michigan City, Indiana.

Old Port Washington Light was extinguished on October 31, 1903 after the north pierhead light was deemed sufficient to mark the harbor entrance. The dwelling remained in use as the keeper was still responsible for the pier light. The assistant keeper, however, lived elsewhere. The buildings remained unchanged until 1934, when the lantern room and tower were removed from the roof. At this time, the house was also converted into a duplex so the assistant keeper could live onsite. Other changes included the demolition of an old barn behind the house that was replaced with the present generator building. Electric generators were to be used to power the light in a new tower nearing completion at the end of the north breakwater.

Old Port Washington Light—November 13, 1893

United States Coast Guard

Port Washington North Pierhead Light

Port Washington North Pierhead Light was established in 1889. It consisted of a square, tapering, wooden tower with the upper two-thirds enclosed and an open lower framework. A raised catwalk connected the tower to shore. The original optic was a fourth order Fresnel lens. Around 1894, an assistant keeper was assigned to Port Washington to help tend this light, which was a long way from the light on St. Mary's Hill. In 1903, this light became the main light for Port Washington Harbor.

United States Coast Guard

Port Washington North Pierhead Light—September 16, 1914

Port Washington North Breakwater Light

The North Pierhead Light was replaced late in 1934 by the present Port Washington North Breakwater Light, first lit at the start of navigation in 1935. Remotely operated, the new light was electrically powered by a submarine cable that ran back to a generator building behind the old lighthouse on St. Mary's Hill. Constructed atop an arched concrete base, the square steel tower tapers upward to support a light with a focal plane 78 feet above water level. A fourth order Fresnel lens was the original optic housed in a circular black lantern room. The lantern room was removed in a later modernization and the light today is produced by a solar-powered plastic optic mounted on a metal pole.

A light identical to this one at Port Washington was established the same year at Indiana Harbor East Breakwater. Except for the concrete base, within a few years of each other, identical steel towers were built at Conneaut and Huron, Ohio and at Gravelly Shoal in Saginaw Bay on Lake Huron. Design similarities are apparent in the Lake Michigan crib lights at Grays Reef and Minneapolis Shoal. These towers are considered Art Deco in style, reflecting the design preferences of the mid-1930s.

Port Washington North Breakwater Light

Port Washington Historical Society

The old lighthouse on St. Mary's Hill continued to be used as a residence after the new breakwater light went into service. The keeper and assistant were still needed to operate generators that powered the new tower and the fog signal equipment housed in its base. Complete automation came in 1975. Thereafter, the building continued to serve as housing for Coast Guard personnel stationed in Milwaukee. In 1992, the site was leased to the city for use as a local history museum operated by the Port Washington Historical Society. A caretaker continues to live in the upstairs apartment. Formal ownership of the site was transferred to the city in 1998. The museum is open free to the public on Sundays from 1 to 4 p.m., Memorial Day through Labor Day. The Society hopes to someday restore the old lighthouse to its original appearance.

Port Washington Historical Society
P.O. Box 491
Port Washington, WI 53074
Phone: 262-284-7240

Status: *1860 Lighthouse: Inactive. Open to public as a museum. Breakwater Light: Active. Not open to public.*

Access: *From I-43, take exit 96 and go east on State Hwy. 33. Hwy. 33 becomes Grand Ave. Continue east on Grand Ave. to Franklin St.*

For the Breakwater Light*: Turn north (left) on Franklin St. (Hwy. 32 north) for a few blocks and turn east (right) onto Pier St. Follow Pier St. to its end at the marina parking lot. Access to the base of the north breakwater is one block to the north at the foot of Jackson St.*

For the 1860 lighthouse*: Turn north (left) on Franklin St. (Hwy. 32 north) for less than one-half mile and turn east (right) onto Woodruff St. Continue right onto N. Catalpa St., jog left briefly on E. Van Buren St., and turn right again on Johnson St. The Port Washington Historical Society museum is located on the left about two blocks down at 311 Johnson St.*

Old Port Washington Light—serves as the Port Washington Historical Society Museum

Sheboygan Harbor

Sheboygan Harbor is located 51 miles north of Milwaukee Harbor at the mouth of the Sheboygan River. The land was opened for settlement in 1835 and for many years the only connection to the outside world was maintained by means of lake shipping. Prior to the commencement of harbor improvements in the early 1840s, the Sheboygan River never had a depth of more than 7 feet or a width greater than 150 feet. Today, a dredged entrance channel leads northwestward from deep water in Lake Michigan between a breakwater on the north and a long pier on the south to an outer turning basin. The channel leads across the south side of the basin to the mouth of the river and from there upstream for about one mile.

Sheboygan (Chippewagan) Light

A little over one-half mile north of the river's mouth is a prominent bluff referred to as North Point. Sheboygan Light was established at the eastern edge of the point in 1839. A rubble-stone tower, the height from its base to the lantern deck was only 30 feet. Eleven Argand lamps and 14" reflectors were the light source, reduced in number to eight by 1848 as a fuel saving measure. Little else is known about this first lighthouse and no photographs of it are known to exist. Threatened by erosion, it was razed and a new lighthouse established in 1860, this time set back farther from the edge of the bluff.

Sheboygan North Point Light

North Point Light consisted of a two-story wood-framed dwelling with a square wooden light tower emerging from the roof peak. This design was repeated at several locations around the lakes and especially on Lake Michigan. Within a few years of each other, nearly identical lighthouses were built at Cheboygan Point on Lake Huron and on Lake Michigan at Tail Point, the Kalamazoo River (Saugatuck), and St. Joseph. The first two lighthouses at North Point served mainly as landfall lights, helping navigators find the town along a dark wilderness shoreline. Located as they were north of the actual harbor entrance, both were of questionable value to navigators unfamiliar with the area. Groundings occurred when ships came too close to shore before realizing the error.

Sheboygan North Point Light—circa 1885

By 1900 the entrance to the harbor was well lit and North Point Light was discontinued on August 29, 1904. The building and 13-acre site were sold at public auction on December 18, 1906 to a local physician, Dr. William Gunther, for a mere $1,415. Dr. Gunther rented the house out for almost ten years. In 1916, the old lighthouse was moved into town, split down the middle, expanded and converted into a double flat. There it remains at 124-126 Lighthouse Court between N. 1st and N. 2nd Streets.

Sheboygan North Pier Light

The first lighthouse on Sheboygan's north pier was established in December 1873. It consisted of a square, wooden, pyramidal structure with an open lower framework. Fire was always a danger in wooden towers and the pier light burned on March 17, 1880. It was quickly replaced with a similar structure. A fog signal building was constructed on the pier close behind the wooden light tower. A raised catwalk connected both structures to shore. After the north pier was extended into deeper water one last time, a conical cast-iron tower replaced the wooden lighthouse during the summer of 1906. This tower and fog signal building remained connected to shore by a raised catwalk. As the south pier was extended to better protect the harbor entrance, the north pier decreased in importance. Once quite long, the north pier actually shrank in length as the area next to it was backfilled. Harbor improvements resulted in the construction of a north breakwater that came to provide most of the protection from wind and waves out of the north through east. Eventually the north pier light was moved to the end of the north breakwater and served as the main light for Sheboygan Harbor.

National Archives

Fog signal building and North Pier Light—circa 1910. Note the first North Breakwater Light at the far right

Harbor Entrance and Lighthouse, Sheboygan, Wis.

Sheboygan North Pier Light—September 6, 1914

Sheboygan North Breakwater Light

The first light at the end of the north breakwater was established between 1898 and 1900. It was a "pagoda style" light, a design repeated on Lake Michigan at Kenosha, Milwaukee, and Racine in Wisconsin; Waukegan, Illinois and Petoskey, Michigan. These lights housed lenses of the lowest order and were hexagonal towers, fully enclosed, with steeply sloping corrugated

First Sheboygan North Breakwater Light in foreground, with its eventual replacement, the North Pier Light, in the background—circa 1912

sheet metal sides up to a small lantern deck. A projecting dormer provided an access door with a window above for interior lighting. A slightly oversized lantern room dome gave the appearance of a mushroom cap. This light was discontinued on June 23, 1915. In August 1915, the conical cast-iron tower at the end of the north pier was moved to its present location at the outer end of the north breakwater in order to serve as the main light for Sheboygan Harbor. Old photographs viewed sequentially suggest the lantern room was removed during a modernization around 1950, but the exact date remains unknown. Besides a modern plastic optic, the decapitated tower sprouts an array of solar panels and weather monitoring equipment.

The City of Sheboygan has done a beautiful job developing its waterfront. Unfortunately, Sheboygan North Breakwater Light remains one of the ugliest towers on the Great Lakes. Someday perhaps, civic pride will demand that the light tower be restored to its original appearance.

Status: *Active. Not open to public.*

Access: *From I-43, take exit 126 and go east on Kohler Memorial Dr., which will turn into Erie Ave. Continue east on Erie Ave. to N. 7th St. Turn north (left) on N. 7th St. to Michigan Ave. Turn east (right) on Michigan Ave. to Broughton Dr. Turn south (right) on Broughton Dr. Watch on your left for the entrance to Deland Park and Harbor Centre Marina. The base of the north breakwater is accessed at the north end of the marina parking lot.*

Sheboygan North Breakwater Light

Manitowoc Harbor

Manitowoc Harbor formed at the mouth of the Manitowoc River, about 75 miles north of Milwaukee. The river was originally obstructed at its mouth by a sand bar with a least depth of about four feet of water. Harbor improvements were initiated in the mid-1840s. By 1885, long north and south piers protected a dredged entrance channel. Construction of converging north and south breakwaters to create a protected inner stilling basin commenced in the mid-1880s, and by 1918 the configuration of the present harbor had largely evolved.

Manitowoc quickly became an important trading and manufacturing city with growth spurred even more by the arrival of the railroads in 1873. Early in its history, Manitowoc became renowned as a major shipbuilding center. During the Second World War, 28 Navy submarines were produced here for the war effort. Large ships are no longer built in Manitowoc. However, the Manitowoc Company, the diversified successor of the original Manitowoc Shipbuilding Company, continues its involvement with shipbuilding activity at other ports on Lake Michigan.

Manitowoc's central location along the west shore of Lake Michigan caused it to become a transportation hub for freight and passenger traffic on the lake. The Goodrich Steamboat Line was synonymous with travel by steamer on the lake for over 75 years ending in 1933. For most of those years, that company maintained an extensive operations base and repair facility just inside the harbor entrance. Other companies established cross-lake railroad car ferry links to ports on the eastern shore of the lake. The tradition of cross-lake passenger travel continues today. The *S.S. Badger*, operated by the Lake Michigan Carferry Company, links Manitowoc and Ludington, Michigan. In service every day from mid-May through mid-October, the *Badger* is the last of its kind. The four-hour crossing in either direction is a unique experience and highly recommended. For additional information call 800-841-4243 or 888-947-3377; or visit their website: www.ssbadger.com.

Manitowoc Light

One of the earliest lighthouses on Lake Michigan was established at Manitowoc in 1839. Located on high ground north of the river's mouth, it consisted of a conical brick tower with a detached, one and one-half-story brick keeper's dwelling. The height of the tower from its base to the lantern room deck was 30 feet. Eleven Argand lamps and 14" reflectors provided the light

Manitowoc Light—circa 1890

source, reduced in number to six by 1848 as a measure to save on fuel costs. The light in this tower was discontinued in 1877 when the North Pierhead Light, established in 1850, was deemed sufficient to mark the harbor entrance. The dwelling continued to be occupied by the keeper, who was now responsible only for the Pierhead Light.

The old light tower and dwelling were demolished in 1895 and the grounds regraded to make way for the construction of a new, two-story duplex meant to house the keeper and an assistant. Wood-framed on a brick foundation and sheathed in clapboard siding, the new dwelling was completed on December 27, 1895. Construction of the duplex and the assignment of an assistant keeper to the station coincided with the establishment in November of a new light and fog signal at the end of the north breakwater.

Manitowoc North Pierhead Light

The first light at the end of the north pier was established in 1850. It consisted of a square, wooden, pyramidal structure about 35 feet tall with an open lower framework. A raised catwalk connected it to the shore. In 1877, the North Pierhead Light was deemed sufficient to mark the harbor entrance and the 1839 Manitowoc Light was darkened. A fog bell struck by machinery was erected against the lakeward face of the wooden light tower in 1881.

Manitowoc North Pierhead Light was substantially rebuilt in 1892. Slightly taller than before, the square tapering form was retained but the lower portion of the tower was now fully enclosed. The catwalk was retained after the rebuild. Over time, the better protection afforded by the north breakwater made the long north pier redundant. Around 1918, in order to clear the harbor area behind the breakwater, the north

Manitowoc North Pierhead Light—circa 1920

pier was substantially shortened. As a result, the North Pierhead Light was relocated closer to the base of the pier near the river's mouth. The lighthouse remained in service until 1937 when it was destroyed by a storm. Since then, a series of minor lights have marked the site.

Manitowoc North Breakwater Light

A light and steam-powered fog signal were established at the southeast end of the north breakwater on November 30, 1895. The building was wood-framed and sheathed in cast-iron plates for durability. An enclosed lantern room was placed upon the gable end of the building facing the lake. No mention of the original optic has been found, but a fifth order Fresnel lens was installed in 1902. Surprisingly, no catwalk was provided for the keeper to get out to this structure. A rowboat was the only way to get back and forth. For this reason, a boat shed was built on the breakwater just behind the lighthouse. A crane was later added so the keeper could at least hoist the boat out of the water to keep it from being smashed against the breakwater. During periods of rough weather, the

The first Manitowoc North Breakwater Light—circa 1912. Note the North Pierhead Light and its catwalk in the background

United States Coast Guard—9th District

possibility of being stranded out on the breakwater was ever-present.

The current Manitowoc North Breakwater Light was established in 1918, replacing the earlier structure. Framed in steel and encased in steel plates, the rectangular structure rests on a base of reinforced

Manitowoc North Breakwater Light

concrete eleven feet high. The lighthouse was painted a deep reddish-brown in color at the time of its completion, which explains its dark appearance in the old photographs. Unlike its predecessor, this lighthouse was originally connected to shore by a raised catwalk, since removed. The first level of the building originally housed fog signal equipment. The watchroom, which comprises the second level, is surmounted by a round light tower that supports a black lantern room. The original optic was a fourth order Fresnel lens later reduced in intensity to the present fifth order lens. It produces a light with a focal plane 52 feet above water level. The light was electrified in the early 1920s and a radio beacon, now gone, was installed in 1927. The station was automated in 1971.

Not to be missed while in Manitowoc is a visit to the Wisconsin Maritime Museum, one of the best on the Great Lakes. Outstanding exhibits bring alive more than a century and a half of Great Lakes mari-

Manitowoc North Breakwater Light—circa 1929

time history. Moored adjacent to the museum and open for tours is the *U.S.S. Cobia*, a World War II Navy submarine of the same class as twenty-eight similar craft constructed at the shipyards in Manitowoc during the war.

Wisconsin Maritime Museum
75 Maritime Drive
Manitowoc, WI 54220-6843
Phone: 920-684-0218

Status: *Active. Not open to public.*

Access: *From I-43, take exit 149 and go east on Hwy. 151, which turns into Calumet Ave. At S. 26th St. turn north (left) for one block and then east (right) onto Custer St. Continue east on Custer, which turns into Washington St. Stay on Washington St. to S. 8th St.*

Turn north (left) onto S. 8th St. and continue over the bridge that crosses the Manitowoc River. Turn east (right) on the first street past the bridge, which is Maritime Dr. Proceed past the Wisconsin Maritime Museum on your right and park in the lot for Manitowoc Marina, which will be on your right. Access to the base of the north breakwater is possible at this point.

To view the lighthouse from the south breakwater opposite: From the intersection of Washington St. and S. 8th St., turn south (right) onto S. 8th St. and east (left) again on Madison St., which turns into Lakeview Dr. and leads past the car ferry dock. Access to the south breakwater is available from the parking lot at the end of Lakeview Dr.

Two Rivers North Pierhead Light

Appropriately named, Two Rivers Harbor is situated near the junction of the East Twin River and the West Twin River, which unite a short distance from the lakeshore. The harbor is located just over 5 miles north of Manitowoc and 80 miles north of Milwaukee. A dredged entrance channel leads northwest from deep water in Lake Michigan between parallel piers. Timber and sawmills gave way to commercial fishing as an important local industry. Today, a few fish tugs remain but the harbor is used mainly by pleasure craft.

Life Saving Crew Entering Boat, Two Rivers, Wis.

Two Rivers North Pier—circa 1910

The surviving Two Rivers North Pierhead Light was established in 1886. It consists of a square, wooden, pyramidal tower with an open lower framework. A long, raised catwalk originally connected the tower to shore. A sixth order Fresnel lens produced a fixed red light about 36 feet above water level. Extensively renovated in 1928, the light was finally retired in 1969 when it was replaced with a modern steel tower. The Coast Guard donated the upper portions of the structure to the Two Rivers Historical Society. Unfortunately, the Fresnel lens was broken during the move.

The restored lighthouse now forms the centerpiece of the Rogers Street Fishing Village Museum located on the east bank of the East Twin River just south of the 22nd Street Bridge. An observation deck has been built around the base of the enclosed watchroom, which is open to the public when the museum is open. The museum operates on dona-

Two Rivers North Pierhead Light—circa 1918

tions and focuses on the history of commercial fishing in the area.

Rogers Street Fishing Village Museum
2102 Jackson St., P.O. Box 33
Two Rivers, WI 54241
Phone: 920-793-5905

Status: *Inactive. Open to public as museum.*

Access: *From the north on State Hwy. 42: continue north on Hwy. 42 (across the West Twin River bridge), which turns into Washington St. in town. Turn east (right) on 22nd St., cross the bridge that spans the East Twin River and turn south (right) onto Jackson St. The lighthouse and museum will be on your immediate right.*

From the south on State Hwy. 42: Continue south on Hwy. 42 into town. Turn west (right) onto 22nd St. and then south (left) onto Jackson St. a short distance ahead. The lighthouse and museum will be on your immediate right.

Two Rivers North Pierhead Light

Rawley Point (Twin River Point) Light

Broad, rounding, and heavily wooded, Rawley Point is one of the most prominent points of land on the western shore of Lake Michigan. It lies just over five miles northeast of the harbor at Two Rivers, Wisconsin. The point takes its name from Peter Rowley, who first settled in the area around 1835 and operated a successful trading post for many years. Just when the

Rawley Point Light—circa 1910

spelling of the name Rowley changed to Rawley in reference to the point remains unknown. Rawley Point has been the location of an important coastal light since 1853. The present light station site is encompassed by Point Beach State Forest, which includes more than 2,900 acres of forest land bordered on the east by six miles of sand beach on Lake Michigan.

The first beacon light was erected on the point in 1853, about one and one-half miles south of the present lighthouse. With an overall height of 75 feet, it consisted of little more than a square, tapering, open wooden framework. It had a large lantern at the top that was hoisted up and down by pulleys for servicing. Although it was poorly situated as an aid to navigation, the beacon continued in service for almost 20 years.

The first major coastal light at Rawley Point was relocated about one and one-half miles north of the previous beacon. Constructed in 1873 and first lit early in 1874, the new lighthouse consisted of an 85-foot tall conical brick tower with an attached two and one-half-story brick keeper's dwelling capable of housing three families. The dwelling remains in use today, but the brick light tower attached to the north side of the building was cut down to the level of the roof peak and capped by a hipped roof. The lower three floors of the tower were then incorporated into the living quarters. The top portion of the

tower was removed after the transfer of the light, late in 1894, to a taller tower erected just to the west of the house. Surprisingly, no photographs of the lighthouse with its original brick tower intact have ever been found. Photos do exist, however, of damage done to the house by a fire on January 1, 1962.

The present light tower at Rawley Point was first lit on November 20, 1894. This tower dated from

Rawley Point Light—January 1962

172

July 1859 and had originally been erected at the mouth of the Chicago River in Chicago where it remained in service until discontinued on November 15, 1893. Dismantled shortly thereafter, the tower was heightened, renovated, shipped to Wisconsin and re-erected for service at Rawley Point.

Rawley Point Light consists of a skeletal cast-iron tower with eight outer legs arranged in an octagonal pattern and an enclosed central tube containing a spiral staircase. There are

United States Coast Guard—9th District

Rawley Point keeper's dwelling viewed from the light tower—January 1962

Rawley Point Light

173

two watchrooms at the top of the tower, which has an overall height of 111 feet. The original optic was a third order Fresnel lens that produced a light with a focal plane 113 feet above lake level. Electrified in the 1920s, the Fresnel lens was removed in 1952 after one of its prisms was damaged. An aeronautical style beacon occupies the lantern room today.

In the days when Rawley Point Light Station was still manned, a keeper and two assistants were necessary to oversee the operation and maintenance of the light, fog signal, and radiobeacon at the site. Introduced in the early 1920s, radiobeacons were the first electronic aids to navigation available on the Great Lakes. Radiobeacon signals were assigned to the most important lighthouses on Lake Michigan and Green Bay. Rawley Point had the added responsibility of serving as a radiobeacon monitoring station to ensure the accuracy of signals being transmitted by other stations around the lake. There are no longer any radiobeacons on the Great Lakes. Over time, they were rendered obsolete by radar, racons, loran-C, and most recently, differential GPS.

Rawley Point Light Station was finally automated in 1979 after use of the fog signal was discontinued. Coast Guard personnel stationed at the base in Two Rivers continue to reside in the old brick house and several rooms in one apartment are available as rental units to military veterans traveling on vacation. Please respect the privacy of the current occupants when visiting the surrounding grounds.

Rawley Point Light

Status: *Active. Not open to public.*

Access: *From the south in Two Rivers: At the intersection of State Hwy. 42 and 22nd St., go east on 22nd St. a short distance and turn north (left) onto County Road O (also called Sandy Bay Rd.). Continue north on County Road O about 4½ miles to the entrance to Point Beach State Park. A daily or annual permit is needed to enter the park. Just past the registration booth, the lighthouse will come into view a short distance to the southeast.*

From the north on Hwy. 42: Continue north on Hwy. 42 to County Road V. Turn east (left) on County Road V until it intersects County Road O. Turn south (right) onto County Road O to the state park entrance as above.

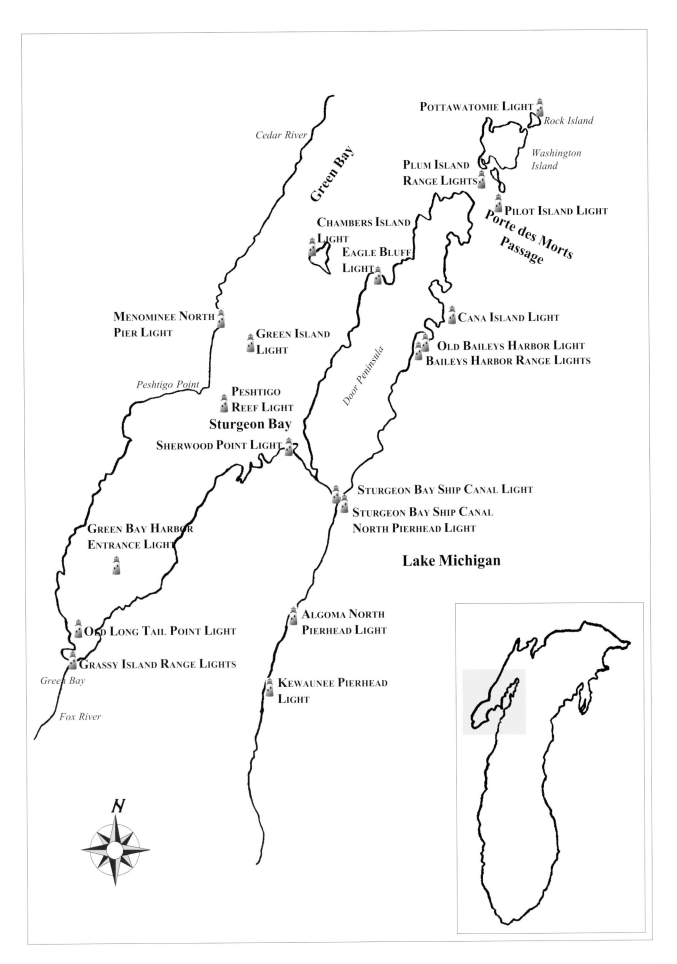

Cedar River

Green Bay

POTTAWATOMIE LIGHT

Rock Island

Washington Island

PLUM ISLAND RANGE LIGHTS

PILOT ISLAND LIGHT

Porte des Morts Passage

CHAMBERS ISLAND LIGHT

EAGLE BLUFF LIGHT

CANA ISLAND LIGHT

OLD BAILEYS HARBOR LIGHT
BAILEYS HARBOR RANGE LIGHTS

MENOMINEE NORTH PIER LIGHT

GREEN ISLAND LIGHT

Door Peninsula

Peshtigo Point

PESHTIGO REEF LIGHT

Sturgeon Bay

SHERWOOD POINT LIGHT

STURGEON BAY SHIP CANAL LIGHT

STURGEON BAY SHIP CANAL NORTH PIERHEAD LIGHT

Lake Michigan

GREEN BAY HARBOR ENTRANCE LIGHT

ALGOMA NORTH PIERHEAD LIGHT

OLD LONG TAIL POINT LIGHT

GRASSY ISLAND RANGE LIGHTS

Green Bay

KEWAUNEE PIERHEAD LIGHT

Fox River

N

Kewaunee Harbor

Kewaunee Harbor is located at the mouth of the Kewaunee River, about 102 miles north of Milwaukee and 25 miles south of the entrance to the Sturgeon Bay Ship Canal. Like so many other small towns founded along the lake, lumber and sawmills were the mainstay of the early local economy. Shallow water severely hampered the development of the port and commerce was conducted from unprotected piers run out into the deeper offshore waters.

Serious harbor improvements were not undertaken until the mid-1880s. A dredged entrance channel leads from deep water in Lake Michigan northwest to an outer harbor basin protected by a detached breakwater on the northeast and a pier on the south side. From the outer basin, the channel leads between piers at the mouth of the river to a turning basin inside the mouth and northerly from there inside the shoreline to a well-protected north inner basin. Kewaunee was the western terminus of a cross-lake railroad car ferry service for many years. That traffic ended in 1990. Today the harbor is used mainly by pleasure craft.

Kewaunee Pierhead Light

A pair of range lights was established on the south pier at Kewaunee in 1891. It is likely that the front range light consisted of little more than a lantern suspended from a wooden pole, but few details regarding these first range lights have been found. As the port became more important to cross-lake railroad car ferry traffic, better lighting at the harbor entrance proved necessary. The front range light was replaced

United States Coast Guard

Kewaunee Pierhead Light—circa 1930

Kewaunee Pierhead Light—viewed from the northern detached breakwater

Kewaunee Pierhead Light—viewed from the northwest

in 1895 with a taller structure that consisted of a square, tapering, cast-iron tower with an open lower framework. The fog signal building that would later become the present lighthouse was constructed immediately behind this tower in 1909. An enclosed passageway extending from the roof level of this building connected it to the back of the light tower. Both structures were painted white and connected to shore by a raised catwalk. The rear range light was replaced in 1912 by an even taller steel skeleton tower.

The 1909 fog signal building was wood-framed and the lower half sheathed in cast-iron plates for durability. The upper portion was sheathed in cedar shingles. At one time there were living quarters for the keeper on the second floor. Nearly identical structures were built within a few years of each other at Waukegan, Illinois and Holland, Michigan.

Late in 1930, the light tower in front of the fog

signal building was damaged by a railroad car ferry that collided with the end of the pier. In 1931 it was removed from service. Its lantern room and fifth order Fresnel lens were transferred to the top of a square tower that was built through the gabled roof at the eastern end of the fog signal building. The rear range light was discontinued in October 1941.

Kewaunee Pierhead Light was finally automated in 1981. The fifth order Fresnel lens remains in place and produces a light with a focal plane 45 feet above water level. The catwalk has not survived into the present.

Status: *Active. Not open to public.*

Access: *State Hwy. 42 runs straight through downtown Kewaunee. From Hwy. 42, turn east onto Ellis St. Ellis St. is less than half a mile south of the Kewaunee River. Take Ellis St. to its end at the beach. The base of the south pier lies just to the north.*

Algoma North Pierhead Light

Algoma Harbor lies at the mouth of the Ahnapee River, about 112 miles north of Milwaukee and 14 miles south-southwest of the entrance to the Sturgeon Bay Ship Canal. Algoma was originally called Ahnapee when it was first settled around 1851. The north pier was constructed in 1856. Modern harbor improvements consist of a dredged entrance channel leading from the deep water in the lake. It runs between a north pier with a detached outer section and a south breakwater to a protected outer harbor basin. Commercial fishing was an important local industry for many years. Today, a few fish tugs remain but pleasure craft mainly use the harbor.

The Ahnapee Light Station, as it was first called when established in 1893, consisted of a set of range lights on the north pier connected to shore by a raised catwalk. The keeper lived

Algoma North Pierhead Light—circa 1907

in a house on a low bluff a short distance away, north of the river's mouth. The front range light was a simple lantern suspended from a wooden pole, the use of which was eliminated around 1908. The rear range light consisted of a square, wooden, pyramidal tower with an open lower framework. The original optic was a fifth order Fresnel lens.

In 1908, Algoma North Pierhead Light was completely rebuilt and consisted of a conical cast-iron tower with an overall height of just 26 feet. The fifth order Fresnel lens from the wooden tower was retained. A fog signal powered with compressed air was added in 1910. The detached outer section of the north pier was completed in 1932. Repositioned at its outer end, the entire light structure was raised to a height of 42 feet by placing the 1908 tower on a new cylindrical steel base. Automation came in 1973. Today a modern plastic optic produces a light with a focal plane 48 feet above water level. Unlike so many other sites along the western shore of Lake Michigan, a portion of the raised catwalk has survived into the present.

Status: *Active. Not open to public.*

Access: *State Hwy. 42 runs straight through the small town of Algoma. The waterfront park there is visible just east of Hwy. 42. There is a good view of the tower from the outer end of the south breakwater.*

Algoma North Pierhead Light

Sturgeon Bay Ship Canal

This canal is located on the western shore of Lake Michigan. It lies about 128 miles north of Milwaukee and 40 miles south of Porte des Morts Passage (Death's Door), the southernmost and most dangerous route between the lake and Green Bay. It provides a navigable connection between Lake Michigan and the south end of Green Bay by means of dredged channels and a canal cut across the narrow land divide between the lake and the head of Sturgeon

Sturgeon Bay Ship Canal—circa 1900

Bay, opening from Green Bay. The canal was cut through by the privately organized Sturgeon Bay and Lake Michigan Canal Company from 1872 to 1881. The canal is an open cut without locks or gates measuring 7,200 feet long, 160 feet wide, and about 24 feet deep. The total length of the channel from its Lake Michigan entrance through Sturgeon Bay to its end near Sherwood Point on Green Bay is 8.6 miles. Sturgeon Bay is a natural branch of Green Bay, but the navigation aids that mark the channel through it are placed with respect to vessels proceeding from Lake Michigan through the ship canal to Green Bay.

The company that developed the canal charged a usage toll and there was no shortage of takers. Prior to the canal's opening, vessels bound from ports at the southern end of Lake Michigan for ports at the southern end of Green Bay had no choice but to go around the dangerous tip of the Door Peninsula about 40 miles to the north. Using the canal shaved almost one hundred miles off that route. Mariners were able to avoid the dan-

gers of the Porte des Morts Passage. The canal also made Sturgeon Bay available as a harbor of refuge from storms for vessels on Lake Michigan.

The canal opened in 1881, however, was of limited usefulness due to its small dimensions. Ships were growing larger and more efficient every year. The canal company lacked the financial resources to improve upon their creation. Recognizing the canal's success and future potential if expanded, the Federal government purchased the canal and took possession of it on April 25, 1893. It was placed under the control of the Army Corps of Engineers. All tolls were eliminated. Responsibility for navigation lights along the canal was transferred to the Lighthouse Board in 1896. Over time, the canal was widened and deepened. The entrance from Lake Michigan was protected by a wave-stilling basin

Sturgeon Bay Ship Canal—circa 1910

enclosed between converging breakwaters. Lights first provided by the Lighthouse Board in 1882 were rebuilt as the improvements progressed.

Once a backwoods settlement, the city of Sturgeon Bay rose to prominence as a result of the increased shipping traffic passing through the canal. By the mid-1890s, shipbuilding and repair replaced fishing and lumbering as the main economic activities. In these new pursuits, the protected waters of the Sturgeon Bay waterfront were used to their best advantage. To this day, Sturgeon Bay remains one of the largest shipbuilding and ship repair centers on the Great Lakes, with dry-docks readily able to accommodate the largest lake freighters. As the largest city in Door County, Sturgeon Bay makes a great starting point for tours of the lighthouses and smaller resort communities to the north.

While in Sturgeon Bay, *do not miss* a visit to the Door County Maritime Museum (DCMM) located on the waterfront at the south end of the Michigan Street Bridge. Outstanding exhibits celebrate the county's maritime heritage. This state-of-the-art facility was dedicated on June 28, 1997, and is open seven days a week year-round. It replaced a much smaller museum building operated seasonally since 1969. DCMM continues to operate a second branch

in Gills Rock at the northern tip of the Door Peninsula, where emphasis is placed on commercial fishing and local shipwrecks.

Since 1994, the DCMM has sponsored the Door County Lighthouse Walk held annually in mid-May. Door County has the highest concentration of lighthouses on the Great Lakes, many of which are difficult to reach and seldom open to the public. During the Lighthouse Walk weekend, most of the lighthouses are opened to the public with special land and sea arrangements made to facilitate visits. This is an excellent opportunity to see the more remote island sites. The only drawback, however, is the weather in mid-May, which can be very unpredictable. Due to concerns for public safety, it is not uncommon for boat tours to be cancelled because of high winds and rough seas. Please note that even under the best weather conditions, it is physically impossible to visit all the lighthouses in a single weekend. If possible, plan for an extended stay; Door County is a beautiful destination year-round. For further information, contact:

Door County Maritime Museum
120 North Madison Avenue
Sturgeon Bay, WI 54235
Phone: 920-743-5958

Sturgeon Bay Ship Canal North Pierhead Light

Although the canal opened in 1881, the first north pierhead light was not established until May 15, 1882. It consisted of a square, wooden, pyramidal tower with an open lower framework. Painted white, it was connected to shore by a raised catwalk. Standing 39 feet in height overall, the tower housed a sixth order Fresnel lens that produced a fixed red light at a focal plane 35 feet above the water. Because insufficient funds had been appropriated, no dwelling was built and the first keeper lived on a dredge working on the canal. In August 1884, the first of two duplicate fog signal buildings housing a steam-powered 10" whistle was built on the pier a short distance

behind the light tower. The increased workload of maintaining the fog plant necessitated the assignment of an assistant keeper. The second fog signal

Sturgeon Bay Ship Canal North Pierhead Light—circa 1950

Sturgeon Bay Ship Canal North Pierhead Light and raised catwalk

building was added in 1886, as was, finally, a wood-framed dwelling with quarters for the two keepers. Only one of the fog signals was used, the other serving as a backup.

The present Sturgeon Bay Ship Canal North Pierhead Light is a combination fog signal building and lighthouse built in 1903 to replace the original wooden tower and two fog signal buildings. It consists of a two-story, rectangular, wood-framed building encased in cast-iron plates for durability. A short, conical, cast-iron light tower emerges from the east-ern end of the hipped roof to give the structure an overall height of 39 feet. The sixth order Fresnel lens from the previous tower was placed in the new tower, producing a light with a focal plane 40 feet above water level. Presently, a modern plastic optic is in place. Originally painted white, the north pierhead light was painted red during a later modernization. The structure remains connected to shore by a raised catwalk. The light and fog signal were automated in 1972.

Sturgeon Bay Ship Canal Light

The North Pierhead Light, with its small sixth order lens, was barely adequate to mark a waterway that was becoming increasingly important. A U.S. Life Saving Station was established on the north side of the canal entrance in July 1886. By 1890, shipping interests were calling for the establishment of a more powerful coastal light to mark the entrance.

The resulting tower was an experimental design finally completed in November 1898. As originally constructed, the Sturgeon Bay Ship Canal Light consisted of a 78-foot tall cast-iron cylinder only 8 feet in diameter, which contained a spiral staircase. The cylinder supported a cast-iron watchroom 12 feet in diameter, which itself was topped by a round cast-iron lantern room housing a third order Fresnel lens. The cylinder supported the full weight of the staircase, watchroom, lantern, and lighting apparatus. The tower was minimally stabilized at its base by eight triangular lattice buttresses only 16.5 feet along the side attached to the tower and 6.5 feet long anchored to a concrete foundation. The lantern room was painted black, but the rest of the 98-foot tower was reddish-brown in color.

The architects of the new tower failed to factor into the design stress loads caused by high winds. As a result, the tower vibrated so badly in the wind that it affected the operation of the light. Powered by a weighted clockwork mechanism, the lens rotated to produce alternating white and red flashes, and the vibration impaired this action. In

Sturgeon Bay Canal Coast Guard Station

an effort to stiffen the tower, four wire guy lines were attached to it but the vibration continued. With the problem unsolved, the light officially went into operation on March 17, 1899. The tower was repainted white in 1900, presumably to make it a better daymark.

The vibration problem was finally solved in 1903 by substantially rebuilding the tower, giving it its present appearance. The central cast-iron cylinder was left to support only the weight of the spiral staircase inside it. The original watchroom, lantern room, and lighting apparatus were retained, but their weight was transferred to a new skeletal, cast-iron framework stabilized by larger buttresses. The tower retained an overall height of 98 feet. The original lens remains in place and produces a light with a focal plane 107 feet above water level. It was automated in 1972. The combined buildings of the former life saving and light stations form the core of the present Sturgeon Bay Canal Coast Guard Station.

Status: *Both lights are active. Not open to public.*

Access: *From Hwy. 42/57 in Sturgeon Bay, turn east just north of the Bay View Bridge onto Utah St. Follow Utah St. less than one-half mile, turning south (right) onto Cove Rd. From Cove Rd., turn left (southeast) onto Canal Rd. for about two and one-half miles to the Coast Guard Station. There is a parking area on the right, just before entering the*

station. There is also a trail to the pierhead light leading directly through the entrance to the station, from which the canal light may also be seen. As a visitor on an active Coast Guard base, it is always best to stop at the office as a courtesy so they know your intended purpose and estimated length of stay.

Sturgeon Bay Ship Canal Light

Dunlap Reef Light

Completion of the Sturgeon Bay Ship Canal in 1881 and the resulting increase in shipping traffic passing through Sturgeon Bay necessitated the marking of Dunlap Reef. The reef is a 700-foot long strip of partially submerged limestone lying adjacent to the western edge of the dredged shipping channel. It lies about one-half mile northwest of the Michigan Street Bridge and just north of the city's Bay View Park.

The Dunlap Reef Range Lights, whose orientation was generally north-south, were established in 1881 to mark the reef and guide eastbound vessels into the channel leading to the ship canal. Dunlap Reef Lighthouse was the rear or southernmost range light. Constructed on a stone-filled timber crib foundation, it consisted of a one and one-half-story wood-framed keeper's dwelling with a square wooden light tower built into the front or northern wall of the dwelling. A wooden boathouse was built on the crib immediately behind the lighthouse as the keeper needed a rowboat to service the front light and to go into town. The front range light was a short, square, wooden, pyramidal structure with an open lower framework constructed in shallow water at the northeast edge of the reef.

Channel improvements made the range unnecessary and it was discontinued in 1924. Prior to offering the lighthouse for sale in 1925, the lantern room and lighting apparatus were removed so they could be used elsewhere if necessary. The buyer dismantled the house, cut down the tower, and moved it to an east side Sturgeon Bay neighborhood where it remains today at 411 S. 4th Avenue. There is nothing from the outward appearance of the house to suggest it was ever a lighthouse.

Today, Dunlap Reef is marked by a permanent, modern light structure on its northeast end and by a number of privately maintained buoys placed from April 1 to October 31 to warn off pleasure boaters.

Dunlap Reef Light—circa 1915

Historical Collections of the Great Lakes

Baileys Harbor

Baileys Harbor is located about 22 miles north of the Sturgeon Bay Ship canal and 3 miles south of Cana Island along the eastern shore of Door Peninsula. First settled around 1849, the place was named after Justice Bailey, a schooner captain who found refuge from a storm there late in 1848. Baileys Harbor became a busy logging port, shipping timber, cordwood, cedar posts, poles and tanning bark. Local shipping interests petitioned the Federal government for the establishment of a lighthouse to mark the harbor's entrance. At the time, Baileys Harbor was also the closest natural harbor of refuge north of Milwaukee, a very long way to the south.

Old Baileys Harbor Light

Old Baileys Harbor Light was established in the autumn of 1852 at the eastern entrance to the harbor on a very small island alternately called North Point Island or Lighthouse Island. The island is close offshore the mainland and the water between the two points is very shallow, sometimes making the island a peninsula. From the time the lighthouse was built, lake captains considered it poorly placed, as the actual port was still over a mile to the northwest. Numerous shoals at the harbor's entrance made navigation difficult during the day and almost impossible at night. The lighthouse was of little use when it came to actually entering the harbor. For this reason, the lighthouse was discontinued on December 1, 1869. The next spring, it was replaced by a better positioned set of range lights established onshore just north of town. Thereafter, the lighthouse and its small island were sold to a private individual and the site has remained privately owned ever since. No photograph of the lighthouse while it was an active aid to navigation has ever been found.

Old Baileys Harbor Light consists of a conical, rubble-stone tower about 45 feet in height from its base to the former lantern room deck. Attached is a small, single-story stone keeper's dwelling. Subsequent owners have expanded the living space with roof window dormers and a wood-framed addition that is larger than the original house. Initially fitted with a sixth order Fresnel lens, the optic was upgraded to one of the fifth order in 1858. Old Baileys Harbor Light retains one of only three bird-cage style lantern rooms left on the Great Lakes. The other two are at Waugoshance Light in northern Lake Michigan near the Straits of Mackinac (a ruin) and Selkirk, New York (miracu-

Old Baileys Harbor Light

lously, completely intact and in excellent condition).

After the Lighthouse Board was created late in 1852, they ordered the superior Fresnel lenses for all U.S. lighthouses. The conversion from Argand lamps and silvered reflectors was carried out between 1852 and 1859. At most sites, the change in lighting apparatus usually meant the old style birdcage lantern room was removed. With roofs of hammered copper and many small panes of inferior glass, the lantern rooms were often too small to accommodate the new lenses. Water leakage around the glass panes was a common problem and the metal sashes supporting the panes interfered with light transmission. Instead, an improved style of multisided or polygonal lantern room was substituted. These only had eight to twelve large panes of glass secured in a strong cast-iron framework topped by a solid cast-iron roof.

Old Baileys Harbor Light probably kept its birdcage lantern room because it was still so new at the time of the conversion and only a small lens was needed to mark the harbor. The fact that the light-

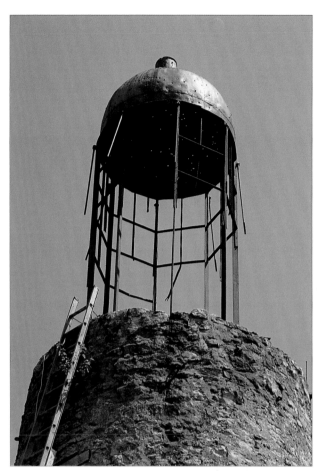

Bird-cage lantern room at Old Baileys Harbor Light

house did not remain in service for very long thereafter made the lantern room's replacement unnecessary. Over time, unfortunately, the top of the tower has been allowed to deteriorate and the rare lantern room is a ruin. The uppermost courses of stone are missing from the tower as is the lantern room deck. Other than this, however, the site is well maintained.

Status: *Inactive. Private residence.* ***Please respect the privacy of the owners.***

Access: *Boat. For most visitors to the area, however, a good view is possible from the nearby mainland. From Hwy. 57 in Baileys Harbor, turn east on Ridges Rd. (watch for the sign directing you to the Baileys Harbor Yacht Club). Follow it for about two and one-half miles out to its very end where there is a large open area. The old lighthouse is visible among the trees on the small island just offshore to the west.*

Old Baileys Harbor Light Tower

Baileys Harbor Range Lights

Due to numerous shoals at the harbor's entrance, entering Baileys Harbor had long been difficult for approaching mariners and best undertaken during daylight hours. Baileys Harbor Range Lights were built on the northwestern shore of the harbor to mark the safest approach. Construction was completed in 1869 and the range lights were first displayed at the start of navigation in 1870. Their establishment rendered obsolete the Old Baileys Harbor Light, which was then discontinued. Six nearly identical sets of range lights were built on the Great Lakes between 1869 and 1873. Of the surviving range lights of this design, Baileys Harbor Range Lights are the only ones still standing in their original positions.

Baileys Harbor Front Range Light consists of a small, white, two-story wooden tower with a square base and an octagonal second story. The tower has an overall height of 21 feet and originally housed a fifth order Fresnel lens that produced a fixed red light with a focal plane 22 feet above water level. The light was displayed from the single window at the top of the tower's front wall. A smaller window on the back of the tower faces the combined dwelling and rear range light. This window allowed the keeper to monitor the operation of the front light from a distance, thus eliminating an unnecessary walk to the front tower. In 1897, the Fresnel lens in the front tower was replaced by a locomotive headlight of greater intensity.

Baileys Harbor Rear Range Light is located 950 feet at a bearing of 340° True from the front range light. It consists of a rectangular, one and one-half-story, wood-framed keeper's dwelling with a covered front porch and a rear kitchen with a lean-to roof. A short, rectangular, wooden tower emerges from the roof peak to give the structure an overall height of 35 feet. The tower originally housed a fifth order Fresnel lens that produced a fixed white light displayed from its single arched window at a focal plane 39 feet above water level. A wooden walkway covers some 600 feet of the total distance to the front range light.

Baileys Harbor Range Lights were automated with acetylene gas lamps in September 1923. The dwelling was vacated and maintenance of the range lights was reassigned to the keepers at Cana Island.

Baileys Harbor Front Range Light

Both range lights were electrified in 1930. At the same time, the town's Lutheran minister and his family received permission to use the empty dwelling as a parsonage. Its use as such continued until around 1959, when it again became vacant. The Coast Guard deactivated the range lights in November 1969 and removed the lighting equipment from both structures. They were replaced by a single directional light mounted atop a skeletal steel tower erected just to the south of the front range light. Baileys Harbor Directional Light, as it is called, serves the same function performed by the old range lights for so many years.

Although the range lights were automated by the mid-1920s, other events would determine their ultimate fate. In 1934, the Bureau of Lighthouses deeded about 30 acres of land and leased the range light buildings to the Door County Park Commission (DCPC). Naturalists were aghast when they learned of plans to develop the property into a trailer park for vacationing motorists. It was known that the property, which consists of about 30 beach "ridges" that parallel the shoreline, was home to over 25 native orchid species and many other rare plants. In order to protect this unique geological and botanical area, concerned citizens formed a nature preserve called the Ridges Sanctuary in 1937. The Sanctuary is a privately held, nonprofit organization. The Sanctuary secured a lease of the land and the buildings from the DCPC, halting future development. In so doing, it also assumed responsibility for the maintenance of the old range light buildings.

Baileys Harbor Rear Range Light

After its use as a parsonage ended, the rear range dwelling remained vacant until 1965. At that time, the Ridges Sanctuary began to use it as an office and a seasonal residence for the preserve's manager. It continues to serve both purposes. Despite the novelty of being located in a protected area, time and the elements gradually took their toll on the old range lights. Both finally underwent a major renovation in 1993. The wooden walkway

Baileys Harbor Rear Range Light

running between them was rebuilt in 1994. Ownership of the range lights was formally conveyed to the DCPC on September 1, 1998. Presently, the Ridges Sanctuary still leases the range lights and surrounding thirty acres from the county, but the Sanctuary now owns and/or manages over one thousand adjacent acres.

Status: *Inactive. Not open to public. The rear range dwelling serves as a seasonal private residence. However, both range lights are open to the public during the annual Door County Lighthouse Walk held in mid-May. Contact the Door County Maritime Museum at 920-743-5958 or the Door County Chamber of Commerce at 920-743-4456 for additional information. The Ridges Sanctuary may be contacted at 920-839-2802.*

Access: *From Hwy. 57 in Baileys Harbor, turn east on Ridges Rd. (watch for the sign directing you to the Baileys Harbor Yacht Club) and go about 0.3 mile. The front range light will be on your immediate left near the edge of the road. The walkway leading back to the rear range light starts a short distance behind it. Parking is allowed along the shoulder of the road.*

Cana Island Light

Cana Island is a low-lying island just under nine acres in size. It lies about halfway between Moonlight Bay and North Bay, two natural harbors of refuge along the eastern shore of Door Peninsula. Cana Island Light was built on the eastern tip of the island to serve as a coastal light and to help mark both harbors.

Cana Island Light was first exhibited at the start of navigation in 1870. The lighthouse consists of a conical, cream-colored brick tower with an overall height of 86 feet. An enclosed passageway connects the tower to a rectangular, one and one-half-story, cream-colored brick keeper's dwelling. The dwelling originally contained quarters for the families of the keeper and his assistant. The arrangement worked especially well during those periods when the assistant was also the keeper's spouse. The original optic, which remains in place, is a third order Fresnel lens that produces a light with a focal plane 83 feet above water level. Protruding as it does into Lake Michigan, Cana Island and its lighthouse are fully exposed to the brunt of storms out of the northeast through the south. The keepers experienced and recorded events related to several dramatic storms. One of the worst storms occurred in October 1880, when gale force winds out of the northeast left the island awash. Water flooded the cellar and ran through the kitchen at the back of the house. Waves at one point were breaking over the house and spray from the surf reached the glass of the lantern room.

The soft-faced Milwaukee brick used in the construction of the tower was no match for the elements. By the turn of the century, the brick was spalling badly. In order to save the deteriorating tower, in 1902 it was encased in cast-iron plates up to the level of the watchroom deck and painted white to make it a more effective daymark. The space between the plates and the tower was filled with concrete. The same process had been used two years earlier to save

Cana Island Light

the tower at Big Sable Point on the opposite side of Lake Michigan.

Cana Island Light Station was originally connected to the mainland by a raised, wooden footbridge built along a naturally occurring rubble-stone causeway about 450 feet in length. Unfortunately, the footbridge did not last long due to wind, waves, and ice. In later years, the causeway was built up with gravel fill. Depending on the wind direction and water level of the lake, the causeway varies between being high and dry to being submerged under two feet of water. Usually, it is covered by less than a foot of water. At one time, a dock and boathouse were located on the island just south of the causeway. Their remnants are still visible in the water.

The rubble-stone fences around the property were completed around 1920 by Keeper Oscar H. Knudsen. Other structures remaining at the site include a brick privy and a very rare octagonal, brick oil storage house. The last signifi-

Cana Island Light

cant structural change to the lighthouse occurred in 1944, when the Coast Guard added an entrance to the south side of the house where a window had been.

Cana Island Light was automated in 1944. Thereafter, the Coast Guard maintained the light and the tower (and continues to do so), but the dwelling and grounds received minimal care. In 1971, the Coast Guard leased the site to the Door County Maritime Museum (DCMM) headquartered in Sturgeon Bay. DCMM opened the grounds to the public and initiated long-needed repairs. Much of the renovation work completed was a result of the involvement of Louis and Rosie Janda and their family. The Jandas were resident caretakers for nineteen summers between 1977 and 1995. Since then, no one has lived at the lighthouse due to environmental concerns related to the lack of running water and sewage disposal facilities.

Cana Island Light Station is one of those places that has changed very little in appearance over the years. The picturesque setting offers a glimpse back in time. Although Cana Island has become one of the most frequently visited tourist sites in Door County, it retains its charm. The grounds are open daily from 10 to 5, mid-May through the end of October. There is a small admission charge. Bring wa-

terproof boots or a change of shoes as the causeway to the island is usually partially submerged. The tower is never open to the public, but the keeper's dwelling may be toured when museum staff are on duty. The dwelling is also opened for the Annual Door County Lighthouse Walk held in mid-May. Contact the DCMM at 920-743-5958 or the Door County Chamber of Commerce at 920-743-4456 for additional information.

Status: *Active. Dwelling only periodically open to public.*

Access: *From Baileys Harbor, go north on Hwy. 57 and turn east (right) onto County Road Q. Stay on CR-Q for about three and one-half miles and turn south (right) onto Cana Island Rd. At the "T" intersection soon encountered, continue right on Cana Island Rd. following signs to the Spikehorn Campground for about one mile. Cana Island Rd. jogs left sharply, narrows, and passes through the campground before ending at the causeway leading to Cana Island. Park on the roadside at the end of the blacktop. Parking space is very limited.* **Please respect the property lines and privacy of local land owners.**

Pilot Island Light (Porte des Morts)

Pilot Island

Green Bay is separated from Lake Michigan by two mainland peninsulas. Garden Peninsula, the northern one, is 20 miles long and Door Peninsula, to the south, is about 70 miles long. The entrance to Green Bay between the two peninsulas is about 28 miles wide. The waterway is so choked with islands and shoals that the passages between them have acquired the deserved reputation of being dangerous. This is no place for a mariner to make a mistake.

There are four main passages through this gauntlet. The northern two lie within the waters of the state of Michigan. The southern two, lying within Wisconsin waters, are at Rock Island and Porte des Morts (Death's Door). Porte des Morts Passage is the southernmost and narrowest of the four. The passage is bordered on the north side by Plum and Pilot Islands and on the south side by the sheer limestone bluffs of the Door Peninsula headland. The shores are rockbound and almost certain destruction to vessels going aground. Numerous shoals border the passage and strong currents set in and out of it according to the wind direction. These conditions, along with frequently reduced visibility due to fog, rain or snow, have been the cause of many marine casualties. Hence the name Death's Door, from which Door County, Wisconsin and the Door Peninsula derive their names.

The entrance to Porte des Morts Passage from Lake Michigan is marked by a pair of range lights on the southwest shore of Plum Island and the light on Pilot Island. Pilot Island consists of little more than three and one-half acres of rocks and lies just under two miles southeast of Plum Island on the northeast side of the entrance to the passage.

The original Porte des Morts Light was actually built on Plum Island in 1848. No photographs of this lighthouse are known to exist and little else is known of it. Shipping interests complained that the light was too far west into the passage and that a light farther out in the lake to the south or east would be more useful. The Lighthouse Board agreed, and in 1858 Porte des Morts Light was rebuilt on Port des Morts Island, the name of

Pilot Island Light

which was changed to Pilot Island around 1875.

The surviving Pilot Island Light of 1858 consists of a two-story keeper's dwelling constructed of cream-colored brick. A short, square, wooden tower emerges from the western end of the roof peak. It supported a lantern room that originally housed a fourth order Fresnel lens having a focal plane 48 feet above water level. A modern, solar-powered plastic optic is in place today. The overall height of the house and tower is 41 feet. The design of this lighthouse was repeated at several other locations on Lake Michigan. All within a few years of each other, nearly identical structures were built in Wisconsin at Green Island, Port Washington and Rock Island; at Grand Traverse and South Manitou Is-

Pilot Island Light—circa 1902

Pilot Island Light

land in Michigan; and at Michigan City, Indiana. Pilot Island Light remained the only lighthouse marking the entrance to Porte des Morts Passage until the range lights on Plum Island were established in 1897.

Pilot Island was frequently shrouded in fog. A fog signal bell was placed in service in 1862 and the first foghorn followed in 1864. Complaints about the poor quality of the fog signal produced led to the establishment of a much louder, steam-powered fog siren in 1875. A duplicate siren was added in a separate building in 1880. Only one of the fog signals was used, the other served as a backup in case of equipment failure. The surviving brick fog signal building dates from 1900, when the sirens were replaced with a 10" steam whistle. A diaphone powered by compressed air later replaced the steam whistle.

Early on, the keeper needed assistants at the station to operate the fog plants, which created a housing crunch. It was alleviated in 1904, when the lighthouse was divided lengthwise down the middle and converted into a duplex to provide separate quarters for the keeper and first assistant. It was at this time that the wing walls on both sides of the building were added to accommodate the new entrances and stairwells. Dual brick kitchens were later added to the back of the lighthouse. An unused fog signal building was then converted into quarters for the second assistant. Other structures on the small island included a barn, boathouse, dock, oil storage house, several privies, and a workshop. All were connected by concrete walkways. All are now gone.

Pilot Island Light was automated in 1962 when use of the fog signal was discontinued. The sight that presents itself today is not a pretty one. Neglect and exposure to the elements have taken their toll on the buildings. The lighthouse is in serious need of rehabilitation. The roof of the fog signal building is sagging and probably will soon collapse. The island is severely overgrown with scrub brush and infested with thousands of cormorants and seagulls whose guano has killed the few remaining trees. Listed by the Coast Guard as excess property, Pilot Island Light Station is one of several locations on the Great Lakes where new stewards are being sought. The Coast Guard plans to maintain the light as an active aid to navigation, but they are trying to get out of the property management business in order to save money and concentrate on their core duties. Whoever eventually takes over the task will not find it an easy one. Access to this rocky island is still very much dictated by the whims of wind and weather.

Status: *Active. Not open to public.*

Access: *Boat. There is a gap between the remains of the old concrete boat dock on the west side of the island and the shoreline that is sometimes spanned by plywood, sometimes not. Proceed with extreme caution only in the calmest weather. A view from the water is sometimes possible from an excursion cruise offered during the annual Door County Lighthouse Walk held in mid-May. Contact the Door County Maritime Museum at 920-743-5958 or the Door County Chamber of Commerce at 920-743-4456 for additional information.*

Plum Island Front Range Light—note Rear Range Light in the distance

Plum Island Rear Range Light

Plum Island Range Lights

Porte des Morts Passage, also known as Death's Door, is the most treacherous and southerly of four main vessel passages separating Green Bay from the open waters of Lake Michigan. The passage is bordered on the north side by Pilot and Plum Islands and on the south side by the sheer limestone bluffs of the Door Peninsula head-

Plum Island Rear Range Light with old keeper's dwelling in foreground

land. Plum Island is about one mile long, .7 mile wide, and heavily wooded. The island supposedly takes its name from the fact that it is located "plumb" in the middle of Death's Door between the Door Peninsula and Washington Island just to the northeast. Somewhere in time, the "b" was dropped. Porte des Morts Light, the first lighthouse to mark the passage, was built on the southwest edge of Plum Island in 1848. Shipping interests considered it too far west into the passage to be of help in making a safe approach. Consequently, the light was moved about two miles to the southeast and reestablished on Pilot Island in 1858. Pilot Island Light remained the only lighthouse marking the entrance to Porte des Morts Passage until 1897, when the range lights on the southwest shore of Plum Island were established.

The Plum Island Range Lights were first lit on May 1, 1897. The front range light consisted of a white two-story wooden tower with a square base and an octagonal upper portion. The design was similar to the front range light at Baileys Harbor, except that it was topped by a small black cast-iron lantern room. The tower housed a sixth order Fresnel lens that produced a fixed red light with a focal plane 32 feet above water level. The wooden tower was replaced with the present skeletal steel structure in

1964. The modern optic in use has a focal plane 41 feet above water level.

The rear range light is located 1,650 feet at a bearing of 330° True from the front range light. The rear range light consists of a skeletal cast-iron tower with four outer legs and an enclosed central tube containing a spiral staircase. A cylindrical watchroom is surmounted by an octagonal lantern room, giving the tower an overall height of 65 feet. The original optic was a fourth order Fresnel lens that produced a fixed red light with a focal plane 80 feet above water level. The light was visible through an arc of 231° so it was visible to vessels already in Porte des Morts Passage as well as down the range to the southeast. A modern, solar-powered plastic optic presently is in use. As a daymark, both the front and rear range lights are fitted with rectangular red dayboards bearing a central white stripe. The keepers lived in a rectangular, two-story duplex constructed of cream-colored brick located close to the rear range tower. A steam-powered fog signal was housed in a brick building, painted white, one-quarter mile to the west on the shoreline. This structure, which received a sizable addition to its lakeward face in November 1955, survives in dilapidated condition. Other structures at the light station included several docks, boathouses, an oil storage house, and a tramway for moving supplies up to the dwelling.

The Plum Island Range Lights were automated in 1969 and use of the fog signal ended in 1975. As active aids to navigation, both of the range lights are well maintained. The remaining dwelling and fog signal building have fallen into a sad state of disrepair. The site is overgrown and slowly being reclaimed by the forces of nature. As property recently "excessed" by the Coast Guard, it is hoped new stewards will soon be found to care for this historic site.

Status: *Active. Not open to public.*

Access: *There is no dock at the light station, but* *there is one at the former Coast Guard station located on the northeast corner of the island. The walk from this dock to the range lights is a little over one-half mile. The range lights may be viewed from a distance from one of the ferries that travel between Northport and Detroit Harbor on Washington Island. During the annual Door County Lighthouse Walk held in mid-May, an excursion cruise is offered that stops at Plum Island and allows those interested to walk over to the range lights. Contact the Door County Maritime Museum at 920-734-5958 or the Door County Chamber of Commerce at 920-743-4456 for additional information.*

Pottawatomie Light

There are four main vessel passages through the gauntlet of islands and shoals that separate Green Bay from Lake Michigan. The northern two lie within the waters of the state of Michigan. The southern two, lying within Wisconsin waters, are at Porte des Morts (Death's Door) and Rock Island. Rock Island is a Wisconsin state park located close to the northeast end of Washington Island. The west, north, and east sides of Rock Island consist of steep limestone bluffs with deep water right up to the rocky beaches. Rock Island Passage, the widest and safest of the four, passes to the north of the island. The state boundary between Michigan and Wisconsin also passes through Rock Island Passage. Pottawatomie Light, located on the northwest corner of the island, marks the southern side of the passage. St. Martin Island Shoals lie to the north.

By the early 1830s, Rock Island Passage was the favored route of sailing vessels traveling between Green Bay and Lake Michigan. The first Pottawatomie Light was largely completed in 1836. Placed in service in 1837, it was the first lighthouse established in Wisconsin on Lake Michigan. It consisted of a conical, rubble-stone tower with a height of 30 feet from its base to the lantern room deck and a detached, one and one-half-story stone keeper's dwelling. Eleven Argand lamps and 14" reflectors provided the light source, reduced in number to eight by 1848 as a fuel saving measure. No photographs of this light are known to exist.

As an interesting aside, the first person chosen to serve as keeper at this remote outpost refused the assignment. The next keeper appointed was David E. Corbin, a War of 1812 veteran. As the story goes, in 1845 the District Inspector visited Corbin and found him to be very competent but lonely as his

Pottawatomie Light—circa 1885

Pottawatomie Light—just before placement of a replica lantern room atop the tower

only companions were a dog and a horse. The Inspector gave Corbin a three-week leave of absence, the longest he had been away from his post in eight years, on the condition that he return with a wife. Corbin failed in this mission and returned empty-handed. After 15 years of service, he died at age 57 while on duty in December 1852. He is buried in a small plot south of the present lighthouse.

Poor mortar led to structural failure of the first lighthouse, which was razed in 1858 before it could collapse. The rebuilt and surviving Pottawatomie Light of 1858 consists of a two-story keeper's dwelling constructed of locally quarried limestone with a large walkout basement. A short, square, wooden tower emerges from the northern roof peak to support a 1999 replica of the original nine-sided lantern room. Overall, the tower has a height of 41 feet. The original optic was a fourth order Fresnel lens. The structure's elevation atop a 120-foot bluff resulted in a light with a focal plane 159 feet above water level. The design of this lighthouse was repeated at several other locations on Lake Michigan. All within

a few years of each other, nearly identical structures were built in Wisconsin at Green Island, Pilot Island, and Port Washington; at Grand Traverse and South Manitou Island in Michigan; and at Michigan City, Indiana.

At one time, other structures at the site included a barn, chicken coop, smokehouse, privy, and an oil storage house. Life was never easy at a remote light station. Cisterns in the basement were used to collect rain water from the roof for drinking purposes. When it did not rain, water had to taken from the lake near the boat dock at the south end of the island and carried, as were other supplies, one and one-quarter miles uphill along a rough, narrow road back to the lighthouse. In 1880, a crew built a wooden staircase up the face of the cliff and a small platform for landing supplies. The keepers and their families, weather permitting, could then climb up 154 steps with water and supplies rather than carry them for over a mile. A well was not drilled until 1910. There is no electricity at the lighthouse to this day.

Pottawatomie Light was automated in 1946.

Around 1980, the badly deteriorated lantern room was removed from the tower and a modern plastic optic atop a metal pole was mounted on the lantern deck. The Fresnel lens was crated up and placed in the basement. Unfortunately, it was later stolen and its whereabouts remain unknown. Battery power gave way to solar panels in 1986. In July 1988, the light was moved to its current location atop a 41-foot skeletal steel tower erected just to the west of the lighthouse.

As part of a state park, the old lighthouse received basic but lifesaving maintenance over the years, at least enough to keep it structurally sound. The park is managed by the Wisconsin Department of Natural Resources (DNR). In 1994, a group called the Friends of Rock Island formed to aid the DNR in enhancing the natural beauty and historic significance of the park. Working under the aegis of the DNR, the Friends group has assumed a major role in the preservation and restoration of the lighthouse. Their first accomplishment was the construction and installation of the replica lantern room in June 1999. Together, it is hoped, they will find the means to completely restore and regularly reopen this historic landmark to visitors.

Friends of Rock Island State Park
126 Country Club Drive
Clintonville, WI 54929
Phone: 715-823-6873

Status: *Inactive. Open to public only sporadically. The lighthouse is open during the annual Door County Lighthouse Walk held in mid-May. Contact the Door County Maritime Museum at 920-743-5958 or the Door County Chamber of Commerce at 920-743-4456 for additional information.*

Access: *For most visitors, two ferries must be used: one from the mainland to Washington Island and another from Washington Island to Rock Island. There is no direct ferry service to Rock Island from the mainland. At the northern end of Hwy. 42 in Gills Rock, a passenger ferry provides service to Washington Island. At the end of Hwy. 42 two miles to the east in Northport, a car ferry also provides service to Washington Island. Both ferries dock at Detroit Harbor at the southern end of Washington Island. It is highly recommended that visitors take their cars over to Washington Island as it is a distance of over nine miles to the second ferry at Jackson Harbor, located at the northeast corner of the island. From Detroit Harbor, go north on County Road W, which is called Main Rd. Near the north end of the island, County Road W turns eastward to become Jackson Harbor Rd. Continue east on Jackson Harbor Rd., watching for the signs pointing to Jackson Harbor. **Karfi** is the name of the second ferry shuttling between Washington Island and Rock Island. Absolutely no vehicles, not even bicycles, may be taken onto Rock Island. The hike from the boat dock at the south end of Rock Island to the lighthouse is about 1.3 miles, most of it uphill. Pack a lunch and plenty to drink. There is no food concession service on the island.*

*By boat: With a small boat **only** in the calmest weather, a beach landing may be made at the base of the cliff below the lighthouse. Reaching the lighthouse is then simply a matter of climbing the wooden staircase.*

Weborg's Wharf at Gills Rock, Wisconsin

Chambers Island Light

Chambers Island Light

Located almost in the middle of Green Bay between the Michigan and Wisconsin shores, Chambers Island lies about 7 miles northwest of Fish Creek and 12 miles northeast of Menominee. Chambers Island Light was built on the northwest tip of the island to mark the main vessel track between the island and the western shore of Green Bay. Then, as now, the largest freighters bound to and from the port of Green Bay passed to the west of the island rather than risk the more hazardous passage known as the Strawberry Channel lying between the island and the mainland to the east.

Chambers Island Light consists of a one and one-half-story rectangular dwelling constructed of cream-colored brick with an at-tached octagonal brick tower at its northeast corner. The tower originally had an overall height of 43 feet and supported a fourth order Fresnel lens that produced a light with a focal plane 68 feet above water level. The light was first displayed on October 1, 1868. The lighthouse was deactivated in 1961 and an automated light established atop a 67-foot tall skeletal steel tower erected just to the south. A mod-

Chambers Island Light—circa 1914

ern, solar-powered, plastic optic remains in service atop the replacement tower, producing a light with a focal plane 97 feet above water level. The lantern room was subsequently removed from the old lighthouse and the lens was eventually donated to a folk museum named Pioneer Village in Minden, Nebraska.

The basic design of Chambers Island Light was repeated at several locations on the Great Lakes, especially on Lakes Michigan and Superior. All within a few years of each other, nearly identical structures, varied only by tower placement and shape, were built on Lake Michigan at Eagle Bluff, McGulpin Point, and White River.

In 1976, the old light station and 40 acres of surrounding property were transferred to the town of Gibraltar for use as a public park. The lighthouse is well maintained. During the peak summer season, caretakers are in residence and the tower and one ground floor office housing a small museum are open to the public.

Status: *Inactive. Seasonally open to public as a museum.*

Chambers Island Light

Commercial fishing boats at Naubinway, Michigan

Access: *Boat. During the annual Door County Lighthouse Walk held in mid-May, a limited number of visitors may arrange to take a day trip to the lighthouse via a small excursion boat named the* **Quo Vadis**, *which departs from the Fish Creek Dock. Advanced reservations are absolutely essential. Contact Door County Maritime Museum at 920-743-5958 or the Door County Chamber of Commerce at 920-743-4456 for additional information.*

Eagle Bluff Light

The Strawberry Islands are a group of four small islands on a shoal bank located about a mile off the Wisconsin shore. The islands parallel what is now the shoreline of Peninsula State Park for a distance of about three and one-half miles. The Strawberry Channel, leading between the island group and the mainland, is marked on the east near its northern entrance by Eagle Bluff Light. Instead of swinging west around Chambers Island to the main ship-

Eagle Bluff Light—circa 1918

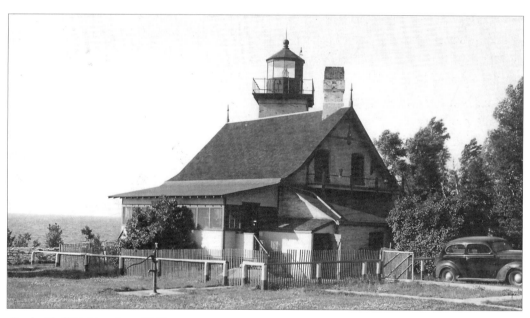

Eagle Bluff Light—circa 1940

ping route, ships traveling between the Port of Green Bay and points to the northeast often used the channel as an alternative, eastern route. The shallowest portion of Strawberry Channel is only 13 feet deep, so its commercial use declined rapidly as ships grew larger. Modern freighters would never consider using it.

Eagle Bluff Light was first exhibited on October 15, 1868. It consists of a one and one-half-story rect-

angular dwelling constructed of cream-colored brick with an attached square brick tower oriented diagonally at its northeast corner. The tower is 43 feet tall overall and supports a lantern room that originally housed a third and one-half order Fresnel lens. The structure's elevation on a 35-foot bluff resulted in a light with a focal plane 76 feet above water level. In 1918, the lens was downgraded to one of the fifth order, no doubt reflecting the diminished importance

Eagle Bluff Light

of the Strawberry Channel to shipping on Green Bay.

The basic design of Eagle Bluff Light was repeated at several locations on the Great Lakes, especially on Lakes Michigan and Superior. All within a few years of each other, nearly identical structures, varied only by tower placement and shape, were built on Lake Michigan at Chambers Island, McGulpin Point, and White River.

Eagle Bluff Light was automated with an acetylene gas lamp in 1926. Thereafter the site was leased to the State of Wisconsin as part of its park system, which eventually became the surrounding Peninsula State Park. After automation, the lighthouse remained vacant except for brief periods when it was rented out as a summer cottage and Boy Scout quarters. Years of neglect took their toll. In 1960, the newly formed Door County Historical Society adopted Eagle Bluff light as its main project. An extensive restoration was started in 1961 and the lighthouse was reopened as a museum in 1963. Many artifacts and original furnishings once used by the families at this lighthouse were donated or recov-

ered and placed on display. Guided tours are offered daily from 10 to 4:30, early June through mid-October. There is a small admission fee. A visit is highly recommended.

Status: *Active. Open to public as a museum.*

Access: *From Hwy. 42, the main entrance to Peninsula State Park is located in the town of Fish Creek. A daily or annual permit is required to enter. A map of the park is available at the office where the permits are sold. Going north on Shore Rd. inside the park, it is approximately four miles to the lighthouse parking area.*

Sherwood Point Light

Sherwood Point Light is located on the southwest side of the entrance to Sturgeon Bay. The lighthouse was built to mark the western approach to the recently completed Sturgeon Bay Ship Canal,

Sherwood Point Light—circa 1908

which resulted in a dramatic increase in shipping traffic through Sturgeon Bay. The light was first displayed on October 10, 1883. Constructed of red-brick, the structure consists of a one and one-half-story keeper's dwelling with an attached square tower that is painted white and has an overall height of 35 feet. This lighthouse is practically identical to Little Traverse Light (Harbor Point) established in 1894 at Harbor Springs, Michigan. The structure's elevation on a limestone bluff results in a light with a focal plane 61 feet above water level.

Sherwood Point Light was originally fitted with a fifth order Fresnel lens that displayed an alternating white and red flash characteristic. The clock-work mechanism that powered the red flash panels apparently was defective and subject to frequent breakdowns. In 1892, the entire lighting apparatus was replaced with the fourth order Fresnel lens that remains in place today. Still standing immediately in front of the lighthouse is a very rare example of a square, pyramidal, wooden fog signal building also built in 1892. It originally supported a fog bell suspended from a bracket on its western side that was automatically struck by machinery housed in the building. In later years, the fog bell was replaced by compressed air foghorns. Presently, the building is

Sherwood Point Light—circa 1912

empty as there is no fog signal at Sherwood Point.

When the Coast Guard automated Sherwood Point Light in August 1983, it was the last manned light station on Lake Michigan and the entire U.S. side of the Great Lakes. Point Betsie Light, automated earlier in 1983, was the last manned light station on the east side of the lake. Since then, the site has been well maintained as the lighthouse continues to be used as a summer vacation residence by Coast Guard personnel. As a private residence, neither the grounds nor the buildings are generally open to the public and visitors are discouraged. However, the grounds only may be toured during the annual Door County Lighthouse Walk held in mid-May. Contact the Door County Maritime Museum at 920-743-5958 or the Door County Chamber of Commerce at 920-743-4456 for additional information.

Sherwood Point Light

Status: *Active. Private residence not open to public.*

Access: *Given its seasonal use as a vacation property, the lighthouse generally is not occupied during the off-peak periods early and late in the year. At these times, discreet visitors are usually able to view the lighthouse from a distance from its access road. If the lighthouse appears to be occupied, however, **please respect the privacy of the residents**.*

Sherwood Point Light is located north of Potawatomi State Park and northwest of the city of Sturgeon Bay. From Hwy. 42/57 on the western edge of town, proceed north on County Road C. CR-C eventually makes a sharp bend to the west and continues west. Turn north onto County Road M and follow it almost to its end. Turn north again onto Sherwood Point Dr. for a short distance to the lighthouse gate. Sherwood Point Dr. is a short, narrow, gravel road that is poorly marked. Some hunting may be necessary to find it.

Green Bay Harbor

Green Bay Harbor is located at the mouth of the Fox River at the south end of Green Bay, about 40 miles southwest from Sturgeon Bay and 75 miles from Porte des Morts Passage. The harbor serves the Wisconsin cities of Green Bay and De Pere. Green Bay is one of the oldest historical points on Lake Michigan. French missionaries touched there as early as 1639 and the first permanent settlement was made in 1745. An American trading post was founded in 1815; in 1816, the Federal government erected Fort Howard. Green Bay has numerous docks and wharves on both sides of the Fox River. The harbor remains one of the most important on Lake Michigan and the Great Lakes. The major commodities handled include coal, limestone, wood pulp, cement, aggregates, and agricultural products.

The lower three miles of the Fox River running through the city of Green Bay is naturally deep and required little improvement. Additional dredging was necessary to deepen the river bed upstream to a turning basin at De Pere. Direct access to the mouth of the Fox River, however, was blocked by areas of shoal water and low-lying islands at the south end of the bay. The natural channel around these obstacles was convoluted and prone to shifting. A straighter channel to the mouth of the river was the goal of harbor improvements begun in 1867. The project was an evolutionary one, with many changes in direction, dimensions, and lighting made to the channel as the ships using it grew larger in size. The present dredged entrance channel leads generally southwest through the shallow water in the south end of Green Bay for about 11½ miles to the mouth of the Fox River. The channel's straight sections and turns are well marked by lighted ranges, lights, and lighted and unlighted buoys.

Old Long Tail Point Light

A series of three lighthouses in the vicinity of Long Tail Point has marked the approach to the harbor at Green Bay. Long Tail Point lies about three and one-half miles north of the Fox River mouth along the western shore of Green Bay. The point is a low ridge of sand and gravel, submerged in places, that extends southeast about three miles from the shoreline starting just south of the mouth of the Suamico River.

Old Long Tail Point Light was established in 1848 on the southeast end of the point. It consisted of a conical rubble-stone tower with a detached, single-story, stone keeper's dwelling. Topped by a bird cage style lantern room, the over-

Old Long Tail Point Light—circa 1910

Old Long Tail Point Light ruins

all height of the tower was about 85 feet. Argand lamps and 14" polished reflectors were the original light source, but the tower was later fitted with a Fresnel lens and a polygonal cast-iron lantern room. By 1859, water was lapping at the base of the tower and it was feared that erosion would soon undermine it. For that reason, the Lighthouse Board discontinued use of the tower in 1859, transferring the lens and lantern room to a new wooden lighthouse constructed on somewhat higher ground several

hundred feet away. The old tower soon fell into disrepair and by the 1870s it was considered an eyesore. A contractor assigned to demolish the tower, either lacking the proper tools or motivation, failed at the task. The hollow shell of the old stone tower remains standing today and the ruins are considered nostalgic. Followed by two later lighthouses, ironically it remains the only one to survive.

Status: *Inactive. In ruins.*

Access: *Boat. The shoreline is a very shallow marsh.*

Tail Point Light #2

The second and third lighthouses in the vicinity of Long Tail Point were referred to by the shorter name of Tail Point. Tail Point Lighthouse was established in 1859 on somewhat higher ground several hundred feet to the northwest of the old stone tower, from which it received its lens and lantern room. It consisted of a two-story, wood-framed dwelling with a square wooden light tower emerging from the roof peak. Old rear view photographs of the station show a boathouse almost next to the building and an access walkway consisting of wooden planks raised just above the surrounding marsh.

The design of this lighthouse was repeated with

minor variations at several locations around the lakes and especially on Lake Michigan. Within a couple of years, nearly identical structures were built at Cheboygan Point on Lake Huron and on Lake Michigan at Sheboygan, St. Joseph, and the Kalamazoo River (Saugatuck).

By 1899, it was felt a light closer to the dredged entrance channel would better serve shipping. On August 1, 1899, the light was transferred to a new Tail Point Light constructed offshore on a timber crib. Keepers who maintained the new light via boat continued to use the old lighthouse as their quarters. Once the crib light was automated in the early 1930s, the old lighthouse was no longer needed. It was later sold to a private individual with the stipulation that it be removed from the area, which had been designated a National Migratory Waterfowl Refuge. The new owner attempted to move it in winter over the ice. Unfortunately, the wheels of the trailer used broke through the ice up to its axles and became stuck. The lighthouse was dismantled then and there before it could break through the ice completely. Much of the salvaged timber was used to build a farm silo.

Tail Point Light #2—July 1913

National Archives

Tail Point Light #3

The third and final Tail Point Light was established on August 1, 1899. It was located offshore closer to the western edge of the dredged entrance channel. Resting on a concrete pier with a timber crib foundation, it consisted of a square, one and one-half-story wood-framed building with a hipped roof. All four sides of the hipped roof were pierced by a dormer window. The roof was surmounted by a round, cast-iron lantern room. The building contained emergency quarters should one of the keepers become stranded there during bad weather, but the keepers con-

Tail Point Light #3—September 1, 1914

tinued to live in the second lighthouse on the point. This Tail Point Light was automated in the early 1930s. Sitting vacant, it remained in service until it was washed off its pier during a severe storm in April 1973. Thereafter a modern pole light was mounted on the same foundation.

Grassy Island Range Lights

What remains of Grassy Island today lies on the east side of the entrance channel four miles northeast of the Fox River mouth. In its natural state, Grassy Island blocked a straight course approach to the Fox River. The low-lying island varied in size considerably depending on the water levels in the bay. One of the earliest parts of the project to improve access to the harbor at Green Bay included a segment of dredged channel 200 feet wide, 15 feet deep, and 2 miles long with a revetted cut across Grassy Island. By 1872, the channel created was finally deep enough to accept vessel traffic.

The surviving Grassy Island Range Lights were established in 1872 to guide vessels into the new channel. They remain two of the oldest wooden light structures on the Great Lakes. Both towers are fully enclosed, square, wooden, pyramidal structures, clad in cedar shingles

Grassy Island Rear Range Light and dwelling—circa 1909

and topped by octagonal lantern rooms. The range lights were located on the revetment on the east side of the channel along with a detached, two and one-half-story, wood-framed keeper's dwelling. The front range light has an overall height of about 25 feet and the rear range light is about 10 feet taller. The range had a generally north-south orientation with the taller rear range light lying to the south. Fixed white lights were originally displayed from both towers. They were changed to a flashing green color characteristic in 1934 so as to better comply with standards established for the lateral system of buoyage used on the Great Lakes.

The range lights remained in operation until 1966, when they were removed to make way for a project to deepen and widen the channel yet again. Fortunately, the towers avoided demolition and were acquired by the Green Bay

Grassy Island Range Lights-circa 1909

Grassy Island Range Lights—circa 1912

Grassy Island Range Lights at the Green Bay Yacht Club

Yacht Club located on the east side of the Fox River just inside its mouth. For over 30 years, the towers sat neglected in the club's parking lot. Finally the first steps were taken toward restoration of these historical structures. In 1999, the towers were moved to their present positions near the entrance to the club's marina basin. Situated as they are, they form a pseudo-range marking the basin entrance. At night, the Grassy Island Range Lights once again display fixed white lights now produced by modern halogen bulbs. As restoration proceeds, the old aluminum siding is coming off and rotten timbers are being replaced.

Status: *Inactive. Not open to public. Privately owned.*

Access: *From I-43 in Green Bay, take exit #187 (Webster Ave.). Turn east onto Webster and go a short distance to a four-way stop sign at N. Irwin Ave. Turn north (left) onto Irwin, which becomes Bay Beach Rd. Continue west on Bay Beach Rd. toward the Fox River. Near the end of the road on your left, watch for the public parking lot near the Coast Guard Station and the Green Bay Yacht Club next door.*

United States Coast Guard

Grassy Island Front Range Light—circa 1905

Grassy Island Front Range Light

Grassy Island Rear Range Light

Green Bay Harbor Entrance Light

The present light marking the approach to the harbor at Green Bay was established in 1935. It is located on the west side of the entrance channel 9.3 miles northeast of the mouth of the Fox River. The cylindrical steel light tower rests on a circular concrete crib foundation. The tower rises in two stages to support a circular lantern room housing a fourth order Fresnel lens with a focal plane 72 feet above water level. The tinted glass panes of the lantern room create the red characteristic of the light. The design of this lighthouse is identical to Peshtigo Reef Light a bit farther to the north. Originally a manned station, the lighthouse was fully automated in 1979.

*Green Bay Harbor Entrance Light—
circa 1940*

Status: *Active. Not open to public.*

Access: *Boat.*

Green Bay Harbor Entrance Light

Peshtigo Reef Light

Peshtigo Point is a low marshy point just east of the mouth of the Peshtigo River, about 40 miles north of Green Bay. Peshtigo Reef extends three miles southeast from the point with depths of water ranging from one to six feet. The reef presented a serious hazard to navigation as it lies just to the west of the main vessel course to Green Bay. The reef was marked seasonally by Lightship No. 77, the Peshtigo Reef Lightship, starting in April 1906.

The present Peshtigo Reef Light replaced the lightship in 1934. Built on the southeast edge of the reef, the cylindrical steel light tower rests on a circular concrete crib foundation. The tower rises in two stages to support a circular lantern room housing a modern plastic optic with a focal plane 72 feet above water level. A red horizontal band painted midway up the tower serves as a daymark. The design of this lighthouse is identical to Green Bay Harbor Entrance Light. Now fully automated, the light was originally operated remotely via radio signals from Sherwood Point Lighthouse, nine miles away in Door County, Wisconsin.

Status: *Active. Not open to public.*

Access: *Boat.*

Peshtigo Reef Light

*Another old laker lives on. Launched in 1914, the **William H. Donner** was converted to a crane ship in 1956 and last sailed in 1969. She now serves as a crane barge/dock at Marinette, Wisconsin, here shown unloading pig-iron from the Canadian vessel **Catherine Desgagnes**.*

Menominee North Pier Light

Menominee, Michigan and Marinette, Wisconsin lie on opposite sides of the Menominee River and are usually considered as one port. Menominee became known for exporting just one product—lumber. Private interests undertook initial harbor improvements; the Federal government did not become involved until 1891. As the turn of the century approached, Menominee began to decline as a port. It survived because of the establishment of a railroad car ferry link between it and harbors on the eastern shore of Lake Michigan. Today, the ferries are long gone and the principal commodities handled are coal, stone, sand, and salt.

Menominee North Pier Light is an octagonal cast-iron tower 25 feet tall dating from 1877. Duplicates of this style of tower also saw service in Cheboygan,

Menominee North Pier Light and fog signal building—circa 1909

Menominee North Pier Light

Michigan; Vermilion and Cleveland, Ohio; and Oswego, New York. In the 1890s, a fog signal building was erected to house the equipment for a steam-powered 10" whistle. The building was wood-framed and sheathed in cast-iron plates for durability. A raised catwalk connected both structures to shore. Over the years, a rear range light on a steel mast was added and deleted (*see photo on page 17*); the fog signal was eliminated; and in 1927 the light tower was placed in its current position on a square base of reinforced concrete. Originally fitted with a fourth order Fresnel lens, the modern plastic optic now in place has a focal plane 46 feet above water level. The light was automated in 1972. Like so many other sites on the west side of Lake Michigan, the catwalk has not survived into the present.

Marinette boasts a state-of-the-art ship building facility operated by Marinette Marine Corporation. The company is currently producing a series of new 175-foot Keeper-Class (coastal) tenders and 225-foot Juniper Class (seagoing) tenders for the U.S. Coast Guard. For a complete discussion of the company and the new ships, refer especially to Chapters 16 and 17 of the book by Frederick Stonehouse entitled ***Lighthouse Keepers and Coast Guard Cutters*** (Avery Color Studios).

Status: *Active. Not open to public.*

Access: *From US-41, turn east on 10th St. until you reach 1st St. Turn south (right) onto 1st St. and east (left) onto Harbor Dr. to its end and the parking area near the base of the pier.*

Green Island Light

Green Island Light is located within Green Bay, almost five miles southeast of the mouth of the Menominee River. Heavily wooded, the island is roughly 87 acres in size and about three-quarters of a mile long. Shoals extend up to a mile from the northwest and southeast ends of the island. The shoal to the southeast presented the greatest hazard to navigation as it was closest to the main route used by ships heading for the Port of Green Bay.

Green Island Lighthouse was established on October 1, 1863 on the southeast edge of the island. It consisted of a two-story dwelling constructed of cream-colored brick. A short, square, wooden tower painted white merged from the peak of the roof to support a lantern room that housed a fourth order Fresnel lens. With a tower height of 40 feet, the focal plane of the light produced was 55 feet above lake level. The design of this lighthouse was repeated at several locations on Lake Michigan. All within a few years of each other, nearly identical structures were built in Wisconsin at Port Washington, Pilot Island, and Rock Island;

Green Island Light—circa 1912

in Michigan at Grand Traverse and South Manitou Island; and at Michigan City, Indiana.

In March 1864, a violent explosion blew the whole lantern room from the top of the tower and destroyed the lens. The subsequent fire also did extensive damage to the interior. A temporary light structure was erected while repairs were underway, which were not completed until June 1865. Surprisingly, official records regarding this incident are decidedly vague. Sperm oil was the official fuel in use at the time of the explosion, although experiments with colza oil, derived from wild cabbage seeds, had been conducted. From 1864 to 1867 lard oil was phased in as the standard fuel, replacing both colza and sperm oils. Records only show that "...in 1864, a Lake Michigan lightkeeper on his own responsibility used a kerosene lamp in his light, but after several nights an explosion scattered oil

Green Island Light—September 12, 1914

all over the keeper and a second violent explosion blew the whole lantern from the tower and destroyed the lens." Kerosene did not become the officially stipulated fuel until the early 1880s. Although Green Island is not directly named as the place where this incident happened, and no mention of disciplinary action against the keeper there has ever

Green Island Lighthouse ruins surrounded by poison ivy

been found, the circumstantial evidence seems very strong.

Green Island Lighthouse was automated with an acetylene gas lamp in 1933. The Coast Guard moved the light to a skeletal steel tower erected nearby in 1956, which itself was rebuilt in 1992 and remains in service today. Old photographs reveal that most

of the old lighthouse was still standing as late as 1976. Sometime after 1976, a fire set by vandals caused the collapse of the tower into the dwelling. Time, fire, and vandals have since destroyed the lighthouse completely. Only a partial brick shell remains.

No discussion of Green Island Light would be complete without mentioning Keeper Frank Drew. Frank Drew was born in the lighthouse on March 11, 1864 while his father, Samuel Drew, was keeper there. After a successful career sailing on lake vessels, Frank entered the Lighthouse Service in 1899. In 1903 he returned to Green Island as the first assistant and was appointed head keeper on July 15, 1909. He

Green Island Lighthouse ruins

remained there until his retirement on April 1, 1929. In the twenty years he served as keeper, Frank Drew was credited with rescuing more than thirty people and rendering other assistance in several incidents around the island. One of the new 175-foot Keeper Class (coastal) tenders built by the Marinette Marine Corporation in nearby Marinette, Wisconsin was named in his honor. The USCGC Frank Drew (WLM 557) was launched on December 5, 1998. Officially delivered to the Coast Guard in July 1999, the vessel's home port is Portsmouth, Virginia.

*Launch of the **USCGC Frank Drew** on December 5, 1998*

Green Island today is deserted. The island is privately owned except for the small wedge of Federally controlled property where the modern light structure stands. The old light station site is covered with a thick blanket of jagged brush and poison ivy—a fact the author discovered the hard way. Be careful if you decide to explore.

Status: *Inactive. In ruins.*

Access: *Boat.*

Cedar River Light

Cedar River is a very small village at the mouth of the Cedar River about 30 miles north of Menominee. Cedar River Light was established in 1889 and discontinued in 1922. Also at the site stood a pair of range lights, little more than lights on poles, established in 1891. The main light was a square, wooden pyramidal structure about 40 feet tall with an open framework for its lower two-thirds and an

Cedar River Light—circa 1890

enclosed watch room just below the lantern deck. Cedar River was a logging port. The main light helped mariners find the port along the dark coast from out on the open waters of Green Bay. The range lights, which were much weaker, helped with the final approach. Note all of the logs in the foreground of the old photograph.

All of these lights are gone today. The two-story brick keeper's house remains as a private residence that is easily viewed from the adjacent street.

Access: *From State Route 35, turn toward the bay (east) onto the dirt road just south of the Cedar River. This road bends to the south (right) just before the old house. **Please respect the privacy of the owners**.*

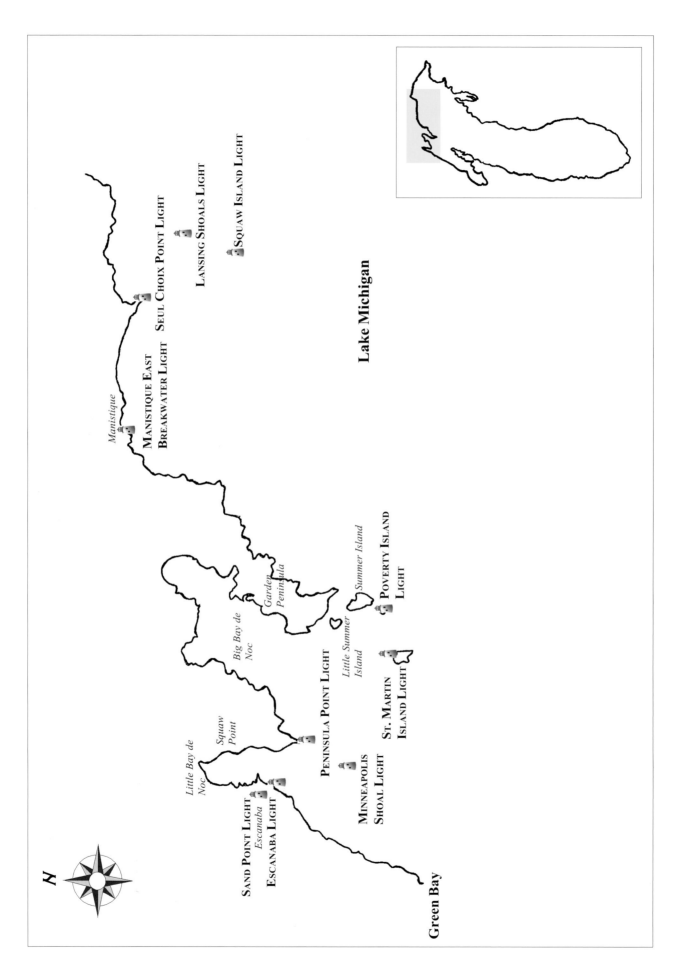

N

Lake Michigan

SQUAW ISLAND LIGHT

LANSING SHOALS LIGHT

SEUL CHOIX POINT LIGHT

MANISTIQUE EAST
BREAKWATER LIGHT

Manistique

*Garden
Peninsula*

*Big Bay de
Noc*

Summer Island

POVERTY ISLAND
LIGHT

*Little Summer
Island*

PENINSULA POINT LIGHT

ST. MARTIN
ISLAND LIGHT

*Squaw
Point*

*Little Bay de
Noc*

MINNEAPOLIS
SHOAL LIGHT

SAND POINT LIGHT
Escanaba
ESCANABA LIGHT

Green Bay

Escanaba Harbor

Escanaba Harbor lies on the west side of Little Bay de Noc at the northern end of Green Bay. Formed by an indentation in the shoreline, the harbor is protected on the south by a small peninsula that extends eastward and terminates at Sand Point. Escanaba was blessed with one of the finest and deepest natural harbors on the Great Lakes, a fact business interests set out to exploit as quickly as possible. Timber was still king in the early 1860s and the lumber barons moved in. There was, however, a more immediate need for iron ore. Industrialization was underway in the larger cities and civil war loomed on the horizon. The railroads had not yet reached as far north as Escanaba from points south, but a rail line was established between the harbor and iron ore mines to the north at Negaunee in Michigan's Upper Peninsula. Men poured into the area seeking work in the mines, in railroad construction, and in lumbering. Four enormous iron ore docks were built at the harbor just north of Sand Point. Escanaba soon became one of the major transshipment ports for iron ore on the Great Lakes. The city billed itself as the "iron port of the world." The largest bulk freighters on the lakes continue to visit this port.

Escanaba Harbor—circa 1906

Escanaba Harbor—circa 1928

Sand Point Light

A lighthouse was needed at Sand Point to mark the harbor entrance and warn of shoal water at the tip of the point. Construction began in 1867 and Sand Point Light was first lit on May 13, 1868. The design was a simple one that would be repeated often around the Great Lakes. The lighthouse consists of a one and one-half-story brick dwelling with an attached brick tower topped by a cast-iron lantern room. The origi-

Sand Point Light—circa 1906

nal optic was a fourth order Fresnel lens that displayed a fixed red light. One curious mistake, however, was made in its construction. The lighthouse was built backwards! Almost all lighthouses face the water and the hazard they were intended to mark. Sand Point Lighthouse faces the city.

Sand Point Lighthouse served mariners continuously until 1939, except for a seven-week period early in 1886 when it was out of service because of a fire of unknown origin that severely damaged the building. The fire also cost the life of Mary Terry, the first keeper at Sand Point and one of the first female lightkeepers on the Great Lakes. In 1939, the Coast Guard moved the light to a new crib structure offshore.

Sand Point Light—circa 1910

Escanaba Light

By 1938, the shape of Sand Point had been changed by dredging and filling, leaving the lighthouse some distance from the hazard it had been built to mark. Located several hundred yards offshore, a new crib light was built in 1938 near the northeast corner of the shallow area extending off the north side of the point. First lit in 1939, this light remains in operation today. Set on a round base, the square steel tower rises in two stages to support a modern plastic optic with a focal plane 45 feet above water level. The light was originally operated remotely from the former Coast Guard Station on shore a short distance away. It was fully automated in 1976.

Escanaba Light

Sand Point Lighthouse Museum

After the old lighthouse was discontinued it was converted into a residence for the Officer-in-Charge of the Aids to Navigation Station that had been established nearby. Over the years, so many alterations were made to the building that it no longer resembled a lighthouse. The lens and lantern room were removed and the tower was cut down. The roof was raised to accommodate a full second story with three bedrooms and a bath. Additional windows were cut through the brick walls and a main floor entryway was added. Adding insult to injury, sheet insulation and aluminum siding were applied over the entire exterior.

Sand Point Light as a residence—circa 1950

Late in 1985, the Coast Guard indicated that use of the building as a residence was to be discontinued and it might be razed. The Delta County Historical Society stepped in and negotiated a lease from the Coast Guard in 1986. After four years of research, fund-raising, and hard work, the lighthouse was restored to its original appearance. A replacement fourth order Fresnel lens was procured from Coast Guard storage and an extra cast-iron lantern room from Poverty Island was used to top off the tower. Interior spaces have been decorated as they would have appeared in the late 1880s. The lighthouse was reopened as a museum in 1990. Daily hours are from 9 to 5, June 1 through the end of August, and 1 to 4 p.m. through September. Also be sure to visit the Delta County Historical Museum next door.

Delta County Historical Society
P.O. Box 484
Escanaba, MI 49824-0484
Phone: 906-786-3428 or 906-786-3763

Status: *Inactive. Open to public as a museum.*

Access: *Sand Point Lighthouse is located in Ludington Park on the city's waterfront due east of the downtown area. Escanaba Light may be seen several hundred yards offshore from the park or viewed up-close from a boat. From the north on US-2/US-41 or from the south on M-35: At the junction of US-2/US-41 and M-35, turn east on Ludington Ave. and take it to its end in the park. The lighthouse will be obvious on the left just past the intersection with Lakeshore Dr.*

Restored Sand Point Lighthouse Museum

Squaw Point Light

Squaw Point lies opposite and just over one mile south of Gladstone, Michigan on the Little Bay de Noc arm of northern Green Bay. A small lighthouse was established there in 1897 to aid vessels making for the ports of Gladstone and Masonville.

Built of cream-colored brick, the

Squaw Point Light—circa 1913

lighthouse consisted of a one and one-half-story dwelling with an attached octagonal tower topped by an octagonal, black lantern room. A fifth order Fresnel lens was displayed with a red-sector to warn ships off the shallows adjacent to the point, which is

mostly sand. Mrs. Katherine "Kate" Marvin became the second keeper of the light in February 1898 upon the death of her husband, Lemeul. He had the post only a little over six months before he died.

Squaw Point Light was automated around 1918 with an acetylene gas lamp. The building was vacant when it burned in a forest fire on August 9, 1921. After the fire the brick walls and the tower were still standing. The remains of the house were demolished and the light re-established in the now free-standing tower. The tower remained active until sometime in 1963 when it too was razed. The U.S. Light List for 1964 shows the light transferred to a metal pole on the point. The pole light lasted until 1993 when it too was discontinued. Today Squaw Point is marked by an offshore buoy appropriately named Squaw Point

Squaw Point Light—circa 1913

Lighted Buoy #12. The site is passed by the road leading to Peninsula Point Light. Nothing remains of the light station and all of the property is privately owned.

For a lighthouse that stood for the better part of 67 years, old photographs are extremely scarce. The best three of six known to exist are displayed here.

Peninsula Point Light

Peninsula Point is the southern tip of the Stonington Peninsula, which separates Little Bay de Noc and Big Bay de Noc at the northern end of Green Bay. Shoals extend for several miles south from the point. Peninsula Point Lighthouse was established in 1865 to warn of these dangers and to provide guidance to the harbors of Gladstone, Escanaba, Fayette, and Nahma.

Like so many others, the building was constructed of cream-colored brick and consisted of a square, 40-foot tower with a one and one-half-story dwelling attached to its northern side. By 1868 the front wall of the dwelling was severely cracked, as was

Squaw Point Light—circa 1960

United States Coast Guard—9th District

the basement, causing a problem with water seepage. The summer of 1903 saw the completion of a major renovation. It included resurfacing the entire exterior of the light tower and dwelling with pressed brick, and the provision of upstairs dormers and windows to enhance the living space. The rebuild explains the radical change in appearance seen in the old photos. The upper portions of the house, including the dormers, were clad in cedar shakes. Note also that the windows on the south face of the tower were heightened and narrowed.

The lighthouse was automated in 1922 with an acetylene gas lamp. Captain James D. Armstrong had become the second keeper in Peninsula Point in 1889. In 1922 he transferred to Escanaba to become keeper of the Sand Point Light. He continued to be responsible for checking the acetylene light and tanks at Peninsula Point, which only needed attention a couple of times each month.

The light was discontinued in 1936, two

National Archives

Peninsula Point Light—August 1883

years after Minneapolis Shoal Light went into service. Ownership of the abandoned lighthouse transferred to the U.S. Forest Service in 1937. The agency continued to maintain the station and established public picnic grounds at the site. Unfortunately, the house portion burned in 1959. The Forest Service cleared the debris and re-

United States Coast Guard

Peninsula Point Light—August 29, 1914

paired the damage to the north side of the tower in 1962.

Today the tower and picnic grounds are part of the Hiawatha National Forest and remain under the stewardship of the Forest Service. The tower is open to visitors who may climb the cast-iron spiral staircase up to the lantern deck for a great view.

Status: *Inactive. Open to public.*

Access: *Take US-2 to County Road 513 (Stonington Exit). The junction is about 3 miles east of Rapid River. Turn south on CR-513, which later becomes Forest Road 2204, for 19 miles to the parking lot. The last mile of the road is not recommended for RVs or trailers over 16 feet long or 8 feet high. A parking area for RVs is available at the beginning of the narrow, winding final mile of road.*

Peninsula Point Light

Minneapolis Shoal Light

Minneapolis Shoal takes its name from the freight steamer *Minneapolis*, one of a fleet of lake boats owned and operated by the Minneapolis, St. Paul and Buffalo Steamship Company, a subsidiary of the Soo Line Railroad. The *Minneapolis*, heavily laden with grain en route from Gladstone to Buffalo, New York, ran aground on this shoal during a heavy September storm in the late 1890s. After the wreck, a lighted bell buoy was placed to mark the shoal.

There was no shortage of hazards to navigation in this area. Minneapolis Shoal lies about 14 miles southeast of Escanaba and 6.25 miles south of Peninsula Point. Shoals extend for several miles in a southerly direction from the point, right in the path of ships headed for Escanaba. Early in its history. Escanaba became, and continues to be, a major transshipment port for iron ore and processed taconite pellets. To warn of these dangers, a lighthouse was established at Peninsula Point in 1865 and Eleven Foot Shoal, 2.25 miles south of the point, was first marked by a lightship in October 1893. As ships grew larger, navigators sought safer water farther south of the point.

Minneapolis Shoal Light was established in 1934. It rests on a timber crib foundation capped by a con-

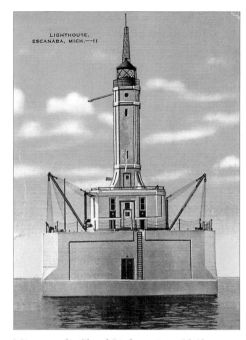

Minneapolis Shoal Light—circa 1942

crete pier 64 feet square. The entire structure is steel-framed and encased in steel plates. The base of the light tower measures 30 feet square and tapers upward to support a cylindrical lantern room. The original optic was a fourth order Fresnel lens, since replaced with a modern plastic optic. The focal plane of the light produced is 82 feet above water level. The station is equipped with a fog horn signal.

Interior spaces were divided into living quarters, storage areas, and machinery spaces. Two main diesel generators and one backup provided power to the station. The lighthouse was usually staffed by a five-man crew that worked four weeks on and two off. The day was divided into four-hour duty watches with eight hours off in between. For better or worse, crew members took turns cooking. The station was resupplied every two weeks during the shipping season when personnel were exchanged. Minneapolis Shoal Light was fully automated in 1979.

Minneapolis Shoal Light has an identical twin at Grays Reef Light on the eastern side of the lake near the Straits of Mackinac. These towers are considered Art Deco in style, reflecting the design preferences of the mid-1930s. Two years after Minneapolis Shoal Light became operational, Peninsula Point Light was discontinued.

Status: *Active. Not open to public.*

Access: *Boat.*

Minneapolis Shoal Light

St. Martin Island Light

Green Bay is separated from Lake Michigan by two mainland peninsulas. Garden Peninsula, the northern one, is 20 miles long, and Door Peninsula, to the south, is about 70 miles long. The entrance to Green Bay between the two peninsulas is about 28 miles wide, but the waterway is so choked with islands and shoals that the passage between them has acquired the deserved reputation of being dangerous. This is no place for a mariner to make a mistake.

There are four main passages through this gauntlet. The southern two lie within the waters of Wisconsin. The northern two, lying within Michigan waters, are at Poverty Island and St. Martin Island. St. Martin Island is a wooded and hilly island located about 4.5 miles north-northeast of Rock Island, Wisconsin. The St. Martin Island Passage passes to the north of the island. St. Martin Island Light was established in 1905 on the northeast point of the island and was built to mark the western end of the passage.

The light tower on St. Martin Island is the only example of a pure exoskeleton tower on the Great Lakes. The hexagonal tower consists of bolted cast-iron panels supported by six exterior channel posts that have latticed buttresses at their bases for added stability. The entire structure rests on a concrete foundation and has an overall height of 75 feet.

United States Coast Guard

St. Martin Island Light—circa 1930

St. Martin Island Light

The hexagonal design gives way to a cylindrical watch room near the top of the tower. The black, cast-iron lantern room presently houses a modern, plastic optic having a focal plane 84 feet above water level. The original fourth order Fresnel lens from this tower is on display at the Point Iroquois Lighthouse Museum located near Brimley, Michigan on Whitefish Bay, Lake Superior.

St. Martin Island Light Station was formally conveyed to the State of Michigan on April 29, 1999. The Station also includes a large, two and one-half-story, cream-colored brick keeper's duplex, a fog signal building, and an oil storage house. All of these buildings are suffering severely from neglect. Perhaps the most unique structure to survive intact at the site is the long tramway that was used to move supplies from the boat dock up the gentle slope to the main buildings. Tramways as complete as this one are very rare on the Great Lakes. One of the old tram cars remains in place, chained to the rails.

Status: *Active. Not open to public.*

Access: *Boat. The remains of the concrete boat dock are crumbling and in bad shape.*

St. Martin Island Light

Surviving tram car on St. Martin Island

Poverty Island Light

There are four main passages through the gauntlet of islands and shoals that separate Green Bay from Lake Michigan. The southern two lie within the waters of Wisconsin. The northern two, lying within Michigan waters, are at St. Martin Island and Poverty Island. Poverty Island Passage is the northernmost of the four and passes to the south of Poverty Island. Poverty Island Light was established in 1875 on the southern edge of the island to mark the passage, which was heavily used by ships bound for the ore docks at Escanaba.

Poverty Island Light consists of a conical, red-brick tower with an overall height of 70 feet. An enclosed passageway connects the tower to a one and one-half-story red-brick keeper's dwelling. Both structures are painted white. The original optic was a fourth order Fresnel lens that produced a light with a focal plane 80 feet above water level. The design of this lighthouse was repeated at three other locations on the Great Lakes. Within a few years of each other, nearly identical structures were built at St. Helena Island in northern Lake Michigan and on Lake Huron at Sturgeon Point and Tawas Point. A fog signal was added as well as a newer dwelling for the assistant keeper.

Around 1950, the Coast Guard removed the Fresnel lens and lantern room from the tower, replacing them with a modern aeronautical style beacon. The lighthouse was automated in 1957 and the station vacated. With no one in residence at this remote location, the buildings soon deteriorated from exposure to the elements, lack of maintenance, and severe damage by vandals. From 1976 to 1982 the light was displayed from a skeletal steel tower erected nearby. A light mounted on a metal pole was transferred back to the top of the old brick tower in 1982. The reason for this action remains unknown. The lighthouse was darkened for good in 1995. A spare lantern room from Poverty Island was used in the restoration of Sand Point Lighthouse in Escanaba.

The scene that presents itself at the old light station today is one of the most pitiful on the Great Lakes. The rocky site is badly overgrown. The decapitated lighthouse is in an advanced state of decay. Paint is peeling, bricks are spalling,

Poverty Island Light—July 1913

United States Coast Guard

Poverty Island—circa 1955

United States Coast Guard

Poverty Island Light

and the interior is a shambles. A quiltwork of plywood patches placed by concerned private individuals covers some of the many holes in the roof. Water leakage will soon compromise the structural integrity of the lighthouse. The assistant keeper's dwelling next door, dating from the early 1930s, has already collapsed in on itself. The dock, boathouse, and fog signal building are all gone. The only other structure remaining at the site, a cylindrical cast-iron oil storage house, is severely corroded.

The rocky shoreline at the base of the light station is a beauty. Unfortunately, those rocks limit access to the site in all but the calmest weather. Could this lighthouse be saved? Yes, with immediate intervention. Is that likely to happen? No.

Status: *Inactive. Nearly in ruins.*

Access: *Boat. No dock.*

Poverty Island Light

Manistique East Breakwater Light

Manistique lies at the mouth of the Manistique River about 80 miles west of St. Ignace and 66 miles east of Escanaba on the north shore of Lake Michigan. Lumbering, and later fishing, were the principal industries. For many years, the town was the western terminus of a railroad car ferry service linking it to Northport, Michigan and several other ports on the eastern shore of Lake Michigan.

The Lighthouse Board recommended a light here as early as 1892 since there were no lights along this shore between Seul Choix Point and Poverty Island. Construction of improved cribbing did not commence until late in 1915 and the light finally went into service early in 1917. The tower is a square, steel, pyramidal structure with an overall height of 45 feet. The tower's position on an elevated concrete base places the focal plane of the light 50 feet above water level. The tower was originally equipped with a fourth order Fresnel lens. The light was automated in 1969.

Manistique remains an inviting resort and retirement community. The city has done a very nice job of making its beach and breakwater accessible via a long wooden boardwalk.

Status: *Active. Not open to public.*

Access: *From US-2, turn south into Lakeview Park, which borders the highway on the south. Lakeview Park is east of the river.*

Manistique East Breakwater Light

Access to the opposite (west) breakwater is available if you are willing to hunt a bit. Turn south west of the river onto the road leading to the waste-water treatment plant. On the right side of the road follow one of the footpaths that lead through the woods down to the beach. The west breakwater is connected to the shore.

Lansing Shoals Light

Lansing Shoals is an extensive area of boulders in northern Lake Michigan about 5 miles north of Squaw Island, 17 miles south of Seul Choix Point, and 40 miles west of the Straits of Mackinac. Some of the water is as shallow as 10 to 12 feet over the shoal—not what one would expect so far out in the lake. Lansing Shoals Light marks an important turning point for ships traveling westward across the north end of the lake bound for ports on Green Bay or ports farther south along the west shore of the lake.

The shoal was first marked by a gas buoy. In July 1900, Lightship No. 55 from Simmons Reef was replaced by a gas buoy and reassigned to Lansing Shoals. The Lighthouse Board recommended a permanent crib light as early as 1908, but the current structure was not built until 1928.

Lansing Shoals Light rests on a timber crib foundation capped by a concrete pier 74 feet square. It consists of a one-story building 32 feet square with a 30-foot high square tower that tapers slightly. The entire structure is steel-framed and encased in steel plates. The original optic was a third order Fresnel lens that produced a light 69 feet above water level.

At most offshore lights of this type the crew quarters were up in the tower area above machinery spaces. Here, just the opposite was the case. Crew quarters and support facilities were located in the crib below the deck. Portholes along the sides of the concrete crib, now blocked off, were for light and could be opened for ventilation. Machinery spaces and work areas were above in the tower and the main structure on deck. The station boat was also kept in the first deck level, hoisted up by a crane and wheeled in through large doors.

Lansing Shoals Light was automated in 1976 and the Fresnel lens removed in 1985, replaced by a modern plastic optic. The lens is on display at the Michigan Historical Museum in Lansing, Michigan.

Status: *Active. Not open to public.*

Access: *Boat.*

Lansing Shoals Light—circa 1955

United States Coast Guard—9th District

Lansing Shoals Light

Squaw Island Light

Squaw Island Light

Squaw Island is the northwesternmost island in the Beaver Island archipelago. Shoals extend all around the small island, but the longest reaches northeasterly two miles from the north end where an abandoned lighthouse awaits salvation. Undoubtedly, the remoteness of this location has helped save the light from vandals.

Squaw Island Light was established in 1892 and consists of a finely detailed red-brick two-story house with an attached octagonal tower. Gracefully arched windows and a covered porch enhance the appearance of the front elevation. Inside, most of the hardwood trim and waist-high wainscoting remain intact. Once in the front door, a spacious two-story foyer leads to a staircase and a railed landing on the second floor. Probably the most unusual feature for government housing: a detached balcony emerges into the upper foyer from a second floor bedroom. It curves to meet a double dormer window for a view of the meadow

Squaw Island Light—circa 1920

outside. Even in its deteriorated state, Squaw Island Light is one of the most unique and beautiful on the Great Lakes.

The light station was discontinued in 1928. Chunks of coal used to fuel the boilers of the steam whistle still litter the floor of the fog signal building. The wood-framed assistant keeper's house remains intact with a chapel still attached to the back, an addition the keepers constructed for religious services.

Certainly vacant, but not a ruin, Squaw Island Light might best be described as having been "stabilized." The island and lighthouse are privately owned by an individual with little interest in historical preservation. Using their own time and money, concerned citizens have stepped in to make critical repairs and maintain the site. From time to time the owner has contributed some money. The house was reroofed in 1998. The building is sealed and fogged with insecticide periodically to prevent termite infestation. Every little bit helps.

Status: *Inactive. Privately owned.*

Access: *Boat. A beach landing is necessary as there is no dock. The water close to shore is shallow and very rocky.*

Squaw Island Light

Seul Choix Point Light

Seul Choix (pronounced: sis-shwa) Point is located on the north shore of Lake Michigan about 25 miles east of Manistique and 60 miles west of St. Ignace. French fur traders called voyageurs found a small bay in the lee of the point to be the only good refuge from storms along the north shore. In reference to this fact, they named the place Seul Choix, which means "only choice." Commercial fishing and logging were important business activities around the point itself, but left unmarked, it remained a hazard to passing vessel traffic. An increasing number of ships were using the north shore route between the Straits of Mackinac and the iron ore docks at Escanaba. For about 100 miles of this route, from St. Helena Island at the western entry to the Straits to Poverty Island off the tip of the Garden Peninsula, there was not a single lighthouse.

The first appropriation for a lighthouse and fog signal at Seul Choix Point was made in 1886. The dollar amount requested proved to be insufficient. Additional funds were approved but work progressed slowly due to a number of delays. The light was placed in service in 1892 but structural problems with the first tower built necessitated its complete demolition. The present tower was finally completed in September 1895.

Seul Choix Point Light consists of a handsome, two and one-half-story red-brick dwelling connected by an enclosed passageway to a tall, conical brick tower. In its original plan, the dwelling held quarters for the families of the keeper and his first assistant. The lighthouse was altered in 1925 when a one-story addition with a hipped roof was placed on the west side of the building to house a

second assistant. Before this addition, the second assistant and his family lived in the station's converted stable. The most unusual architectural features of the dwelling are the gable ends of the roof above the second story windows. Note that they are "bowed" outward and dressed underneath with ornamental brackets. The bowed clapboards give the appearance of a wooden, clinker-built ship's hull. The dwelling is a unique structure whose design was not repeated elsewhere. Another unique feature, for those interested in the paranormal, is the lighthouse's deserved reputation for being one of the most haunted on the Great Lakes.

The light tower, painted white, rises to an overall height of just under 80 feet. The ten-sided cast-iron lantern room originally housed a third order Fresnel lens with a focal plane 80 feet above water level. The tower at Seul Choix is very similar in design to several others constructed on the Great Lakes.

Other structures at the light station included a steam fog signal and boiler house, boathouse, oil house, privy, two docks, and a tramway to transport supplies from the boats up the gentle slope to the station. Seul Choix Point Lighthouse was automated in 1972. At that time, the Fresnel lens was replaced

Seul Choix Point Light—circa 1915

Seul Choix Point Light

by the more modern aeronautical-style beacon that remains in place today. The last Coast Guard personnel left the station in 1973. Thereafter, the buildings and grounds began to deteriorate from neglect.

In June 1977, the Coast Guard allowed the Michigan Department of Natural Resources to purchase the property. The lighthouse grounds were then leased to Mueller Township for use as a park. In 1988, the Gulliver Historical Society obtained a lease on the lighthouse with the goal of restoring this landmark and reopening it as a museum. The restoration effort, led by Marilyn Fischer, President of the Gulliver Historical Society, is largely complete today and the work has been done beautifully. Both the house and the tower are open for viewing. Also, the fog signal building has been converted into a small maritime museum. The lighthouse is open to the public from mid-June to mid-October. Guides are on duty, seven days a week, from noon to 4 p.m. A visit is highly recommended.

Seul Choix Point Lighthouse Park & Museums
Gulliver Historical Society
RR 1, Box 79
Gulliver, MI 49840
Phone: 906-283-3169

Status: *Active. Open to public as a museum.*

Access: *From US-2, turn southeast on County Road 432 at the blinking light in Gulliver (about eleven miles east of Manistique) and go about four miles to County Road 431. Turn south (right) on CR-431, which is a gravel road, for close to five miles following the signs to the lighthouse.*

Mystery Lighthouse #1

When is a lighthouse not really a lighthouse? When it is part of a water intake crib. Chicago, for example, has four very large and several smaller water intake cribs stretched out along its lakefront. Almost all of these cribs are marked by lights of some type maintained as private aids to navigation for the benefit of pleasure craft. Some authors include these structures in lighthouse lists, but I do not because water intake cribs were not built to serve as aids to navigation.

The picture shown, dating from around 1900, sup-posedly shows one of Chicago's water intake cribs. It is hard to tell whether this is really a photograph, an artist's conceptual drawing, or a combination of the two. Nowhere in my research have I come upon a reference to such an elaborate masonry light tower on a water intake crib. The picture was given to me in return for a favor by a nautical antiques dealer in Massachusetts. It had him stumped, and I don't know what to make of it either. The original source of the picture remains unknown.

Stone
THE LAKE CRIB.
309
W. Jackson St.,
CHICAGO.

Mystery Lighthouse #1—circa 1900

Mystery Lighthouse #2

Mystery Lighthouse #2—1893

The picture shown is a scene from the Columbian Exposition (World's Fair) of 1893 held in Chicago. The actual location is Jackson Park Harbor, a basin for small craft located about seven miles south of the mouth of the Chicago River. The view is from the west looking east with Lake Michigan in the background. The building in the foreground with the long boat ramp is the Jackson Park Life Saving Station, which became operational on July 1, 1892. The station was open to the public for display during the Exposition and a number of visitors are visible milling about in the photograph. This old Life Saving Station remains intact and thousands of motorists zip past it daily on Lakeshore Boulevard. Few of those motorists probably realize what the building once was. The larger, square display pavilion in the photograph next to the station no longer exists.

Immediately behind the Life Saving Station stands a tall, skeletal, cast-iron light tower erected for display as part of the exhibit sponsored by the U.S. Lighthouse Service. Close examination of the photograph reveals no lens in the lantern room, so this lighthouse definitely was not functional. At the close of the Exposition, the tower was dismantled but no records have been found to indicate whether it was moved somewhere else, placed in storage, or cannibalized for spare parts. Therein lies the mystery. The Lighthouse Service erected several nearly identical towers around the country in sandy coastal areas where they could be taken down and moved if threatened by erosion. Anclote Key Light near Tarpon Springs, Florida is a prime example, but it was established in 1887. A more likely suspect, based on its establishment date of 1895, is the Crooked River (Carrabelle) Light, also in Florida. However, no direct link between this light tower, or any other, and the one displayed in Chicago has been found.

A couple of sources claim that the dismantled mystery light tower was transported to Rawley Point in Wisconsin and re-erected there, but this scenario is definitely not the case. Rawley Point Light is a rebuild of the old Chicago Light dating from 1859, and like that light, it has eight supporting legs arranged in an octagonal pattern. The mystery light tower, identical to the above mentioned lights in Florida, has eight supporting legs arranged in a square pattern.

Glossary

Automate: to convert from manual to automatic operation.

Beacon: a lighted or unlighted fixed aid to navigation attached directly to the earth's surface. Lighthouses and day beacons both constitute beacons.

Boathouse: building or shed, usually built partly over water, for sheltering a boat or boats and related equipment.

Breakwater: an offshore structure used to protect a harbor or beach from the force of waves.

Buoy: a floating object of defined shape and color that is anchored at a given position and serves as an aid to navigation.

Catwalk: an elevated narrow walkway usually constructed of metal and/or wood on a pier or breakwater to allow safer access to a light during inclement weather.

Characteristic: the audible, visual, or electronic signal displayed by an aid to navigation to assist in its identification. Characteristic refers to lights, sound signals, RACONS, radiobeacons, and day beacons (NOTE: the U.S. Light List for the Great Lakes defines thirteen distinct light characteristics alone. In the text, there is deliberately no mention of light characteristics at most locations as they were frequently changed over time).

Crib: a structure of reinforced timbers placed offshore, filled with stones and capped with concrete or other masonry work to form a foundation of a lighthouse, pier, or breakwater.

"D9" Tower: minor lighted aid to navigation consisting of a cylindrical tower constructed of steel and concrete. The design originated within the Ninth Coast Guard District (i.e., District Nine, or D9) that encompasses the Great Lakes. Usually around 30 feet tall, these replacement towers are highly functional and require little maintenance. Unfortunately, they are not much to look at.

Day Beacon: an unlighted fixed structure that is equipped with a dayboard for daytime identification.

Dayboard: the daytime identifier of an aid to navigation presenting one of several standard shapes and color patterns.

Daymark: the daytime appearance of an aid to navigation consisting of its unique color, shape, architectural style, or dayboard in use.

Depot: a place for storage and repair of lighthouse supplies, lenses, and fuels that were then distributed to individual light stations.

Diaphone: a fog signal using compressed air to produce two sequential tones with the second tone of lower pitch.

Establish: to place an authorized aid to navigation in operation for the first time (NOTE: the date a light was established is the same as the date it was first exhibited, displayed, or lit).

Focal Plane: the vertical distance from the focal point of the lens to the water surface (NOTE: the focal plane is an indication of the light's elevation above the water, which affects its nominal range (SEE BELOW). The focal plane changes as water levels rise and fall).

Fog Signal: a device that transmits sound, intended to provide information to mariners during periods of restricted visibility and foul weather.

Fresnel Lens: a lens developed by Augustin Fresnel using a series of glass prisms that greatly concentrated the light beam and made it visible for many miles.

Fuel or illuminant: a substance burned to produce light: whale oil, fish oil, colza, lard, kerosene, acetylene and others were all used at one time.

Gallery: outdoor railed walkway encircling the watch room.

Geographic Range: the greatest distance the curvature of the earth permits an object of given height to be seen from a particular height of eye without regard to luminous intensity or visibility conditions.

Global Positioning System (GPS): a satellite-based radio navigation system providing continuous worldwide coverage operated by the Department of Defense for military applications. It provides navigation, position, and timing information to air, marine, and land users. Differential GPS (DGPS) is an augmentation to the GPS signal made by the U.S. Coast Guard for the benefit of civilian maritime users. DGPS provides mariners with absolute position accuracy of 1-5 meters in all weather conditions.

Harbor of Refuge: a portion of a body of water along the shore deep enough for anchoring a ship, and so situated with respect to coastal features, whether natural or artificial (i.e., piers and breakwaters), as to provide protection from wind, waves, and currents, especially during severe storms.

Illuminant: see **Fuel** above.

Lantern Deck: the railed, outdoor walkway encircling the lantern room, used to stand on while maintaining the windows.

Lantern Room: a room at the top of a lighthouse, usually surrounded in whole or in part by glass, where the lighting apparatus (lantern and lens) are housed.

Lateral System: a system of aids to navigation in which characteristics of buoys and beacons indicate the sides of the channel or route relative to a conventional direction of buoyage (usually upstream). Virtually all U.S. lateral marks follow the traditional 3R rule of Red, Right, Returning from seaward and proceeding toward the head of navigation (NOTE: on the Great Lakes, the conventional direction of buoyage is generally considered westerly and northerly, except on Lake Michigan, where southerly movement is considered as returning from the sea).

Lens: a transparent material like glass or plastic formed to focus rays of light.

Light: the signal emitted by a lighted aid to navigation; the illuminating apparatus used to emit the light signal; a lighted aid to navigation on a fixed structure.

Lighthouse: a lighted beacon of major importance with an attached or detached dwelling for a resident keeper.

Light List: a publication of the U.S. Government containing a list of aids to navigation, their location and identifying marks, in a specific geographic region.

Lightship or Light Vessel (LV): a ship equipped with a tall mast that serves as a light tower, anchored in an area where building a lighthouse was technically difficult or too expensive.

Light Station: a group of structures in close proximity to a lighthouse built to support its function and the efficiency of a resident keeper. Such structures often included: fog signal building, barn, dock, oil house, privy, kitchen, workshop, boathouse, stable or garage.

LORAN: an acronym for **LO**ng **RA**nge **N**avigation, which is an electronic aid to navigation consisting of shore-based radio transmitters. The LORAN system enables users equipped with a LORAN receiver to determine their position quickly and accurately 24 hours a day in practically any weather (NOTE: LORAN has been made redundant by DGPS and will gradually be phased out of service).

Luminous Range: the greatest distance a light can be expected to be seen given its nominal range and the prevailing meteorological visibility.

Mark: any visual aid to navigation.

Nominal Range: the maximum distance a light can be seen in clear weather (assuming a meteorological visibility of 10 nautical miles). The Light List specifies this range for all lighted aids to navigation except range lights, directional lights, and private aids to navigation NOTE: in general, the nominal range of lighthouses on the Great Lakes varies from 12 to 18 miles, but the largest lights can be seen at even greater distances given the best atmospheric conditions. Variables affecting the distance at which a light may be first seen include: candlepower or intensity of the light source itself; height of the light; height of the observer's eye; cleanliness of the lens and lantern room glass; and the transmissivity of the air. Transmissivity is a measure of the normal quality of the air in a particular location during clear periods without rain, fog, smoke, or snow. Areas of Lake Superior away from cities have a very high percentage of transmissivity. Areas that are perfectly clear are assigned a factor of 1. Areas near the industrial southern end of Lake Michigan have a low percentage of transmissivity.

Oil House: a reinforced brick or cast-iron building used to store large quantities of flammable fuel away from the light tower and dwelling.

Order: the classification by size and strength of Fresnel lenses using a seven step ranking of, from largest to smallest: 1, 2, 3, 3½, 4, 5, 6.

Pier: a structure built to extend from land out into or over water, used as a landing place for ships and/or to protect a harbor entrance.

Pierhead: the end of a pier farthest from the shore.

Privy: outhouse (NOTE: in recent years, a popular place for archeological digs).

Racon: a radar beacon that produces a coded response on a viewer's radar screen when triggered by a radar signal.

Radar: an acronym for **RA**dio **D**etection **A**nd **R**anging, an electronic system designed to transmit radio signals and receive reflected images of those signals from a "target" in order to determine the bearing and distance to the "target".

Radiobeacon: an electronic apparatus that transmits a coded radio signal for use in providing a mariner a line of position (NOTE: radiobeacons first appeared in the 1920s and have been rendered obsolete by newer electronic aids to navigation. All the radiobeacons on the Great Lakes have been discontinued).

Range: a line of reference used in navigation formed by the extension of a line connecting two charted points.

Range Lights: two lights aligned to form a range that often, but not necessarily, indicates a channel centerline. The front range light is lower and nearer to the mariner. The rear light is higher and farther from the mariner. Being "on the range" means having the rear light appear directly over the front light. With the lights so aligned, a mariner knows he is in the middle of a channel or properly positioned to enter a harbor (NOTE: at many Great Lakes ports, the range lights were located along one of the entrance piers or breakwaters. This required the mariner to "leave" the range at some point and maneuver into the channel to avoid collision with the pier).

Reflector: a bowl-shaped surface mirrored or coated with polished silver placed behind a light source to reflect and concentrate its rays in one direction.

Sector: the arc over which a light is visible, described in degrees True, as observed from seaward toward the light. May be used to define the distinctive color difference of two adjoining sectors, or an obscured sector (NOTE: in general, red sectors are used to mark shoals or warn the mariner of other obstructions to navigation or of nearby land. Such lights produce approximate bearing information, since observers may note the change of color as they cross the boundary between sectors).

Service Room: a room usually near the top of a light tower containing enough supplies for the day's use; may also be used as a workshop for emergency repairs.

Skeleton Tower: a tower, usually of steel, constructed of heavy corner members and various horizontal and diagonal bracing members.

Ventilator Ball: a small metal sphere containing vent holes mounted on the top of a lantern room to draw off fumes from the burning fuel.

Watch Room: a room at the top of a light tower immediately below the lantern room from which to monitor the operation of the lighting apparatus (lantern and lens) and the weather.

Bibliography

Books

Bukowski, Douglas. *Navy Pier, A Chicago Landmark*. Chicago, IL: Metropolitan Pier and Exposition Authority, 1996.

Clifford, Mary Louise and J. Candace. *Women Who Kept the Lights, An Illustrated History of Female Lighthouse Keepers*. Williamsburg, VA: Cypress Communications, 1993.

Elliot, James L. *Red Stacks Over the Horizon—The Story of the Goodrich Steamboat Line*. Ellison Bay, WI: Wm. Caxton Ltd, 1967.

Frederickson, Arthur C. and Lucy F. *Frederickson's History of the Ann Arbor Auto and Train Ferries*. Frankfort, MI: Gulls Nest Publishing, 1994.

Great Lakes Lighthouse Keepers Association. *Instructions to Light-Keepers*. Allen Park, MI: GLLKA, 1989.

Great Lakes Lighthouse Keepers Association. *Maritime Heritage Educational Resource Guide. Third Edition, Revised*. Dearborn, MI: GLLKA, 1998.

Hatcher, H. and Walter, E. *A Pictorial History of the Great Lakes*. New York, NY: American Legacy Press, 1963.

Hirthe, Walter M. and Mary K. *Schooner Days in Door County*. Minneapolis, MN: Voyageur Press, 1986.

Holland, Francis Ross, Jr. *America's Lighthouses: An Illustrated History*. New York, NY: Dover Publications, 1988.

Hyde, Charles K. *The Northern Lights, Lighthouses of the Upper Great Lakes*. Lansing, MI: Two Peninsula Press, 1986.

Larson, John W. *History of Great Lakes Navigation,* U.S. Army Corps of Engineers Institute for Water Resources, National Waterways Study. Washington, D.C.: U.S. Government Printing Office, 1983.

Law, W.H. *Deeds of Valor by Heroes and Heroines of the Great Water World*. 1911.

Ludington Daily News. *Ludington's Carferries, The Rise, Decline, and Rebirth of a Great Lakes Fleet*. Ludington, MI: Ludington Daily News, 1997.

Mansfield, J.B. *History of the Great Lakes, Volume 1*. Chicago, IL: J.H. Beers & Co., 1899.

Noble, Dennis. *Lighthouses and Keepers*. Annapolis, MD: U.S. Naval Institute Press, 1997.

O'Brien, T. Michael. *Guardians of the Eighth Sea, A History of the U.S. Coast Guard on the Great Lakes*. Washington D.C.: U.S. Government Printing Office, 1976.

Penrose, Laurie and Bill J. *A Traveler's Guide to 116 Michigan Lighthouses*. Davison, MI: Friede Publications, 1992.

Penrose, Laurie and Bill J. *A Traveler's Guide to 116 Western Great Lakes Lighthouses*. Davison, MI: Friede Publications, 1995.

Putnam, George R. *Lighthouses and Lightships of the United States*. New York, NY: Houghton-Mifflin Company, 1933.

Stonehouse, Frederick. *Wreck Ashore—The United States Life-Saving Service on the Great Lakes.* Duluth, MN: Lake Superior Port Cities, 1994.

Stonehouse, Frederick. *Lighthouse Keepers and Coast Guard Cutters.* Gwinn, MI: Avery Color Studios, 2000.

Terras, Donald J. *The Grosse Point Lighthouse, Landmark to Maritime History and Culture.* Evanston, IL: Windy City Press, 1995.

Wakefield, Larry and Lucille. *Sail and Rail—A Narrative History of Transportation in Western Michigan.* Holt, MI: Thunder Bay Press, 1996.

Wardius, Ken and Barb. *Wisconsin Lighthouses, A Photographic and Historical Guide.* Madison, WI: Prairie Oak Press, 2000.

Booklets

Flint, Willard. *A History of U.S. Lightships.* Washington, D.C.: U.S. Coast Guard Historian's Office, 1993.

Harris, Patricia G. *New Buffalo, MI Lighthouse, 1839-1859.* Michigan City, IN: Gen-Hi-Li, 1992.

Schemel, George W. *Belle City Beacons, Lighthouses of Racine County.* Racine, WI: Tumbleweed Ventures, Ltd.

Tag, Thomas A. *White River Light Station.* Dayton, OH: Data Image, 1996.

Tag, Thomas A. *Little Sable Point Light Station.* Dayton, OH: Data Image, 1996.

Tag, Thomas A. *Big Sable Point Light Station.* Dayton, OH: Data Image, 1997.

Werner, Edward C. *History of the Lighthouses at Kenosha (Southport) Wisconsin.* Kenosha, WI: Kenosha County Historical Society, 1990.

Magazines

Cain, Louis P. "The Creation of Chicago's Sanitary District and Construction of the Sanitary and Ship Canal." *Chicago History*, Summer, 1979.

Edwards, Jack. "Seul Choix Point Lighthouse." *Great Lakes Cruiser Magazine*, July, 1995.

Edwards, Jack. "St. Helena: Yesterday, Today, and Tomorrow." *Great Lakes Cruiser Magazine*, May, 1994.

Edwards, Jack. "Waugoshaunce, A Nautical Gravestone." *Great Lakes Cruiser Magazine*, October, 1994.

Franklin, Dixie. "Saviors of St. Helena." *Michigan Natural Resources Magazine*, Summer, 1991.

Hubbard, Richard. "Another Successful Season for *S.S. Badger*." *Professional Mariner Magazine*, Vol. 16, December/January 1996.

Jenvey, Bruce. "The Lights of Michigan City." *Great Lakes Cruiser Magazine*, May, 1996.

Moehl, Dick. "Developing a New Generation of Preservationists." *Great Lakes Cruiser Magazine,* December, 1995.

Sweet, Tim. "Lighting the Outer Limits." *Wisconsin Natural Resources Magazine,* February, 2000.

Trap, Paul. "Rails Across the Water." *Michigan History Magazine,* November/December, 1993.

Van Hoey, Mike. "Preserving the Lights of the Straits." *Michigan History Magazine*, September/October, 1986.

Newspapers

Ludington Daily News. "Out With the New." June 15, 1996.

Ludington Daily News. "New Light Going Up at Big Point Sable." October 12, 1985.

Racine Review. "Reef Light Two Miles From City Little Known to Racine Residents." May 10, 1929.

Racine Sunday Bulletin. "Old Age Catches Up With Reef Lighthouse." July 23, 1961.

Sheboygan Press. "Residence Replaces Old Lighthouse on North Point." December 13, 1916.

Traverse City Record-Eagle. "Lighthouse Land Transfer Nixed." September 6, 2000.

Government Sources

Record Group 26, NARA Clipping Files.

USCG CG-232. *Historically Famous Lighthouses*. Washington, D.C.: Government Printing Office. 1972.

U.S. Department of Commerce, NOAA. *Great Lakes Coast Pilot No. 6*. Various years.

U.S. Department of Interior, NPS, National Maritime Initiative. *1994 Inventory of Historic Light Stations*. 1994.

U.S. Department of Transportation, USCG. *Great Lakes Light List*. Various years.

Unpublished Material

Karges, Steven. *Bailey's Harbor Range Lights*. Door County Lighthouse Walk, 1995.

Karges, Steven. *Cana Island Light*. Door County Lighthouse Walk, 1996.

Karges, Steven. *Chambers Island Light*. Door County Lighthouse Walk, 1995.

Karges, Steven. *Eagle Bluff Light*. Door County Lighthouse Walk, 1996.

Karges, Steven. *Plum Island Range Lights*. Door County Lighthouse Walk, 1995.

Karges, Steven. *Pilot Island Light*. Door County Lighthouse Walk, 1995.

Karges, Steven. *Pottawatomie Light*. Door County Lighthouse Walk, 1995.

Karges, Steven. *Sherwood Point Light*. Door County Lighthouse Walk, 1996.

Karges, Steven. *Sturgeon Bay Canal Station Light*. Door County Lighthouse Walk, 1996.

Pleger, Thomas C. *"Green Island Light Station, Wisconsin, A Synthesis of Related Historical and Archeological Data."* 1992.

Index

boldface type indicates picture